ALSO BY GEOFFREY C. WARD

Treasures of the World: The Maharajahs

Before the Trumpet: Young Franklin Roosevelt, 1882–1905

A First-Class Temperament: The Emergence of Franklin Roosevelt

The Civil War: An Illustrated History (with Ken Burns and Ric Burns)

American Originals: The Private Worlds of Some Singular Men and Women

Tiger-Wallahs: Encounters with the Men Who Tried to Save the Greatest of Cats
    (with Diane Raines Ward)

Baseball: An Illustrated History (with Ken Burns)

Constant Companion: The Unknown Story of the Intimate Friendship
    Between Franklin Roosevelt and Margaret Suckley

The West: An Illustrated History

The Year of the Tiger

Not for Ourselves Alone: The Story of Elizabeth Cady Stanton and
    Susan B. Anthony (with Ken Burns)

Jazz: A History of America's Music (with Ken Burns)

ALSO BY DAYTON DUNCAN

The West: An Illustrated History for Children

People of the West

Miles from Nowhere

Grass Roots

Out West: An American Journey

Lewis & Clark: The Journey of the Corps of Discovery (with Ken Burns)

ALSO BY KEN BURNS

The Civil War: An Illustrated History (with Geoffrey C. Ward and Ric Burns)

Baseball: An Illustrated History (with Geoffrey C. Ward)

The Shakers: Hands to Work, Hearts to God (with Amy S. Burns)

Lewis & Clark: The Journey of the Corps of Discovery (with Dayton Duncan)

Not for Ourselves Alone: The Story of Elizabeth Cady Stanton and
    Susan B. Anthony (with Geoffrey C. Ward)

Jazz: A History of America's Music (with Geoffrey Ward)

MARK TWAIN

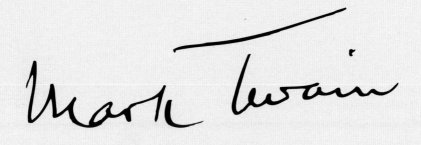

Mark Twain

BY

GEOFFREY C. WARD AND DAYTON DUNCAN

BASED ON A DOCUMENTARY FILM DIRECTED BY

KEN BURNS

WRITTEN BY

DAYTON DUNCAN AND GEOFFREY C. WARD

WITH A PREFACE BY

KEN BURNS

PICTURE RESEARCH BY

SUSANNA STEISEL AND PAM TUBRIDY BAUCOM

AND CONTRIBUTIONS BY

RUSSELL BANKS
JOHN BOYER
JOCELYN CHADWICK
HAL HOLBROOK
RON POWERS

ALFRED A. KNOPF
NEW YORK   2001

THIS IS A BORZOI BOOK
PUBLISHED BY ALFRED A. KNOPF

Library of Congress Cataloging-in-Publication Data
Ward, Geoffrey C.
    Mark Twain / by Geoffrey C. Ward, Dayton Duncan, and
Ken Burns—1st ed.
        p.   cm.
    Includes index.
    ISBN 0-375-40561-5 (alk. paper)
    1. Twain, Mark, 1835–1910. 2. Humorists, American—
19th century—Biography. 3. Authors, American—19th cen-
tury—Biography. 4. Journalists—United States—Biography.
I. Duncan, Dayton. II. Burns, Ken, 1953– III. Title.

PS1331 .W37 2001
818'.409—dc21
[B]   2001033820

Manufactured in the United Kingdom by Butler & Tanner Ltd
First Edition

Endpapers: Halley's comet, the astronom-
ical event that greeted Sam Clemens's
arrival in the world and heralded Mark
Twain's departure from it

Opening page: This cartoon, captioned
"Mark Twain and His Empire—A Laughing
World," appeared in the *New York Com-
mercial Advertiser*, December 22, 1901.

Frontispiece: Samuel Clemens aboard the
USS *Mohican*, in Seattle Harbor early in
his round-the-world lecture tour in the
summer of 1895

Page vii: Samuel Clemens in England,
1900

Pages viii and ix: Mark Twain in his hilltop
writing pavilion at Quarry Farm near
Elmira, New York, 1903

CONTENTS

THE RIGHT WORD

Ours is a useful trade, a worthy calling: with all its lightness and frivolity it has one serious purpose, one aim, one specialty, and it is constant to it—the deriding of shams, the exposure of pretentious falsities, the laughing of stupid superstitions out of existence; and that whoso is by instinct engaged in this sort of warfare is the natural enemy of royalties, nobilities, privileges and all kindred swindles, and the natural friend of human rights and human liberties.

—Mark Twain

Most of us, whether we know it or not, are in the business of words, and we hope, with some reasonable expectation, that those words will last. But alas, especially today, those words often evaporate; their precision blunted by neglect; their insight diminished by the sheer volume of their ever-increasing brethren; their force diluted by ancient animosities that seem to set each group, each faction, each interest against the other. We wonder, in an age when the present moment consumes and overshadows all else, what finally does endure? We struggle continually to comprehend and reconcile and express in words a complicated and often contradictory world—in both the broadest national sense and at an intensely private and psychological level—and we fail miserably most of the time. Imprisoned by our need to accentuate simplistic opposites, our public discourses and feeble attempts at self-discovery lack the mitigating wisdom that transcends those opposites and tolerates, with subtle irony or humorous self-deprecation, those inevitable contradictions.

Mark Twain, nearly alone among American writers, seems to have escaped, despite a personal life and literary career filled with gigantic contradictions and glaring instability, the literary prison of myopic exposition and indulgent introspection. He *endures*: as a gifted, continuously hilarious and accurate humorist (where most of his contemporaries are simply no

longer funny); as a devastatingly truthful social critic, painfully aware of the potentially derailing issues of race and space this favored land contends with daily (where the fashion of cause has metastasized for many into embarrassing self-righteousness); and as the apotheosis of what it means to *be* an American, courageously searching for personal, indeed spiritual, redemption and national self-definition all at the same time (where some of us are content to fertilize less ambitious fields).

And he understood the language. The difference between the right word and almost the right word, Mark Twain said, is the difference between lightning and the lightning bug.

This book is a companion to a two-part, four-hour documentary film on the life of Samuel Langhorne Clemens and his famously, irrepressibly rambunctious alter ego Mark Twain. That film is in turn part of a broader series of biographical portraits on noteworthy Americans that have been broadcast from time to time on national public television. Over the last seven years we have grappled with and tried to come to grips with many extraordinary human beings, including the enigmatic Thomas Jefferson, the heroic and spellbinding story of Lewis and Clark, the utterly American architect Frank Lloyd Wright, and the little-known but monumentally influential careers of Elizabeth Cady Stanton and Susan B. Anthony. With each film we sought to engage a true, honest, complicated past, unafraid of controversy or tragedy, but equally drawn to those stories and moments that suggest an abiding faith in the human spirit and particularly the unique role this remarkable republic has in the positive progress of mankind.

We were not, however, completely prepared for Mark Twain—and his delicate relationship with Sam Clemens. While Twain, the literary invention, became the "most conspicuous person on the planet," Clemens found himself torn between the two worlds and the two identities he inhabited—torn between fame and fam-

ily, between humor and bitterness, bottomless hunger for success and haunting fears of failure. It became our mission, in this, we believe, our funniest and saddest film, to try to parse the difference between the two personalities; to try to understand the genius of Twain's exquisite use of language and his absolutely honest, zenlike, often painful, but also knee-slapping, head-shaking humor; to try (in vain, of course) to experience and fathom the many gut-wrenching tragedies and losses of Clemens's life; to try to see the way Twain, alone among writers in the nineteenth century, and continually at war with himself, bravely confronted his demons and those of his countrymen and almost single-handedly invented American literature; to try, in the end, to accompany an aging, often bitter, obviously mortal Sam Clemens in his final "agony days," just as his literary twin achieved an artistic immortality reserved only for the best of us.

I am the human race compacted and crammed into a single suit of clothes but quite able to represent its entire massed multitude in all its moods and inspirations. . . .
   I am only human—although I regret it.

He was a Southerner and a Northerner, a Westerner and a New England Yankee—a tireless wanderer who lived in a thousand places all around the world. But he would call just two of them home: the small Mississippi River town where he grew up, which he would transform with his imagination into the idealized hometown of every American boy; and the magnificent Connecticut house he built for his wife and children, which he hoped would shelter them from hardship, but where sadness and heartbreak found them nonetheless.

During his long life he was a printer's apprentice and a riverboat pilot, a prospector who never struck gold and a Confederate soldier who never fought a battle. He was considered in his day the funniest man on earth—a brilliant performer on the lecture circuit who could size up and entertain almost any audience—and a spectacularly inept businessman whose countless schemes to get rich quick threatened again and again to bring him to ruin.

But above all, Mark Twain was a writer—a natural-born storyteller and a self-taught genius with words, who understood before anyone else that art could be created out of the *American* language.

"The genius was for speaking the *voice* of America," his biographer Ron Powers told us, "for internalizing and then flawlessly reproducing the voice of the American people."

"He wrote as though there had been no literature before him, as though he had discovered the art of telling a story about these folks that inhabit this continent," the playwright Arthur Miller said in an interview for our film. "And that there was no other continent; [that this country] was like something that rose up out of the sea and had no history. And he was just telling what he ran into."

He wrote constantly—newspaper stories, poetry, plays, political diatribes, travel pieces, irreverent musings about religion—and a series of autobiographical sketches noted as much, he admitted, for the tall tales they spun as for the truth they told. And he wrote books—books read by millions all over the world—including his masterpiece, *Adventures of Huckleberry Finn*, a deceptively simple story of a backwoods boy and a runaway slave that showed his people a new way to think about themselves. Years later Ernest Hemingway would call it "the best book we've ever had. There was nothing before. There's been nothing as good since."

Like the nation he would come to embody, Twain was always reinventing himself, always restless, always full of contradictions. "I am not *an* American," he once said. "I am *the* American."

> *I was made merely in the image of God but not otherwise resembling him enough to be mistaken for him by anybody but a very near-sighted person. . . .*
> *I believe that our Heavenly Father invented man because He was disappointed in the monkey.*

Unlike the collaborative nature of film—and this film and book are collaborations of the best kind—the art of writing is by its nature singular and personal, resisting collective interpretation and true understanding of the mysteries of its mechanics.

Our aesthetic appreciation of the act of writing, especially in Twain's case, tends to be eclipsed by the drama of biography and the distraction of social issues like race and imperialism. But Twain's style, his joyous, careening collisions of words, his surprising use of verbs, his muscular and elaborate metaphors, his confidence in vernacular rhythms and truths, his anthropomorphizing of everything (animals, houses, planets, nations, rivers, even ideas), his repetition, and his godlike sense of time, create a music so stunning and so unique in American letters that it is hard to find even the most primitive tools to deconstruct its magic.

As documentary makers who have consciously eschewed the misguided consensus of many of our colleagues that film is the enemy of the word, we have instead, across the arc of more than a score of productions chiefly in American history, embraced the poetry in prose and narrative, and have found in Twain's example inspiration, brotherhood, and enormous sympathy. There is a universal appeal to Twain's writing, his characters, his plotting, and his humor, of course, but also to his observational genius (Ron Powers calls Twain "an enormous noticer"), and the clarity, common sense, and attractive anger of his outrage and political attack. For Twain, the ordinariness of life and things and events has a kind of mystical possibility—he loved the image of cattle grazing on a sod roof, "peerless sunsets," the smell of an "old, rank, delicious pipe," "ham and hard-boiled eggs"; it is, he warned, "what all the ages have struggled for." The opposite of all that, the pretensions, cruelties, and inattentions of human behavior, brought out a ferocious democratic fairness in Twain which found beautiful, touching, and elegant expression in withering criticism of police brutality, racism, anti-Semitism, religious hypocrisy, governmental arrogance, petty tyrants, and safe bourgeois life.

For Clemens, for Twain, it all began with speaking and the sound of words—his mother called his gift for gab "Sammy's long talk"—and it was a gift inherited from the improbable young nation and the mysterious country he was born into, from Sunday school and Bible readings, from slave stories and gospel singing, from the palpable danger and vivifying experiences of life and loss on the frontier. His art gathered momentum in a boyhood filled with delights, adventures, characters, lies, guilts, and excruciating doubts. Like the "lawless" Mississippi River—the principal highway of his imagination—that remained no matter where he went, Clemens's life and Twain's art were filled with undercurrents and unseen treacheries. "His exuberant and almost irrepressible humor is always colored," William Styron told us, "by this understanding that life is not just one big yuck, but is a serious event in which horrible things happen." They did happen.

Twain wrote with an almost biblical certainty and authority, combining an aw-shucks, utterly American sense of humor and timing with a seemingly effortless and yet obviously sophisticated choice of words. He knew from the start that God was the greatest dramatist, and much of his genius can be found in his simply getting out of the way of a good story. He took for granted that God was everywhere, but his own search disappointed him continually. As a result, on the surface of things he railed—against God, injustice, bigotry, greed—but inside it seems he accepted, surrendered, and even, despite the intense bitterness in his later writings, reconciled the mountain of evidence, beautiful and ugly, that was his world and the grist for his art. He saw more. He acknowledged the contradictions in himself and in his country, between white and black, Puritanism and excess, modesty and hubris, and with a self-deprecating wink made himself the butt of his jokes as often as others. All of this, tethered dangerously to a life lived constantly on the edge—filled with deaths, failures and blasted trusts, riches, love, and recognition beyond example—conspired to make Mark Twain this avatar of American literature.

I think we never become really and genuinely our entire and honest selves until we are dead— and not then until we have been dead years and years. People ought to start dead and then they would be honest so much earlier.

In the end, all along, Mark Twain made people laugh, his humor hitting the "yes and no" of things simultaneously, its implied and embedded understanding so true, so arresting, so funny. The jokes and stories, anecdotes and vivid characterizations, seem less about pleasing his audiences, though they nonetheless nearly always did, than about abolishing the pain in the awful truth of life, offering the antidote that mitigating wisdom and a twinkle in the eye always is, an antidote the human race so desperately craves. And he never lost that twinkle. Or the wisdom: "Ah well, I am a great and sublime fool. But then I am God's fool, and all His works must be contemplated with respect."

"Lecturing," Twain (or Clemens, it doesn't matter) wrote, "is gymnastics, chest-expander, medicine, mind-healer, blues-destroyer, all in one." He could have easily been speaking about writing. All his life he would return to the solitude of his work place—the third-floor billiards room in Hartford, the top of the stagecoach while he was roughing it, his Elmira, New York, octagon with the "retreating range of distant blue hills," even his exile in Europe; he would return to the careful crafting of words and the holy corrective that writing was for all the ills, improbabilities, and joys of his world. "The secret source of humor itself," Twain also wrote, "is not joy, but sorrow. There is no humor in heaven."

[Our] race, in its poverty, has unquestionably one really effective weapon—laughter. . . . Against the assault of laughter nothing can stand.

Ken Burns
Walpole, New Hampshire

PROLOGUE

Late in the afternoon on Thursday, May 29, 1902, Will Sutton, desk clerk of the Windsor Hotel in Hannibal, Missouri, was lounging behind his counter, just as he did every weekday, when two strangers walked in and asked for rooms. They were just off the 5:35 train from St. Louis. Sutton didn't recognize the first man: he turned out to be a young newspaper reporter named Robertus Love, on assignment for the *St. Louis Post-Dispatch.* But Love's much older companion—small and slender with a drooping moustache, a tangle of light gray hair, and a suit to match—was the most readily recognizable American on earth: his real name was Samuel Langhorne Clemens, but he was better known even here, in his old hometown, by his pen name, Mark Twain.

Sutton stammered with excitement as the old man signed the register: "Mr. Clemens, I was born close to your birthplace . . . and have been in the house where you were born, often."

"I was not born often—only once," Clemens drawled, "but I'm glad to see you, all the same."

They shook hands, and Sutton handed over a room key. Clemens climbed the stairs, unlocked his door, and closed it behind him. He was sixty-six years old and weary. He hadn't been back to the town where he'd spent his boyhood in years and had told no one he was coming—the visit had been an afterthought, an unplanned stop on the long train journey from his current home in the Bronx, just north of Manhattan, to Columbia, Missouri, where the state university was to give him an honorary degree—and he knew he would need rest before the excitement that was sure to follow him wherever he went the following morning. He climbed into bed, lit a cigar, and read till he grew sleepy.

Hannibal had been home to a little more than 3,000 souls when seventeen-year-old Sam Clemens had left it to make his fortune in the summer of 1853. Steamboats had provided its only contact with the wider world then; a Hannibal citizen's first visit to the metropolis of St. Louis (population 30,000), just 150 miles downriver, had been enough, Clemens recalled, for him to talk "St. Louis, and nothing but [St. Louis] and its wonders for months and months afterward." Now the village where Clemens had spent his formative years had itself become a small industrial city, with more than 12,000 citizens. Steamboats seldom visited its riverfront anymore, but fifty-six passenger trains stopped there every day; so did thirty-four freight trains. There were scores of factories in town, including the largest cement plant in the world, and streetcars plied streets where young Sam Clemens had once walked barefoot.

He, too, had changed almost beyond recognition since he'd first left Hannibal, and he had crowded into the intervening five decades enough experiences for half a dozen ordinary lifetimes. He'd been a printer and a riverboat pilot before the Civil War, then served briefly as a Confederate militiaman. He'd gone west and tried silver mining; become a hard-drinking newspaperman in Virginia City and a humorous lecturer in San Francisco. He had witnessed firsthand the corruption and greed that gripped Washington, D.C., during the era he was the first to call the Gilded Age, and had himself lived the gaudy life of a would-be millionaire before his own overreaching drove him and his family into bankruptcy and exile overseas. He had redeemed his reputation and rebuilt his fortune through his own hard work, only to suffer the loss of his dearest child. He had recovered from that as well, and since 1900 had somehow managed to make himself simultaneously an outspoken critic of American adventurism abroad and America's best-loved public figure.

But above all, he had been a writer, pouring forth torrents of words: twenty-four volumes of fiction and essays so far, with still more books in the works, along with plays and occasional poetry, political diatribes, irreverent musings about God and man, and thousands of private letters that revealed his innermost desires and deepest insecurities. But he was still best known for two novels of boyhood set in a small Mississippi River town very like Hannibal: *The Adventures of Tom Sawyer,* in which he transformed his own often difficult early years into an idyll that became the envy of generations of American boys and girls; and *Adventures of Huckleberry Finn,* which proved for the first time that art could be created out of the American language and laid bare the contradictions at the heart of American life—slavery and racism.

"If you attempt to create & build a wholly imaginary incident, adventure or situation," he once wrote in a notebook, "you will go astray, & the artificiality of the thing will be detectable. But if you found on a *fact* in your personal experience, it is an acorn, a root, & every created adornment that grows up out of it & spreads its foliage & blossoms to the sun will seem realities, not inventions. You will not be likely to grow astray; your compass of fact is there to keep

Prodigal's return: Hannibal citizens surround their town's favorite son (wearing bow tie) during his surprise visit in the spring of 1902.

you on the right course." During his long, astonishingly prolific literary career, he had drawn upon experiences from every part of his life, but his memories of Hannibal had always remained the true north of his compass of fact, and it was good to be home again.

Word spread overnight that Hannibal's favorite son had returned, and a sizable crowd was waiting outside when he and Robertus Love emerged from their hotel at 9:30 a.m. and started off on foot for Clemens's old family home at 206 Hill Street—"the house I lived in when I whitewashed the fence 53 years ago," he called it in a letter to his wife, Livy. "It all seems so small to me," he said when he and the jostling crowd got there. "I suppose if I should come back here ten years from now, it would be the size of a birdhouse."

Mrs. Henry Garth, the well-to-do widow of one of his closest childhood friends, took him out to the Mount Olivet cemetery in her carriage so that he could visit the graves of those he called "my people": his mother, Jane, dead twelve years now; his luckless older brother, Orion; his younger brother, Henry, for whose accidental death forty-four years before he still blamed himself; and his father, John Marshall Clemens, whose early death had forced young Sam to go to work while still a schoolboy.

That afternoon, an informal reception for Clemens was held at the Farmers and Merchants Bank. Old schoolmates crowded in to shake his hand.

"How are you doing, Eddie?" he asked one.

"Like yourself, Sam," the old man said, "like a cow's tail going down." Clemens laughed; gritty turns of phrase like that were his literary stock-in-trade.

He went on to attend a Memorial Day ceremony at his mother's old Presbyterian church and dined that evening at Mrs. Garth's with Laura Hawkins

Townspeople—including at least three photographers—turn out to see Mark Twain return to what he remembered as the "large white house" on Hill Street, in which he spent much of his boyhood. It "isn't large now," he wrote later, "although it hasn't lost a plank; I saw it a year ago and noticed that shrinkage."

Frazier—his childhood sweetheart and the model for the golden-curled object of Tom Sawyer's affections, Becky Thatcher—who was now a stout widow with false teeth, in charge of Hannibal's Home for the Friendless. Then he hurried to the Opera House to hand out diplomas at the Hannibal High School commencement. "Take one," he told the students. "Pick out a good one. Don't take two, but be sure you get a good one."

"It has been a rushing day," he wrote home to Livy that evening, and the next three days were almost as busy. Some members of the throng that continued to follow him around town had now chosen to dress up as characters from his books. "Today, Hannibal is full of Huck Finns, Tom Sawyers and Beckys," Robertus Love reported to his readers. "There are more 'originals' of Huck, Tom and Becky in this town since Mark Twain arrived than one would expect to meet in a staid old town with 23 respectable Sunday schools and a Salvation Army. You don't need to bait your hook if you go fishing for a Huck. Just make a cast anywhere around town, and there's your Huckleberry."

On Saturday evening, Clemens agreed to speak before a hastily arranged meeting of the ladies' Labinnah Club (Hannibal spelled backward). He was the country's most popular platform performer as well as its best-known writer, and audiences like this one were ordinarily child's play for him. But this crowd was different: seated among the five hundred townspeople who had squeezed into the hall to hear him were seven of his boyhood friends, white-haired now and bent with age. At first things went well, and he had everyone laughing at a story from his youth in which his late mother played a part. Then, suddenly, he bowed his head to hide his tears. "I realize that this must be my last visit to Hannibal," he told his anxious listeners when he could bring himself to speak again, "and in bidding you hail I also bid you farewell." Robertus Love wrote:

His voice was choked, his utterance was broken. It was the almost wailing voice of an old man who realized that his years were behind him. . . . Mark Twain . . . had forgotten his world-wide fame, the plaudits of princes, the friendship of emperors, the adulation of the multitudes of many lands. He had forgotten his books and his splendid home in the East. Nothing remained to him save the past of half a century ago and the insistent clamor of that inward voice crying across the years: "Farewell, farewell."

By the next morning, Clemens's customary impishness had returned. He dropped in at several Sunday schools attached to churches that had not even existed in his time, and gravely assured each group of children that he had once been one of them, even pointing out the chair in each classroom in which he had supposedly sat. He climbed with an old friend named John Briggs up Holliday's Hill—Cardiff Hill in *The Adventures of Tom Sawyer.* "Down there by the island is the place we used to swim," he said when they got to the top, "and yonder is where a man was drowned, and there's where the steamboat sank. Down there on Lover's Leap is where the Millerites put on their robes one night to go to heaven. None of them went that night, but I suppose most of them have gone by now."

When it was time for him to take the train to Columbia the next morning, a large throng gathered at the depot to see him off. He spotted an old schoolmate named Tom Nash in the crowd, deaf since developing scarlet fever after falling through the ice while skating with Clemens forty years before. "He was old and white-headed," Clemens recalled, "but the boy of 15 was still visible in him. He came up to me, made a trumpet of his hand at my ear, nodded his head toward the citizens and said confidentially—in a yell like a fog horn—'Same damned fools, Sam. Same damned fools.'"

Twain says a final goodbye to the hometown his writings had already made immortal, June 1, 1902.

CHAPTER ONE

A BOY'S PARADISE

*I was born the 30th of November, 1835, in the almost invisible vil-
lage of Florida, Monroe County, Missouri. . . . The village contained a hundred people and I increased the population by 1 per
cent. It is more than many of the best men in history could have
done for a town. . . . There is no record of a person doing as much—
not even Shakespeare. But I did it for Florida, Missouri, and it
shows I could have done it for any place—even London, I suppose.*
—*Chapters from My Autobiography, 1906*

Samuel Clemens was born in a two-room rented shack some thirty-five
miles southeast of Hannibal in Florida, Missouri, the fourth son and the
sixth of seven children born to John Marshall and Jane Lampton
Clemens. One infant son had died before Sam's birth—only four of the
children would survive to adulthood—and Sam, born two months prema-
ture, was so thin and sickly, his mother remembered, that "I could see
no promise in him." But Halley's comet had blazed in the sky the night
of his birth, and she clung to the hope that it might be a bright omen for
her baby's future. He was christened Samuel Langhorne Clemens—
Samuel was his paternal grandfather's name, Langhorne the family name
of old friends of his father's—but in his early years, because of his size
and fragility, everyone called him "Little Sammy."

His health was just one of his parents' worries. John Marshall
Clemens was a merchant and lawyer, descended from a prominent Virginia family, concerned always with keeping up appearances but chroni-
cally unable to make a go of things. Like thousands of other ambitious
young men of his time and place, he moved westward with his growing
family again and again—five times in a dozen
years—betting that first one raw frontier settlement
and then another would flourish and he with it. He
had managed along the way to buy more than seventy
thousand mountainous acres of pine forest in Tennessee, which he believed would one day make his
family rich beyond their dreams, but in the interim
none of his plans ever quite worked out. He was
always well respected by his neighbors and warm and
loving toward his eldest daughter, Pamela, but toward
his sons he remained "stern, unsmiling," according to
Sam. "My father and I," he wrote, "were always on

(opposite) **The earliest known portrait
of Sam Clemens, a daguerreotype
made when he was fifteen and working
as a printer's apprentice. The camera
reversed the image but Sam outwitted
it by spelling his name backward in
moveable type so that it could be read
correctly.**

(below) **The Florida, Missouri, shack in
which Samuel Langhorne Clemens was
born. "Heretofore," he wrote after seeing
this picture, "I have always stated it was
a palace, but I shall be more guarded
now."**

the most distant terms when I was a boy—a sort of armed neutrality, so to speak." He remembered that he never saw his father laugh.

Jane Clemens was different. "My mother [was] very much alive," Sam would remember, "fond of excitement, fond of novelties, fond of anything going that was of a sort proper for members of the church to indulge in. . . . Always ready for Fourth of July processions, Sunday-school processions, lectures, conventions, camp-meetings, revivals in the church . . . and never missed a funeral." She loved dancing and music, too, enjoyed having as many as nineteen cats and kittens under-foot, and delighted in storytelling—"she was the most eloquent person I ever met in all my life," her son recalled—all qualities he would inherit, along with his mother's thick red hair.

By 1839, when Sam was four, it had become clear even to John Clemens that Florida, like all the other outposts he had tried, was never going to prosper, and he moved his family once again, this time to the Mississippi River town of Hannibal. Its future looked bright. It was already home to one thousand people; three steamboats came and went each day; there was even talk of a railroad. Clemens bought a small hotel, called the Virginia House, just one hundred yards from the river-front, but he would suffer disappointments here, too: the town did grow but too slowly to provide enough guests to keep his hotel going. He bor-rowed money to stock a dry-goods store that also went under; struggled to support his family on the meager fees he earned as a justice of the peace; and finally pulled his eldest son, Orion, out of school and packed him off downriver to St. Louis to learn the printer's trade so that he could help keep the family afloat. A distant cousin bought a narrow lot on Hill Street and allowed Clemens to build on it the house Sam visited in his old age; but when Sam was eleven, the family had to sell off most of its furnishings to pay its debts and moved across the street to rooms above a pharmacy, where Jane did the cooking for the owner's family in lieu of rent.

Jane Clemens constantly worried about money as her family teetered between near-prosperity and genteel poverty. And although Sam's health slowly improved, she had to endure the death of two more children—a daughter, Margaret, and then a son, Benjamin—in the space of three years. When Benjamin died, she had six-year-old Sam touch the head of his older brother's corpse in farewell—an experience that gave him ter-rifying nightmares and led him to believe himself somehow responsible for his sibling's death.

Nonetheless, Sam remembered Hannibal as "a boy's paradise." "In [Hannibal] when I was a boy," he remembered, "everybody was poor but didn't know it; and everybody was comfortable and did know it." In the nearby oak forests, he and his young friends pretended to be Indians or

Jane Lampton Clemens, Sam's mother: Despite the death of her husband and three of her children, her son wrote, she remained "of a sunshiny disposition," and "always had the heart of a young girl."

(Below) Bird Street between First and Main, looking toward the Mississippi. Judge Clemens's law office was located in the next block, on the left side of the street.

Sam's first schoolteacher, Elizabeth Horr: She was "a New England lady of middle age with New England ways and principles," he wrote, who predicted that her six-year-old pupil would one day be "President of the United States, and would stand in the presence of kings unabashed"—or so he claimed.

There were no public schools in Missouri in Clemens's boyhood, but he is known to have attended at least three private ones. This schoolhouse stood on Center Street.

pirates, Robin Hood and his Merry Men, and, later, treasure hunters like the hopeful young men who began streaming through Hannibal after gold was discovered in California. The boys explored a deep limestone cave where the corpse of a fourteen-year-old girl was preserved for a time in a copper cylinder, and where a local ne'er-do-well named Injun Joe was said once to have gotten lost, surviving only on bats. They spent whole days alone on an island in the Mississippi, fishing, smoking corn-cob pipes and an especially rank brand of cigars known locally as "Garth's damndest," inventing elaborate pranks to play on the townspeople, and swimming naked in the big river. Nine times Sam was pulled from the water in what he recalled as "a substantially drowned condition." His mother tried to laugh off the narrow escapes by telling him, "People who are born to be hanged are safe in water."

One of Sam's closest boyhood friends was Tom Blankenship, the son of the town drunkard, who lived not far from the Clemens home in a dilapidated old house. "He was ignorant, unwashed, insufficiently fed," Clemens wrote later, "but he had as good a heart as ever any boy had."

His liberties were totally unrestricted. He was the only really independent person—boy or man—in the community, and by consequence he was tranquilly and continuously happy and was envied by all the rest of us. We liked him; we enjoyed his society. And as his society was forbidden us by our parents the prohibition trebled and quadrupled its value, and therefore we sought and got more of his society than of any other boy's.

The derelict house on Hill Street, where Tom Blankenship, the inspiration for Huckleberry Finn, lived. "*Blankenships*," Twain wrote in notes for a portrait of Hannibal he never completed. "The parents paupers and drunkards; the girls charged with prostitution—not proven. Tom, a kindly young heathen."

After dark, whenever Sam heard Tom's secret catcall, he would slip out the bedroom window for a night of adventures. But even without Tom Blankenship's influence, Sam was restless and high-spirited. He considered going to church a punishment and frequently skipped the evening prayer services his mother ordered him to attend—though he memorized Bible verses to convince her he had, in fact, showed up. Sam objected especially to the sermons that "dealt in limitless fire and brimstone, and thinned the predestined elect down to a company so small as to be hardly worth sav-

White Town Drowsing

Life in the Mississippi River town of Hannibal, Missouri, armed Mark Twain with a lifetime's worth of memories. Perhaps his most memorable portrait of the town—and the role the river played in his boy's imagination—comes from his 1883 book, Life on the Mississippi.

After all these years I can picture that old time to myself now, just as it was then: the white town drowsing in the sunshine of a summer's morning; the streets empty, or pretty nearly so; one or two clerks sitting in front of the Water Street stores, with their splint-bottomed chairs tilted back against the wall, chins on breasts, hats slouched over their faces, asleep—with shingle-shavings enough around to show what broke them down; a sow and a litter of pigs loafing along the sidewalk, doing a good business in watermelon rinds and seeds; two or three lonely little freight piles scattered about the "levee;" a pile of "skids" on the slope of the stone-paved wharf, and the fragrant town drunkard asleep in the shadow of them; two or three wood flats at the head of the wharf, but nobody to listen to the peaceful lapping of the wavelets against them; the great Mississippi, the majestic, the magnificent Mississippi, rolling its mile-wide tide along, shining in the sun; the dense forest away on the other side; the "point" above the town, and the "point" below, bounding the river-glimpse and turning it into a sort of sea, and withal a very still and brilliant and lonely one.

Presently a film of dark smoke appears above one of those remote "points;" instantly a negro drayman, famous for his quick eye and prodigious voice, lifts up the cry, "S-t-e-a-m-boat a-comin'!" and the scene changes! The town drunkard stirs, the clerks wake up, . . . every house and store pours out a human contribution, and all in a twinkling the dead town is alive and moving. Drays, carts, men, boys, all go hurrying from many quarters to a common center, the wharf. Assembled there, the people fasten their eyes upon the coming boat as upon a wonder they are seeing for the first time. And the boat *is* rather a handsome sight, too. She is long and sharp and trim and pretty; she has two tall, fancy-topped chimneys, with a gilded device of some kind swung between them; a fanciful pilot-house, all glass and "gingerbread," perched on top of the "texas" deck behind them; the paddle-boxes are gorgeous with a picture or with gilded rays above the boat's name; the boiler deck, the hurricane deck, and the texas deck are fenced and ornamented with clean white railings; there is a flag gallantly flying from the jack-staff; . . . the upper decks are black with passengers; the captain stands by the big bell, calm, imposing, the envy of all; great volumes of the blackest smoke are rolling and tumbling out

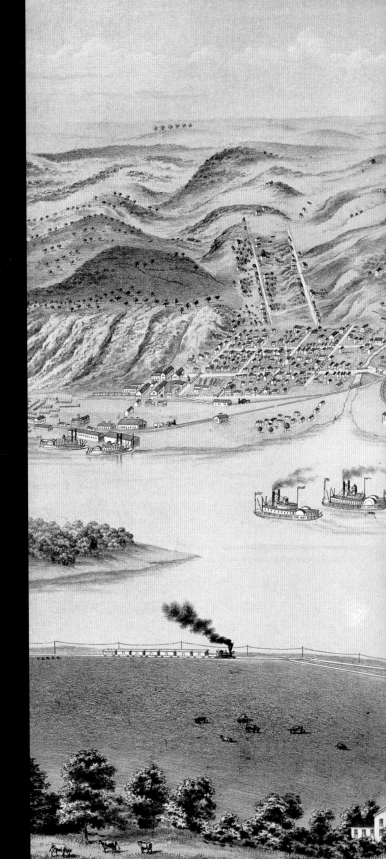

f the chimneys—a husbanded grandeur created
with a bit of pitch pine just before arriving at a
own; the crew are grouped on the forecastle;
he broad stage is run far out over the port bow,
nd an envied deckhand stands picturesquely
on the end of it with a coil of rope in his hand;
he pent steam is screaming through the gauge-
ocks; the captain lifts his hand, a bell rings,
he wheels stop; then they turn back, churning
he water to foam, and the steamer is at rest.
hen such a scramble as there is to get aboard,
nd to get ashore, and to take in freight and
o discharge freight, all at one and the same
ime; and such a yelling and cursing as the
mates facilitate it all with! Ten minutes later
he steamer is under way again, with no flag on
he jack-staff and no black smoke issuing from
he chimneys. After ten more minutes the town
s dead again, and the town drunkard asleep by
he skids once more.

Hannibal, as it looked to the lithographic artist
Albert Ruger in 1869, sixteen years after Sam Clemens
had moved on. Railroad passengers alighting at the
depot on the Illinois side of the river were borne by
steam ferry to what would later become the most
celebrated steamboat landing in American literature.
Bear Creek, in which young Sam nearly drowned, is at
the left, on the town's southern edge. The Clemens
home stands one block from the riverfront; it is the first
structure on the right side of Hill Street, just past Main

ing," but he absorbed enough strict Presbyterianism that late-night thunderstorms seemed to his vivid imagination to be God's warning to him to mend his ways:

> With every glare of lightning I shrivelled and shrunk together in mortal terror, and in the interval of black darkness that followed I poured out my lamentings over my lost condition, and my supplications for just one more chance, with an energy and feeling and sincerity quite foreign to my nature. But in the morning I saw that it was a false alarm and concluded to resume business at the old stand and wait for another reminder.

He loved to read—*Robinson Crusoe* and *The Arabian Nights* were special favorites—and was an excellent speller, but he was otherwise a mediocre student who often played hooky and once stowed away on a steamboat before being caught and returned to his home. "You gave me more uneasiness," his mother told him, "than any child I had."

For several months each summer, she sent him—along with a favorite cat or two carried in a basket—to the farm of his well-to-do uncle John Quarles. There, he and his cousins scoured the woods and fields for wild berries, gorged themselves on his aunt's country cooking, and spent as much time as they could among the cabins in which his uncle's thirty slaves lived. "All the negroes were friends of ours," Clemens wrote of his boyhood in slaveholding Missouri, "and with those of our own age we were in effect comrades. I say in effect [because] we were comrades and yet not comrades; color and condition interposed a subtle line which both parties were conscious of and which rendered complete fusion impossible." Among the African-Americans Sam knew best were a woman named Aunt Hannah, who seemed so old to him and his playmates that they believed she must have known Moses; a slave girl his own age named Mary Quarles, who was his closest companion at his uncle's farm; and Jerry, a twelve-year-old boy who, when his owners were not looking, liked to climb on the woodpile and lampoon the local preacher. "You tell me whar a man gits his corn-pone," Jerry liked to say, "en I'll tell you what his 'pinions is."

But above all, Sam remembered "Uncle Dan'l," his "good friend, ally and adviser . . . whose sympathies were wide and warm," who taught him to sing the spirituals and jubilees he would love throughout his life, and in the evenings, around the dying kitchen fire, loved to tell a ghost story with a startling surprise ending that Sam would many years later turn into one of his most effective performance pieces, "The Golden Arm." "It was on the farm that I got a strong liking for [Uncle Dan'l's] race," Clemens would write as an old man, "and my appreciation of certain of its fine qualities. This feeling and this estimate have stood the test of

Mary Quarles, Sam's boyhood playmate, photographed many years after she and the rest of the slaves who had belonged to the Quarles family had been freed

Sam Clemens spent several boyhood summers on his uncle John A. Quarles's farm (above), four miles from Florida, Missouri. It was, he wrote, "a heavenly place for a boy."

sixty years and more and have suffered no impairment. The black face is as welcome to me now as it was then."

That appreciation grew slowly, Clemens recalled.

In my schoolboy days I had no aversion to slavery. I was not aware that there was anything wrong about it. The local papers said nothing against it; the local pulpit taught us that God approved it, that it was a holy thing, and that the doubter need only look in the Bible if he wished to settle his mind—and then the texts were read aloud to us to make the matter sure; if the slaves themselves had an aversion to slavery they were wise and said nothing.

As a young boy, Sam saw his father administer a beating to Jennie, the Clemenses' only slave, for talking back to her mistress; later the boy wept when she was sold down the river. His father sold other slaves as well, once exchanging a man remembered only as "Charley" for ten barrels of tar, to be delivered on or before the following Christmas. And in 1841 he served on a circuit court jury that sentenced three abolitionists to twelve years in jail for daring to help five slaves flee toward Canada and freedom. Sam himself looked on at the age of ten as a white overseer

11

hurled a chunk of iron ore at a slave "for merely doing something awkwardly" and killed him. "Everybody seemed indifferent about it—as regards the slave," he wrote, "though considerable sympathy was felt for the slave's owner, who had been bereft of valuable property by a worthless person who was not able to pay for it." One of his most lasting childhood memories was of a dozen black men and women chained together, waiting to be shipped downriver to the slave market at New Orleans. "Those," he said, "were the saddest faces I have ever seen."

In 1847, John Clemens seemed finally to be on the brink of the success that had always eluded him. He was the leading candidate to become clerk of the county court, a job that promised at last to provide him with both the dignity and the steady income he'd been seeking for so long. But he was caught in a sleet storm while campaigning and developed a fatal case of pneumonia. "Cling to the land and wait," he told his family from his deathbed; "let nothing beguile it away from you." Far from being a blessing, the land in Tennessee would become a "curse" for his family, his son wrote later, because it always gave them the sense of being *prospectively* rich" while they were actually "condemned . . . to a long and discouraging struggle with the world for a livelihood."

Orion, ten years older than Sam and now the head of the family, was already sending home what money he could from St. Louis. But to make ends meet, Jane Clemens now had to take in boarders in their rented quarters. Sam's sister Pamela began giving piano lessons. It was "pretty tough sledding," Sam remembered, and he, too, would eventually be called upon to help. "From the time that my father died, March 24, 1847, when I was past eleven years old, until the . . . first days of 1857," he remembered, "I worked—not diligently, not willingly, but fretfully, lazily, repiningly, complainingly, disgustedly, and always shirking the work when I was not watched. The statistics show that I was a worker about ten years." He was exaggerating but only slightly. He stayed in school for at least three years after his father died, but he did hold after-school and summer jobs—as an errand boy, a grocery clerk, and an apprentice to the town blacksmith—before he, too, had to leave school and go to work at the *Missouri Courier* as a printer's apprentice. The editor and proprietor of the paper, he remembered, "allowed me the usual emolument of the office of apprentice—that is to say board and clothes, but no money. The clothes consisted of two suits a year, but one of the suits always failed to materialize and the other suit was not purchased so long as [the proprietor's] old clothes held out. I was only about half as big as [he was], consequently his shirts gave me the uncomfortable sense of living in a circus tent, and I had to turn up his pants to my ears to make them short enough."

**Orion Clemens,
Sam's hapless older brother**

"LOCAL" RESOLVES TO COMMIT SUICIDE.

'Local,' disconsolate from receiving no further notice from 'A Dog-be-Deviled Citizen,' contemplates Suicide. His 'pocket-pistol' (i. e. the *bottle*,) failing in the patriotic work of ridding the country of a nuisance, he resolves to 'extinguish his chunk' by feeding his carcass to the fishes of Bear Creek, while friend and foe are wrapt in sleep. Fearing, however, that he may get out of his depth, he *sounds the stream with his walking-stick.*

The artist has, you will perceive, Mr. Editor, caught the gentleman's countenance as correctly as the thing could have been done with the real *dog*-gerytype apparatus. Ain't he pretty? and don't he step along through the mud with an air? 'Peace to his *re*-manes.'

'A Dog-be-Deviled Citizen.'

In what Twain later called "my first literary venture," he used his brother's newspaper to launch this crude assault on the editor of a competing paper who had tried to drown himself. "I thought it was desperately funny," he remembered, "and was densely unconscious that there was any moral obliquity about such a publication." When the aggrieved editor threatened to shoot him, he ridiculed him for that, too (right).

**Pamela Clemens Moffett,
Sam's older sister**

"PICTURE" DEPARTMENT.

" LOCAL" discovers something interesting in the *Journal,* and becomes excited.

[" LOCAL," determined upon the destruction of the great enemy of the canine race, charters an old swivel (a six pounder) and declares war. *Lead* being scarce, he loads his cannon with *Tri-Weekly Messengers.*]

" LOCAL" is somewhat astonished at the effect of the discharge, and is under the impression that there was something the matter with the apparatus—thinks the hole must have been drilled in the wrong end of the artillery. He finds, however, that although he missed the " DOG-BE-DEVILED CITIZEN," he nevertheless hit the man " who has not the decency of a gentleman nor the honor of a blackguard," and thinks it best to stop the controversy.

MR. EDITOR:

I have now dropped this farce, and all attempts to again call me forth will be useless.
        A DOG-BE-DEVILED CITIZEN.

Then, in the spring of 1850, he got a job at the *Hannibal Journal,* now owned by his older brother. Orion Clemens shared many of his younger brother's qualities—energy, restlessness, excitability—but none of his genius or extraordinary powers of concentration. He was "as unstable as water," Sam remembered, "the strangest compound that ever got mixed in a human mold. . . . He woke with an eagerness about some matter or other every morning; it consumed him all day; it perished in the night and he was on fire with a fresh new interest next morning before he could get his clothes on. He exploited in this way three hundred and sixty-five red-hot new eagernesses every year of his life." His eagerness never seemed to pay off; over the course of the two years Sam worked for the *Journal,* Orion was not once able to come up with the three and a half dollars a week he had promised his younger brother.

But Sam made the most of the experience. He had discovered that he liked to write: crude light verse as well as rough-hewn humorous sketches under the pseudonym of W. Epaminondas Adrastus Blab—anything, he later said, "to make the paper lively." Once, left in charge while Orion was out of town, he poked heavy-handed fun at some of the town's leading citizens, including the high-strung editor of a competing paper, who was already the object of town gossip for having attempted suicide after being jilted by a girlfriend. Like nearly everything else from his boyhood, Clemens would later turn the incident into a story:

For once the Hannibal Journal *was in demand—a novelty it had not experienced before. The whole town was stirred. Higgins dropped in with a double-barrelled shot-gun early in the forenoon. When he found that it was an infant (as he called me) that had done him the damage, he simply pulled my ears and went away. . . .*

[Orion] was very angry when he got back—unreasonably so, I thought, considering what an impetus I had given the paper, and considering also that gratitude for his preservation ought to have been uppermost in his mind, inasmuch as by his delay he had so wonderfully escaped dissection, tomahawking, libel, and getting his head shot off.

"My literature attracted the town's attention," Sam later remembered, "but not its admiration."

He was seventeen in the spring of 1853, and both Hannibal and his brother's failing newspaper now seemed too confining. After gravely promising his mother not to drink or gamble, Sam packed his bags and set off to see more of the world. It was the beginning of a lifetime of wandering. "All I do know or feel," he would write his mother a few years later, "is that I am wild with impatience to move—move—*Move!* . . . Curse the endless delays! . . . I wish I never had to stop *any*where a month."

He found work in St. Louis first, setting type for the *Evening News*. Then, with a few coins in his pocket and a ten-dollar bill sewn into his coat lining, he boarded a train for the first time and took it all the way to New York. There he earned four dollars a week working in a print shop, spent his evenings devouring the books in the printer's library, and tried to adjust to life in a big city. In one of a number of letters Orion printed in his newspaper, he reported home:

> *In going to and from my meals, I go by the way of Broadway—and to cross Broadway is the rub—but once across it is the rub for two or three squares. My plan—and how could I choose another, when there is no other—is to get into the crowd and when I get in I am borne and rubbed and crowded along, and need scarcely trouble myself about using my own legs; and when I get out it seems like I had been pulled to pieces and very badly put together again.*

He soon moved on to Philadelphia, where he visited the grave of Benjamin Franklin—a hero to him and Orion because Franklin, like them, had begun his career as a printer's apprentice—and earned a reputation as a swift and accurate compositor for the *Inquirer*. He spent a long weekend in Washington, D.C., where he found the broad avenues impressive but not the United States senators, "who give the people the benefit of their wisdom and learning for a little glory and eight dollars a day." His views were still those of a small-town Missouri boy far from home: Philadelphia was filled with far too many "abominable foreigners," he told his mother, and he could not get used to the presence of free African-Americans. "I reckon I had better black my face," he wrote, "for in these Eastern States niggers are considerably better than white people."

By the spring of 1854, Sam had had enough of life in the East. He had kept his pledge to his mother not to drink or gamble, but he had managed to send her only a single dollar from his earnings, and now had no home to which to return. His mother and younger brother, Henry, had left Hannibal and moved first to Muscatine, Iowa, and then to Keokuk, where Orion and a new bride now lived and where Orion had opened a print shop. Sam worked there until he realized that his brother would once again be unable to make good on the promise of a weekly salary, then arranged for his first paying job as a writer—a series of travel letters at five dollars each for the *Keokuk Post*, under the pen name of

Samuel L. Clemens in 1851 or 1852, not long before he set out to see the world on his own

Thomas Jefferson Snodgrass—before moving on again to St. Louis, Chicago, and Cincinnati.

In February of 1857, at the age of twenty-one, Sam boarded the steamboat *Paul Jones* bound for New Orleans with the grand ambition of booking passage to Brazil to make his fortune trading in coca plants. Coca was a "vegetable product of miraculous powers," he had been told, "so nourishing and so strength-giving that the natives of the mountains of the Madeira region would tramp up-hill and down all day on a pinch of powdered coca and require no other substance." It was the first of a host of get-rich-quick schemes that would capture his imagination over the coming years. But on his way down the river, an older dream was reawakened—a dream that would permanently alter the direction of his life.

The riverfront at Keokuk, Iowa, as it looked in 1860, five years after Sam moved there briefly to help Orion with a dubious new venture. "He bought a little bit of a job-printing plant," Twain recalled, "—on credit of course—and at once put prices down to where not even the apprentices could get a living out of it."

LIFE ON
THE MISSISSIPPI

When I was a boy, there was but one permanent ambition among my comrades in our village on the west bank of the Mississippi River. That was, to be a steamboatman. We had transient ambitions of other sorts, but they were only transient. When a circus came and went, it left us all burning to become clowns; the first negro minstrel show that came to our section left us all suffering to try that kind of life; now and then we had a hope that if we lived and were good, God would permit us to be pirates. These ambitions faded out, each in its turn; but the ambition to be a steamboatman always remained
—*Life on the Mississippi, 1883*

(opposite) The crowded St. Louis river-front about 1860. "The first time I ever saw St. Louis," Mark Twain recalled, "I could have bought it for six million dollars and it was the mistake of my life that I did not do it."

(below) Horace Bixby points out a dangerous reef to the young Sam, in an illustration by John Harley from Mark Twain's *Life on the Mississippi*, 1883.

Several of Sam Clemens's boyhood friends had already become riverboat pilots—a job that carried with it both status and a handsome salary—and Sam now decided that he should be one, too. It took some persuasion, but Horace Bixby, the pilot of the *Paul Jones*, finally agreed to take him on as a cub pilot, in exchange for the first $500 of his wages.

"I entered upon the small enterprise of 'learning' twelve or thirteen hundred miles of the great Mississippi River with the easy confidence of my time of life," Clemens remembered. "I supposed that all a pilot had to do was to keep his boat in the river, and I did not consider that that could be much of a trick, since it was so wide." But under Bixby's grim and exacting guidance, Sam soon realized just how wrong he had been. A riverboat pilot needed to commit to memory every landmark on both sides of the big river, from New Orleans north to St. Louis and back again. He was also required to anticipate the force of the current going upstream and downstream; know the difference between riffles on the water's surface caused by the wind and those created by dangerous reefs; be able to find the safest channel both in dangerously low water and during the spring "rise," when the whole stream sometimes seemed choked with trees that had fallen in from the constantly changing banks; and make mental notes of the changing depths at every crucial spot where the leadsmen dropped their knotted ropelines into the water and sang out their measurements: "quarter-twain," "half-twain," and the most pleasant sound of all to a pilot, "mark twain," meaning two fathoms or twelve feet—safe water.

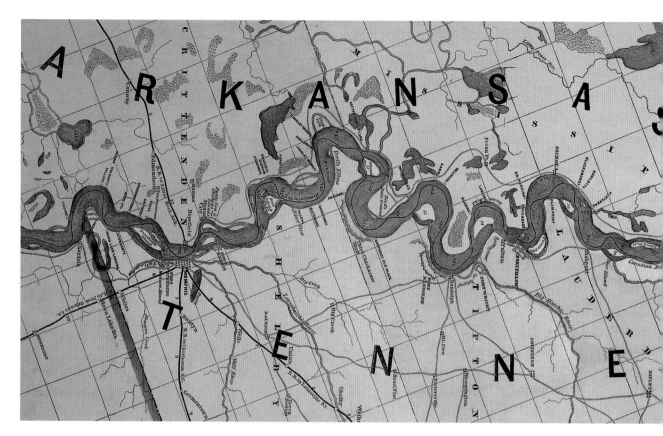

A pilot had to digest all this information—and then be able to apply it, day and night, in clear weather and impenetrable fog. It was like learning the Old and New Testaments by heart, Clemens wrote, and having to be prepared "to recite them glibly, forward or backward, or begin at random anywhere in the book and recite both ways and never trip or make a mistake."

The face of the water, in time, became a wonderful book—a book that was a dead language to the uneducated passenger, but which told its mind to me without reserve, delivering its most cherished secrets as clearly as if it uttered them with a voice. And it was not a book to be read once and thrown aside, for it had a new story to tell every day.

Throughout the long twelve hundred miles there was never a page that was void of interest, never one that you could leave unread, without loss, never one that you would want to skip, thinking you could find higher enjoyment in some other thing. There never was so wonderful a book written by man; never one whose interest was so absorbing, so unflagging, so sparklingly renewed with every re-perusal. . . . In truth, the passenger who could not read this book saw nothing but all manner of pretty pictures in it, painted

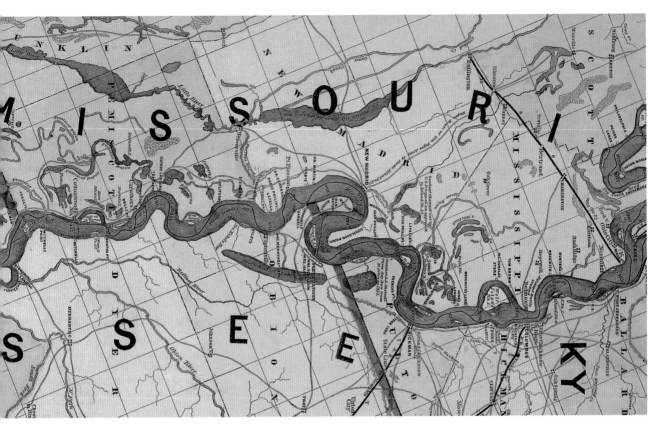

It took five detailed panels like this to trace the twisting course of the Mississippi young Sam Clemens had to memorize in order to become a steamboat pilot. This section, from an 1862 map, begins just above Fort Jefferson, Kentucky, and ends a few miles below Memphis, Tennessee. "The Mississippi," Mark Twain wrote, "is not a commonplace river, but on the contrary is in all ways remarkable. Considering the Missouri its main branch, it is the longest river in the world. . . . It seems safe to say that it is also the crookedest . . . since in one part of its journey it uses up one thousand three hundred miles to cover the same ground that the crow would fly over in six hundred and seventy five."

by the sun and shaded by the clouds, whereas to the trained eye these were not pictures at all, but the grimmest and most dead-earnest of reading-matter.

In the spring of 1858, Orion's mismanaged newspaper and printing business in Iowa had collapsed, and Sam's nineteen-year-old younger brother, Henry, was in need of a new job. Sam, now a cub pilot on the swift side-wheeler *Pennsylvania*, persuaded him to sign on as a clerk. He was grateful for Henry's companionship and happy to get him started on a career, despite a disturbing dream he'd had. In it, he'd seen Henry's corpse in a metal coffin, dressed in one of Sam's own suits with a bouquet of white roses and one red rose on his breast.

On the next trip downriver, Sam got into a violent quarrel with the chief pilot, who he believed had mistreated Henry, and when they arrived at New Orleans Sam was transferred to another riverboat. The brothers agreed to meet at their sister's house in St. Louis, then Henry set out upriver on the *Pennsylvania*.

Sam followed two days later aboard another steamboat, the *A. T. Lacey*. At Greenville, Mississippi, someone shouted from shore that the *Pennsylvania*'s boilers had blown up and she had gone down near Memphis. Some 150 people were said to have perished. In Arkansas, Sam was relieved when he got a newspaper that listed Henry among the uninjured. But farther upriver, he saw corpses bobbing in the water, and another paper listed Henry as hurt beyond hope.

When he finally reached Memphis and rushed to the makeshift hospital where the survivors of the disaster had been taken, Sam found his brother on a pallet on the floor, still alive but badly burned and not expected to survive. Henry had been blown into the water, his lungs scalded by inhaled steam, but had swum back to help save the wounded before a second explosion engulfed him in flames. Some bystanders at the makeshift hospital tried to console Sam, calling him "lucky" because he had not been on the *Pennsylvania* during that fateful trip. "May God forgive them," he wrote his sister-in-law, "for they know not what they say."

Instead, he blamed himself bitterly—for having lured Henry onto the river in the first place, and especially for not being on the scene when his little brother had needed him most. "Long before this reaches you," he wrote to his sister-in-law on June 18,

Henry Clemens, Sam's younger brother, and (below) a portion of the *Missouri Republican*'s June 16, 1858, account of the explosion aboard the steamboat *Philadelphia* that brought about his death

> *my poor Henry, my darling, my pride, my glory, my all, will have finished his blameless career, and the light of my life will have gone out in utter darkness. . . . O, God! this is hard to bear. . . . The horrors of three days have swept over me. They have blasted my youth and left me an old man before my time. Mollie, there are gray hairs in my head tonight. For forty-eight hours I labored at the bedside of my poor burned and bruised but uncomplaining brother, and then the star of my hope went out and left me in the gloom of despair.*
>
> *. . . Pray for me, Mollie, and pray for my poor sinless brother.*
>
> > *Your unfortunate Brother,*
> > *Saml. L. Clemens*

Sam looked on helplessly as his brother drifted in and out of sleep. A physician urged him to ask that an eighth of a grain of morphine be administered if Henry began to toss and turn too much—rest was essential if he was to survive his burns. And so, when the patient awakened and began to writhe in pain on the evening of June 21, Sam stopped a passing doctor—"hardly out of medical school," he recalled—who initially refused to give him the drug because he had no means of measuring out the proper dose. Sam insisted, and the doctor finally poured what Sam remembered as a "vast quantity" of morphine onto the blade of a knife and forced it to Henry's lips. Henry soon drifted back to sleep, then slipped into a coma and finally died. Again, Sam blamed himself, convinced somehow that it was his call for morphine, not the terrible explosion, that had caused his brother's death.

When he came to collect Henry's body for the long, sad journey home, he found that all the dead victims of the disaster had been placed

Additional Particulars
OF THE
Explosion and Burning of the
PENNSYLVANIA!
Two Hundred Lost and Missing.
STATEMENT OF PASSENGERS.
Incidents of the Disaster, &c.

We published yesterday morning a telegraphic statement of the late terrible disaster to the steamer Pennsylvania, bound from New Orleans to this port.

From passengers of the Pennsylvania who arrived in this city by railroad last evening, we have received full statements, to be found below. They embrace all that was known here last evening concerning this awful calamity, but give very few additional names of the lost, missing or saved.

STATEMENT OF MR. W. G. MEPHAM.

The steamer Pennsylvania left New Orleans on the 9th inst., with one hundred and twenty-five cabin passengers and one hundred and fifty-eight deckers She afterwards took on board, at Baton Rouge, Nathez and Vicksburg, 62 passengers, and at Napoleon 10. There were 40 deck hands and firemen; 24 of the steward's crew, and 16 officers—making in all 450 souls.

Out of this number, 182 were rescued by a wood boat, and about 70 others escaped in various ways. These numbers include the wounded and scalded. About 200 are lost and missing.

At about 6 o'clock on the morning of the 13th inst., when the boat was about 70 miles below Memphis, she exploded four of her boilers, while under way. At the time of the explosion, she was near 300 yards from shore. The cabin was torn to pieces forward of her wheel houses. Very few of the passengers were out of their staterooms at the time. The passengers in the after part of the cabin—men, women and chil-in unpainted pine coffins—all but one: the women of Memphis had been so moved by Henry's story that they had raised sixty dollars to buy him a metal casket. Because his clothes had been badly burned, they had asked for some of Sam's clothes to lay him out in. And just as Sam began to recognize this imagery from his earlier dream, an elderly woman appeared bearing a bouquet of white roses with a single red one in the center, and gently placed it on Henry's breast.

A year later, in the spring of 1859, Sam received his official riverboat pilot's certificate. He was soon earning $250 a month—as much, he liked to point out, as the vice president of the United States and certainly far more than Orion, or his father, had ever earned. He became vain about his looks, he recalled, bought expensive clothes, began speculating in commodities, and treated his mother to a trip to New Orleans, where he had developed a taste for fine food—and for whiskey, now that she had released him from his promise to abstain from alcohol.

Sam Clemens's pilot's certificate, issued to him at St. Louis on April 9, 1859

"A pilot, in those days, was the only unfettered and entirely independent human being that lived in the earth," he later recalled. "His movements were entirely free; he consulted no one, he received commands from nobody, he promptly resented even the merest suggestions. . . . So here was the novelty of a king without a keeper, an absolute monarch who was absolute in sober truth and not by a fiction of words."

Nearly a thousand steamboats then plied the Mississippi and its tributaries, carrying more cargo than all the nation's oceangoing vessels combined. Sam would serve on at least eighteen of them, including the *White Cloud,* the *Crescent City,* the *Arago,* the *Aleck Scott,* the *City of Memphis,* and the *John J. Roe,* a boat so slow, he later wrote, that "we used to forget what year it was we left port in. Ferryboats used to lose valuable trips because their passengers grew old and died, waiting for us to get by. . . . She was dismally slow; still, we often had pretty exciting times racing with islands, and rafts, and such things."

Sam also continued to write, producing satirical sketches for newspapers along the Mississippi— one under the pseudonym of Sergeant Fathom—and storing up valuable memories of places, scenes, and people.

When *A Midnight Race on the Missis-sippi* was published by Currier & Ives in 1890, such sights were already history. But in "the flush times of steamboating," Mark Twain recalled, "a race between two notoriously fleet steamers was an event of vast importance." In 1853, the *Eclipse*, shown here running bow-to-bow with the *Natchez*, set a record by running from New Orleans to Cairo, Illinois, in three days, three hours, and twenty minutes. When the *Robert E. Lee* claimed in 1870 to have broken that record, Twain disagreed, pointing out that in the intervening years the ever-changing river had shortened the course by fifty miles.

Steamboating Days

Looking back in Life on the Mississippi *many years later, Mark Twain would lovingly revisit the days when Sam Clemens had been a riverboat pilot.*

If I have seemed to love my subject, it is no surprising thing, for I loved the profession far better than any I have followed since, and I took a measureless pride in it. The reason is plain: a pilot, in those days, was the only unfettered and entirely independent human being that lived in the earth. Kings are but the hampered servants of parliament and people; parliaments sit in chains forged by their constituency; the editor of a newspaper cannot be independent, but must work with one hand tied behind him by party and patrons, and be content to utter only half or two-thirds of his mind; no clergyman is a free man and may speak the whole truth, regardless of his parish's opinions; writers of all kinds are manacled servants of the public. We write frankly and fearlessly, but then we "modify" before we print. In truth, every man and woman and child has a master, and worries and frets in servitude; but in the day I write of, the Mississippi pilot had none. The captain could stand upon the hurricane deck, in the pomp of a very brief authority, and give him five or six orders while the vessel backed into the stream, and then that skipper's reign was over. The moment that the boat was under way in the river, she was under the sole and unquestioned control of the pilot. He could do with her exactly as he pleased, run her when and whither he chose, and tie her up to the bank whenever his judgment said that that course was best. His movements were entirely free; he consulted no one, he received commands from nobody, he promptly resented even the merest suggestions. Indeed, the law of the United States forbade him to listen to commands or suggestions, rightly considering that the pilot necessarily knew better how to handle the boat than anybody could tell him. So here was the novelty of a king without a keeper, an absolute monarch who was absolute in sober truth and not by a fiction of words. I have seen a boy of eighteen taking a great steamer serenely into what seemed almost certain destruction, and the aged captain standing mutely by, filled with apprehension but powerless to interfere. . . . It will easily be guessed, considering the pilot's boundless authority, that he was a great personage in the old steamboating days. He was treated with marked courtesy by the captain and with marked deference by all the officers and servants; and this deferential spirit was quickly communicated to the passengers, too. I think pilots were about the only people I ever knew who failed to show, in some degree, embarrassment in the presence of traveling foreign princes. But then, people in one's own grade of life are not usually embarrassing objects.

By long habit, pilots came to put all their wishes in the form of commands. It "gravels" me, to this day, to put my will in the weak shape of a request, instead of launching it in the crisp language of an order.

The famously slow *John J. Roe* (above), aboard which young Sam Clemens served as pilot: "She was never able to overtake the current," Twain recalled. "But she was a love of a steamboat."

Black firemen stoke a steamboat's boiler. "Mississippi steamboatmen," Twain wrote, "were important in landsmen's eyes (and in their own, too) according to the dignity of the boat they were on. . . . Negro firemen, deck-hands and barbers belonging to these boats were distinguished personages in their grade of life, and they were well aware of that fact, too."

In that brief, sharp schooling, I got personally and familiarly acquainted with about all the different types of human nature that are to be found in fiction, biography, or history. . . . The average shore-employment requires as much as forty years to equip a man with this sort of an education. . . . When I find a well-drawn character in fiction or biography, I generally take a warm personal interest in him, for the reason that I have known him before—met him on the river.

"I loved the profession far better than any I have followed since," Sam later wrote about his riverboat days, "and I took a measureless pride in it." He had assumed then that he would live out his days as a pilot and "die at the wheel when my mission was ended."

But the Civil War began on April 12, 1861. All commercial traffic on the Mississippi stopped. Sam was aboard one of the last steamboats to make it from New Orleans to St. Louis; a shell fired from a Union outpost shattered the glass in her pilothouse as she raced by. Some of his friends, including his old mentor, Horace Bixby, enlisted as pilots for the Union; others, like his boyhood friend Sam Bowen, volunteered their skills to the Confederacy. The Clemens family, too, was divided. Sam's mother made no secret of her hatred for Yankees, but his brother Orion had become a Republican and campaigned for Abraham Lincoln. Sam himself had voted for John Bell of Tennessee—who had run on the platform of preserving both the Union *and* slavery—and he was now ambivalent about the impending conflict, hoping only that it would be over soon so he could return to the river.

Eventually, he went back to Hannibal, where some of the young men with whom he'd once played Robin Hood had formed a small Confederate militia unit called the Marion Rangers. Sam signed on, too, mostly

Sam Clemens, 1858. "Two things seemed pretty apparent to me," he remembered. "One was, that in order to be a pilot a man had got to learn more than any one man ought to be allowed to know; and the other was, that he must learn it all over again in a different way every twenty-four hours."

(above left) The *City of Memphis*, which Clemens helped pilot in the spring of 1860: She is "the largest boat," he wrote home to Orion, "and the hardest to pilot, and consequently I can get a *reputation* on her. . . . The young pilots who used to tell me, patronizingly, that I could never learn the river, cannot keep from showing a little of their chagrin at seeing me so far ahead of them . . . And I must confess that when I go to pay my dues, I rather like to let the d——d rascals get a glimpse of a hundred dollar bill peeping out from among notes of smaller dimensions, whose faces I do *not* exhibit!"

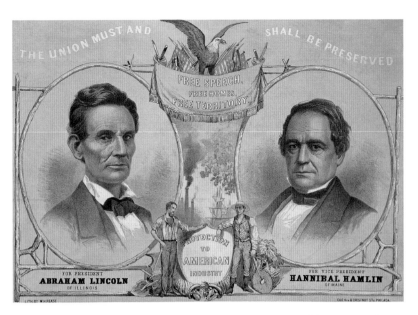

The victory of the national Republican ticket advertised on this lithographed poster in 1860 sparked the Civil War—and indirectly helped turn Sam Clemens from steamboating to literature.

just for something to do. His friends elected him second lieutenant, he remembered; there was no first lieutenant. He was not with them long. Factual details of his time as a rebel soldier are few, but the Marion Rangers seem to have spent most of their time hiding in the woods and fleeing from even the rumor of advancing Union troops. Within two weeks, the homegrown unit disbanded. Most of Sam's friends went on to enlist in the regular Confederate Army. Sam did not. He "skedaddled."

He later wrote:

When I retired from the rebel army in '61 I retired . . . in good order, at least in good enough order for a person who had not yet learned how to retreat according to the rules for war, and had to trust to native genius. It seemed to me that for a first attempt at a retreat it was not badly done. I had done no advancing in all that campaign that was at all equal to it. . . . I knew more about retreating, than the man that invented retreating.

Meanwhile, Orion had befriended Edward Bates, a prominent St. Louis attorney who had become Abraham Lincoln's attorney general, and as a reward for his work on behalf of the Republican Party, Bates had urged the secretary of state to appoint Orion secretary of the new Territory of Nevada. Bates's endorsement had been less than enthusiastic—the best he could bring himself to say for his nominee was that he was "an honest man of fair mediocrity of talents & learning"—but it had been enough to persuade William H. Seward to make the appointment. Sam, now twenty-five years old, begged his brother to take him along—even agreed to pay the stagecoach fare for both of them. Others could go to war. Sam Clemens was going west.

HANNIBAL'S SAM CLEMENS
RON POWERS

Place formed Mark Twain as it has no other American writer. When the seventeen-year-old Sammy Clemens boarded a night packet and slipped off down the Mississippi to St. Louis in June of 1853, he was not leaving his Edenic Hannibal behind (though he would revisit it only six times over the rest of his long life); he had it tightly bundled and stored, inside his prodigious memory.

Hannibal and its environs never left Sam. The town never left him, nor the river, nor the enveloping wilderness. Nor did the voices that floated through these environs like invisible actors on a great dioramic stage. This preserved universe formed a sanctuary for Twain against his epic griefs and rages.

"I can see the farm yet, with perfect clearness," he declares near the beginning of his autobiography, speaking of the acreage owned by his uncle John Quarles. "I can see all its belongings, all its details. The life which I led there . . . was full of charm, and so is the memory of it yet."

Here is a sixty-one-year-old man of the industrialized Gilded Age, writing in Vienna of images that he began storing at age four, on an obscure prairie homestead two decades before the Civil War. Publicly revered now as a literary sage and prophet, privately despairing over bankruptcy and the recent death from meningitis of his beloved eldest daughter, Susy, Mark Twain chooses to reminisce of soil and trees.

"I can call back the prairie, and its loneliness and peace, and a vast hawk hanging motionless in the sky," he writes.

I can see the woods in their autumn dress, the oaks purple, the hickories washed with gold . . . and I can hear the rustle made by the fallen leaves as we plowed through them. I can see the blue clusters of wild grapes hanging among the foliage of the saplings. I know how the wild blackberries looked, and how they tasted . . . and I can feel the thumping rain, upon my head, of hickory nuts and walnuts when we were out in the frosty dawn . . . and the gusts of wind loosed them and sent them down.

He has dined with Kaiser Wilhelm and been toasted as "the Belle of New York." His many works have been collected in a uniform edition. And he is dreaming of hickory nuts.

"I can call it all back," writes Mark Twain, "and make it as real as it ever was, and as blessed."

This trancelike state of old reverie is no digression. It is not a substitute for the writer's necessary work. It is nothing less than the work itself. To Mark Twain, that long-ago farm in Missouri, and the riverside town to which his family soon removed, held the roots of his identity. The farm, the town, the river gestated his literary awakening, and his political and theological formation as well. The boy's native place became an extension of the man.

But not entirely through its "blessed" qualities. If young Sammy Clemens's world had been merely "full of charm," the mature writer might have remained merely the fond "humorist" that many still mistake him to be. Fortunately for American literature, the blessings of that terrain coexisted with curses; the "heavenly place for a boy," as Twain himself described it, sometimes revealed its proximity to hell. Often the two realms were indistinguishable.

With every fresh loss in a lifetime of losses, Mark Twain went rushing back into his past. He seemed bent on recovering a purity in it, a purity banished from the America of speculators and scoundrels, from what he called the "United States of Lyncherdom." But with each new inventorying of his remembered paradise, Mark Twain reencountered images of its dark companion town: a nighttime Hannibal of anxiety, cruelty, murder, and a wrathful God, who spread death in sheets of fire and water. Acknowledging the horrors that lay coiled in his Eden may not have salved Twain's many sorrows, but it lifted his reveries from self-indulgence into literature.

The sunlit Hannibal of Sammy's boyhood was certainly no fiction: a vivid little midcontinent hive of sawmills, slaughterhouses, saloons, tanyards, and sturdy row houses, it lay tucked into a floodplain between two dramatic limestone bluffs overlooking the Mississippi. Circuses passed through town in the summer, and "mesmerizers" and minstrel shows and colorful scoundrels of all kinds, alighting from the steamboats that crowded the levee. Hannibal may have been isolated from the world, but the river brought the world to Hannibal.

Beyond the town's perimeters lay hillside forests of oak and walnut and sycamore, open fields awash in dandelion and columbine and wild ginger. A boy and his friends could commandeer those silent spaces and re-create in them the departed pageants, with themselves as the ringmasters and hypnotists. Not far downriver, snaking beneath several miles of elevated limestone, lay the "crooked aisles" of a vast cave system; a dual source of fascination and terror for a child, the tangible extension of an ambiguous dream.

But Sammy's Hannibal was also a dangerous place. Night-venturing boys could and did drown in that gorgeous river or in the creeks that fed it, entangled in the unseen coopers' hoop-poles set to soak below the surface. (Sammy felt responsible.) Fire claimed other victims: a jailbird, dropping a match spark on his bedding, could be roasted alive in his cell, while Sammy, among others, looked on helplessly. (Sammy always remembered that he had supplied the fatal match.) The high-strung boy also looked on as men shot one another at point-blank range; as a slave-owner brained his human chattel with a lump of iron ore. He studied the bodies of a sister, then a brother, and then of his grim, failed father, all of whom died in their household beds before he reached mid-adolescence. ("Dead brother Ben. My treachery to him," he wrote, cryptically, as an aging man.) He saw

a corpse rise suddenly from its entanglement in the river's sloughs, freed by a shift in the current, to terrify him and his friends as they searched for pecans and berries by the shore.

As surely as Hannibal's sunny delights shaped Mark Twain's metaphors and vision, so did its dark terrors, presided over by the stern and unforgiving God of the local Presbyterian church. They (along with his lifelong guilt) lent the dignity of suffering to his memories of place, and profundity to his antic wit. "The secret source of Humor itself is not joy, but sorrow," the revered "humorist" would write. "There is no humor in heaven."

The power of Sammy's "place" was not limited to its features of terrain or to the pageants and episodes that played themselves out on its surface. An equally great influence on him was the voices: the many and transporting human voices that saturated his consciousness from the cradle onward.

His mother's voice led the rest. Jane Lampton Clemens was an early version of Mark Twain himself. A small, fiery, red-haired backwoods woman, she lacked formal education but was clearly brilliant in a mercurial and quick-witted way. Jane told Sammy bloodcurdling tales of Indian massacres in her frontier past and chilled him with warnings of God's dark wrath. But she also jollied the boy with a dry, wise-cracking patter; the two sparred verbally throughout his boyhood. (Told that Sammy had nearly drowned in Bear Creek one day, she drawled, "People born to be hanged are safe in the water.") Jane gave Sammy a sense of playfulness that his icy, striving father could not. And she gave him the great sense of moral indignation on behalf of the dispossessed that he never lost.

But the voices that truly transformed Sammy—and through him, American literature and American consciousness—were the voices of black men and women and children: his uncle John Quarles's slaves.

Quarles kept about thirty slaves on his farm at Florida, Missouri, a hamlet some thirty miles southwest of Hannibal, where John Marshall and Jane Lampton Clemens arrived in June 1835 from Tennessee. Sammy was born in Florida in November of that year. Sickly and frail through his infancy, he was allowed the run of his relatives' acreage as soon as he was old enough to walk, and some tug of enchantment led the tiny red-haired boy directly into his slaves' demimonde: the fields where they worked and sang by day, the shacks where they cooked and talked by night.

The constant singing, talking voices of the slaves were familiar enough to their white masters, but few of these folks actually listened to the ambient thrum. Sammy listened. He listened at close quarters, perched with clusters of black and white children before the bed where lay the ancient balding Aunt Hannah, a confederate of Moses, it was said, who told of witches. And he sat in the kitchen of Uncle Dan'l, a bright, generous man "whose sympathies were wide and warm and whose heart was honest and simple and knew no guile." While winter flames from the fireplace threw their shadows against the wall, Uncle Dan'l told the children about ghosts and talking animals and magic spells. As the boy gained acceptance in the demimonde, he began to hear less fanciful tales: true laments for husbands and wives and children separated at auction; allusions to escape from bondage; fantasies of vengeance delivered by armies of angels in fiery chariots. "I listened as one who receives a revelation," he later wrote.

The revelations continued by day, in the pantries and the fields, as the slaves sang. Like their captive brethren throughout America, those Missouri slaves sang. And beneath the rhythms and exotic imagery of their songs lay urgency and deep significance. Embedded in the spirituals and jubilees was the complex, deeply coded language formed by a captive culture over two and a quarter centuries. The language, like that of Aunt Hannah and Uncle Dan'l, spoke of the things that mattered most: the separation and distant deaths of loved ones; of visitations from the spirit world; of the hideous floggings they had heard of or endured.

Samuel Clemens never stopped hearing that special language of his native place, or that incantatory music. Nor did he ever question the authenticity of its content. (After all, black people and black voices were the norm in his childhood world, well before he learned from society that they were marginal, infe-

rior.) Like his stored images of the farm and the town, the language of those slaves seems to have remained locked inside his memory, to be released almost verbatim when the writer Mark Twain demanded it.

Twain used that remembered language to bring black Americans into storytelling as characters on an equal footing with white characters. In doing so, he explored the moral dimensions of a race largely considered by white America, until then, as having no moral dimensions. And thus he elevated into legitimacy a race of depersonalized beings, and demonstrated their accountability to fate, their capacity to suffer. It is clear, to take the most famous example, that the great tidal cadences of Jim's voice in *Adventures of Huckleberry Finn* had their origin in Uncle Dan'l's storytelling.

Finally, there was the great synthesizing force in Mark Twain's boyhood place. There was the river.

The Mississippi River prefigured everything else in Sammy's universe. It had drawn the first settlers of Hannibal to its floodplain; it had shaped the character of the young town; and slowly, inexorably, over the thirteen years he lived within sight of it, the Mississippi summoned Sam Clemens onto its all-embracing life.

How could he have resisted? The Mississippi was a wondrous interruption in that landlocked prairie, a fabulous anomaly, a constant *event,* motion in the midst of stasis. To an impressionable, furiously noticing boy, the river touched the deepest symbolic chords: river of life, river of time, river of immortality, river of oblivion.

River as *story.*

The boy and the river understood each other right away.

"The face of the water, in time, became a wonderful book," he wrote of his early steamboating days—"a book that was a dead language to the uneducated passenger, but which told its mind to me without reserve, delivering its most cherished secrets as clearly as if it uttered them with a voice. And it was not a book to be read once and thrown aside, for it had a new story to tell every day."

"Tom at Home," opening-page illustration by True Williams from
The Adventures of Tom Sawyer, 1876

The small boy had fantasized a life on the Mississippi as a pirate or a lion tamer in the circus. In the early 1850s, the young man memorized the river as a prospective pilot. He memorized its bends and depths and nuances over 1,200 miles from St. Louis to New Orleans, and he memorized the reverse of these over the 1,200 miles back. And like the voices of the slaves on his uncle's farm, the river yielded up its deeply coded secrets to him.

"There never was so wonderful a book written by man," he wrote; "never one whose interest was so absorbing, so unflagging, so sparklingly renewed with every re-perusal. The passenger who could not read it was charmed with a peculiar sort of faint dimple on its surface . . . but to the pilot that was an *italicized* passage . . . for it meant that a wreck of a rock was buried there that could tear the life out of the strongest vessel that ever floated."

Learning this great text that was the river, Sam also learned something about learning: "Now when I had mastered the language of this water and had come to know every trifling feature that bordered the great river as familiarly as I knew the letters of the alphabet, I had made a valuable acquisition. But I had lost something too. I had lost something which could never be restored to me while I lived. All the grace, the beauty, the poetry had gone out of the majestic river!"

Here was a uniquely New World perspective: a reverence for the wonderment of innocent experience, and a disenchantment with the rigid conventions of "academic" knowledge, the very kind of suffocating formalism that passed for high culture in old Europe. Like Emerson and Whitman before him, Mark Twain helped liberate American letters from subservience to this past-obsessed ideal. The Mississippi, surging forward and always shifting its channels, became a metaphor for his literary genius. He wrote in a great improvisational flow, on the currents of human voices. His sentences were carefully crafted, stripped of ornamentation and taut with energy. But the structure of his books had the feel of a wayward tide—one event leading meanderingly to another, the plotlines interrupted by digressions like unexpected tributaries, the narrative always overflowing the frame of the story, infinite and dreamy. Like a song in the fields, or a rambling fable in front of a kitchen fireplace. Like a river.

"After all these years I can picture that old time to myself now, just as it was then," wrote Mark Twain from the vantage point of urbane middle age: "the white town drowsing in the sunshine of a summer's morning; the streets empty, or pretty nearly so; one or two clerks sitting in front of the Water Street stores, with their splint-bottomed chairs tilted back against the wall, chins on breasts . . . asleep . . . [and] the great Mississippi, the majestic, the magnificent Mississippi, rolling its mile-wide tide along."

Mark Twain's capacity to conjure up the universe of that white town transformed the literature of America and the world. But that was hardly surprising that he remembered. After all, he had the town tightly bundled and stored, inside his prodigious memory.

CHAPTER THREE

ROUGHING IT

We jumped into the stage, the driver cracked his whip, and we bowled away and left "the States" behind us. . . . There was a freshness and breeziness . . . and an exhilarating sense of emancipation . . . that almost made us feel that the years we had spent in the close, hot city, toiling and slaving, had been wasted and thrown away.

—*Roughing It,* 1872

On July 26, 1861, the Clemens brothers left St. Joseph, Missouri, on the Central Overland and Pike's Peak Express Company stagecoach. Each ticket had cost Sam $150, and they were restricted to fifty pounds of baggage between them. Orion insisted on bringing law books and a six-pound unabridged dictionary. Sam stowed away his pipes, five pounds of tobacco, and a pistol, he said, that "only had one fault—you could not hit anything with it."

They crossed the plains of Kansas, then Nebraska, stopping for five minutes every ten to fifteen miles to change horses at station houses made of sod. "It was the first time," Sam noted, "we had ever seen a man's front yard on top of his house."

We crossed the sand hills near the scene of the Indian mail robbery and massacre of 1856, wherein the driver and conductor perished, and also all the passengers but one, it was supposed; but this must have been a mistake, for at different times afterward on the Pacific coast I was personally acquainted with a hundred and thirty-three or four people who were wounded during that massacre, and barely escaped with their lives. There was no doubt of the truth of it—I had it from their own lips. One of these parties told me that he kept coming across arrow-heads in his system for nearly seven years after the massacre; and another of them told me that he was struck so literally full of arrows that after the Indians were gone and he could raise up and examine himself, he could not restrain his tears, for his clothes were completely ruined.

As the stage rolled through the nights, they slept on the mailbags crammed inside the coach. On warm days, Sam perched on top, clad only in his underwear, drinking in the fresh air and admiring the scenery:

(opposite) Carson City, Nevada Territory, 1865. "It never rains here," Clemens wrote home to his mother after he and Orion got there, "and the dew never falls. No flowers grow here, and no green thing gladdens the eye. The birds that fly over the land carry their provisions with them."

(below) "Worth a Million": Sam Clemens and a fellow silver miner celebrate what turns out to be an illusory fortune, in an illustration from *Roughing It* drawn by True Williams.

*It was comfort . . . to sit up and contemplate the majestic panorama
of mountains and valleys spread out below us and eat ham and
hard boiled eggs while our spiritual natures revelled alternately in
rainbows, thunderstorms, and peerless sunsets. Nothing helps
scenery like ham and eggs. Ham and eggs, and after these a pipe—
an old, rank, delicious pipe—ham and eggs and scenery, a "down-
grade," a flying coach, a fragrant pipe and a contented heart—
these make happiness. It is what all the ages have struggled for.*

He saw his first jackrabbit, his first antelope, his first buffalo and coyote.
Crossing the Continental Divide at South Pass, he saw his first snow in
summertime on the nearby mountains. He shared a meal with a real-life
outlaw, encountered a tribe of Indians, shouted for joy as a Pony Express
rider galloped past. He was having the time of his life.

Then the stage pushed on into the great deserts of Utah and
Nevada.

*Imagine a vast, waveless ocean stricken dead and turned to ashes;
imagine this solemn waste tufted with ash-dusted sage-bushes;
imagine the lifeless silence and solitude that belong to such a
place; imagine a coach, creeping like a bug through the midst of
this shoreless level, and sending up tumbled volumes of dust as if it
were a bug that went by steam; imagine this aching monotony of
toiling and plowing kept up hour after hour, and the shore still as
far away as ever, apparently; imagine team, driver, coach and passengers so deeply coated with ashes that they are all one colorless
color; imagine ash-drifts roosting above moustaches and eyebrows
like snow accumulations on boughs and bushes. This is the reality
of it.*

*. . . There is not the faintest breath of air stirring; there is not a
merciful shred of cloud in all the brilliant firmament; there is not a
living creature visible in any direction whither one searches the
blank level that stretches its monotonous miles on every hand; there
is not a sound—not a sigh—not a whisper—not a buzz, or a whir
of wings, or distant pipe of bird—not even a sob from the lost souls
that doubtless people that dead air.*

When they finally reached the far end of the desert, "we were glad, for
the first time, that the dictionary was along," Sam wrote, "because we
never could have found language to tell how glad we were, in any sort
of dictionary but an unabridged one with pictures in it."

Three weeks after leaving Missouri, the Clemens brothers at last
pulled into Carson City, the raw settlement that was the capital of
Nevada Territory.

(above) The official seal of Nevada Territory, designed by Orion Clemens in the
autumn of 1861. Its Latin inscription—
Volens et Potens—was meant to suggest
both "loyalty to the Union and the wealth
to sustain it."

(opposite) Sam Clemens flanked by two
members of the third Nevada Territorial
Legislature in 1864. At left is Representative William H. Clagett; the man on
the right is Speaker A. J. Simmons, a
sometime silver miner who, Sam told
his mother, was also "the ablest public
speaker in the territory." The inscription,
apparently an allusion to the trio's
raffish appearance, is in Sam's hand.

My dear Mother,

Our city lies in the midst of a desert of the purest, most unadulterated and compromising sand, *in which infernal soil nothing but that fag-end of vegetable creation, "sage-brush," ventures to grow. . . . It . . . is the ugliest plant that was ever conceived of. . . . When crushed, sage brush emits an odor which isn't exactly magnolia and equally isn't exactly polecat, but is a sort of compromise between the two.*

I overheard a gentleman say the other day that this was "the damnedest country under the sun." And that comprehensive conception I fully subscribe to. . . . The country is fabulously rich in gold, silver, copper, lead, coal, iron, quicksilver, . . . thieves, murderers, desperadoes . . . lawyers, Christians, Indians, Chinamen, Spaniards, gamblers, sharpers, coyotes, poets, preachers and jackass rabbits.

Three of the suspected men still in confinement at Aurora. Mark Twain—

As Orion settled in as territorial secretary, Sam quickly came to see that being "secretary to the secretary" was a job with no duties and no pay. Still expecting the Civil War to be over in a few months, and with nothing else to do, he went with a friend to explore Lake Tahoe, a place so beautiful, he wrote his sister, that "whenever I think of it I want to go there and *die.*" They staked a series of timber claims on a stretch of shore they christened Sam Clemens Bay and began dreaming of becoming lumber kings with grand houses overlooking the lake. But on the fourth day, Sam was careless with a campfire, igniting a forest fire that reduced their dreams to ashes. He would have to try something else.

"By and by," he remembered, "I was smitten with the silver fever. . . . Plainly this was the road to fortune. . . . Day in and day out the talk pelted our ears and the excitement waxed hotter and hotter around us. . . . Cart-loads of solid silver bricks, as large as pigs of lead, were arriving from the mills every day, and such sights as that gave substance to the wild talk about me. I succumbed and grew as frenzied as the craziest."

With Orion bankrolling him, Sam joined the hundreds of other men combing the Nevada hills for instant riches—expecting, he confessed, "to find masses of silver lying all about the ground." His search took him to the Esmeralda district, then to the Humboldt region, always with the same result.

> We prospected and took up new claims, put "notices" on them and gave them grandiloquent names. . . . In a little while we owned largely in the "Gray Eagle," the "Columbiana," the "Branch Mint," the "Maria Jane," the "Universe," the "Root-Hog-or-Die," the "Samson and Delilah," the "Treasure Trove," the "Golconda," the "Sultana," the "Boomerang," the "Great Republic," the "Grand Mogul," and fifty other "mines" that had never been molested by a shovel or scratched with a pick. . . . We were stark mad with excitement—drunk with happiness—smothered under mountains of prospective wealth—arrogantly compassionate toward the plodding millions who knew not our marvellous canyon—but our credit was not good at the grocer's.

He stuck to it for more than six months, including one miserable week during which he was forced to take a job in a quartz mill, screening sand with a long-handled shovel. "I was discharged just at the moment that I was going to resign," he wrote. "I could not endure the heavy labor; and on the company's side they did not feel justified in paying me to shovel sand down my back." He would later claim that he and his partners were briefly owners of a multimillion-dollar silver mine—until they lost it to a band of armed claim jumpers. But by September of 1862, all Sam had to show for his time as a prospector was a sore back, blistered hands, and a pile of unpaid debts.

Still, he was determined to make a name and fortune for himself in the West. "I shall never look upon Ma's face again," he wrote Orion, "until I am a rich man." And to his sister Pamela, he bravely reported, "My livelihood must be made in this country—and if I have to wait longer than I expected, let it be so—I have no fear of failure."

Privately, however, as he surveyed his life just before his twenty-seventh birthday, Sam was wracked by self-doubt.

> What to do next?
>
> It was a momentous question. . . . I had gained a livelihood in various vocations, but had not dazzled anybody with my successes; still the list was before me, and the amplest liberty in the matter of choosing, provided I wanted to work—which I did not. . . . I had once been a grocery clerk, for one day, but had consumed so much sugar in that time that I was relieved from further duty by the proprietor. . . . I had studied law an entire week, and then given it up because it was so prosy and tiresome. I had engaged briefly in the study of blacksmithing, but wasted so much time trying to fix the bellows so that it would blow itself, that the master turned me adrift

in disgrace. . . . I had been a bookseller's clerk for awhile, but the customers bothered me so much I could not read with any comfort, and so the proprietor gave me a furlough and forgot to put a limit to it. I had clerked in a drug store part of a summer, but my prescriptions were unlucky, and we appeared to sell more stomach pumps than soda water. . . . I had been a private secretary, a silver miner and a silver mill operative, and amounted to less than nothing in each, and now—

What to do next?

A stagecoach about to set forth from the Wells Fargo Express Office on C Street in Virginia City, 1866. "Money was as plenty as dust," Twain recalled of his days there; "every individual considered himself wealthy, and a melancholy countenance was nowhere to be seen. . . . The 'flush times' were in magnificent flower!"

MARK TWAIN

He would find his answer in Virginia City, a Nevada boomtown built atop the richest body of silver ore ever discovered in America, the Comstock Lode. The wide-open town was home to a dozen breweries, saloons at every turn, a half-dozen jailhouses, he wrote, "and [there was] some talk of building a church."

Virginia City was also the home of the *Territorial Enterprise,* Nevada's first and most successful newspaper, with the largest circulation of any paper between Chicago and San Francisco. Sam had contributed a few stories to the *Enterprise* during his mining days. Now he was offered the full-time job of local reporter at twenty-five dollars a week. He threw himself into the work.

> *I canvassed the city . . . and found one wretched old hay truck dragging in from the country. But I made affluent use of it. I multiplied it by sixteen, brought it into town from sixteen different directions, made sixteen separate items out of it, and got up such a sweat about hay as Virginia City had never seen in the world before.*
>
> *This was encouraging. . . . Presently, when things began to look dismal again, a desperado killed a man in a saloon and joy returned once more. I never was so glad over any mere trifle in my life. . . .*
>
> *Next I discovered some emigrant wagons going into camp on the plaza and found that they had lately come through the hostile Indian country and had fared rather roughly. I made the best of the item that the circumstances permitted, and felt that if I were not confined within rigid limits by the presence of the reporters of the other papers I could add particulars that would make the article much more interesting. However, I found one wagon that was going on to California, and made some judicious inquiries of the proprietor. When I learned . . . that he . . . would not be in the city the next day to make trouble, I got ahead of the other papers, for I took down his list of names and added his party to the killed and wounded. Having more scope here, I put this wagon through an Indian fight that to this day has no parallel in history.*
>
> *My two columns were filled. When I read them over in the morning I felt that I had found my legitimate occupation at last. I reasoned within myself that news, and stirring news, too, was what a paper needed, and I felt that I was peculiarly endowed with the ability to furnish it. . . . I felt that I could take my pen and murder all the immigrants on the plains if need be and the interests of the paper demanded it.*

Sam Clemens loved the reporter's life. He haunted saloons, theaters, whorehouses, and police stations for bits of information; drank, smoked, and played cards and billiards with other newsmen late into the night;

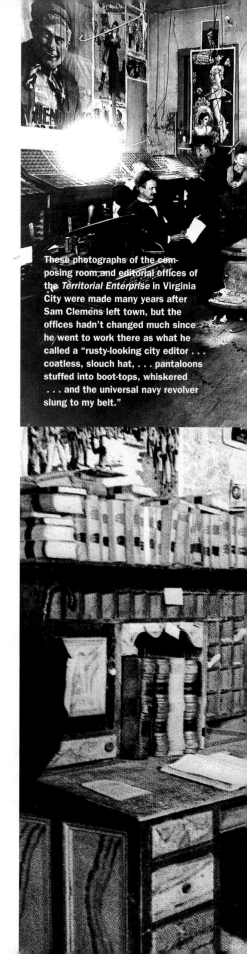

These photographs of the composing room and editorial offices of the *Territorial Enterprise* in Virginia City were made many years after Sam Clemens left town, but the offices hadn't changed much since he went to work there as what he called a "rusty-looking city editor . . . coatless, slouch hat, . . . pantaloons stuffed into boot-tops, whiskered . . . and the universal navy revolver slung to my belt."

A Profound Sensation

The most celebrated of Sam Clemens's hoaxes was this story, printed in the Territorial Enterprise *on October 4, 1862.*

A petrified man was found some time ago in the mountains south of Gravelly Ford. Every limb and feature of the stony mummy was perfect, not even excepting the left leg, which had evidently been a wooden one during the lifetime of the owner— which lifetime, by the way, came to a close about a century ago, in the opinion of a savant who has examined the defunct. The body was in a sitting posture, and leaning against a huge mass of croppings; the attitude was pensive, the right thumb resting against the side of the nose; the left thumb partially supported the chin, the fore-finger pressing the inner corner of the left eye and drawing it partly open; the right eye was closed and the fingers of the right hand spread apart. This strange freak of nature created a profound sensation in the vicinity, and our informant states that by request, Justice Sewell or Sowell, of Humboldt City, at once proceeded to the spot and held an inquest on the body. The verdict of the jury was that "deceased came to his death from protracted expo- sure," etc. The people of the neighborhood volunteered to bury the poor unfortunate, and were even anxious to do so; but it was discovered, when they attempted to remove him, that the water which had dripped upon him for ages from the crag above, had coursed down his back and deposited a limestone sediment under him which had glued him to the bedrock upon which he sat, as with a cement of adamant, and Judge S. refused to allow the charitable citizens to blast him from his position. The opinion expressed by his Honor that such a course would be little less than sacrilege, was eminently just and proper. Everybody goes to see the stone man, as many as three hundred having visited the hardened creature during the past five or six weeks.

New Year's Day

Territorial Enterprise, **January 1, 1863**   Now is the accepted time to make your regular annual good resolutions. Next week you can begin paving hell with them as usual. Yesterday, everybody smoked his last cigar, took his last drink, and swore his last oath. To-day, we are a pious and exemplary community. Thirty days from now, we shall have cast our reformation to the winds and gone to cutting our ancient short comings considerably shorter than ever. We shall also reflect pleasantly upon how we did the same old thing last year about this time. However, go in, community. New Year's is a harmless annual institution, of no particular use to anybody save as a scapegoat for promiscuous drunks, and friendly calls, and humbug resolutions, and we wish you to enjoy it with a looseness suited to the greatness of the occasion.

and poked fun at politicians and rival reporters in his columns. And when there was no news, he had a good time making some up. Once he reported the discovery of a "petrified man" in Nevada—a corpse supposedly preserved for a century by limestone sediments. Close readers noted that the corpse was frozen in a posture of thumbing its nose and winking one eye and understood that the story was a hoax, but gullible newspaper editors around the nation reprinted it as if it were true.

Artemus Ward, then the most popular humorist in America, passed through town on a lecture tour, ended up staying for three weeks after striking up a friendship with Sam, and tried to persuade him to take his budding talents back east. Meanwhile, Sam's standing at the *Territorial Enterprise* continued to grow. His editor raised his salary—to six dollars a day, he wrote his mother, for only three dollars' worth of work. "I am prone to boast of having the widest reputation as a local editor, of any man on the Pacific coast," he told her. "Everybody knows me, & I fare like a prince wherever I go, be it on this side of the mountains or the other. And I am proud to say I am the most conceited ass in the Territory."

With his new career taking off, Sam Clemens decided to take on a new pen name. In his younger days he had signed his newspaper stories with a variety of pseudonyms: W. Epaminondas Adrastus Blab, Thomas Jefferson Snodgrass, Rambler, Sergeant Fathom. More recently, his Nevada stories had appeared under the name Josh. But on February 3, 1863, Clemens tried out a different pen name, drawn from his days on the Mississippi—one that would stick with him the rest of his life and eventually become the most celebrated in American literature. At the

The humorist "Artemus Ward"—whose real name was Charles Farrar Browne—had begun his career setting type, just as Sam Clemens had. His writings—filled with terrible puns and exaggerated misspellings—were much admired by Abraham Lincoln, and he was among the first to encourage Clemens to become a writer. After he died at thirty-three, Mark Twain remembered him as "one of the gentlest and kindest men in the world."

end of a humorous dispatch from Carson City to the *Territorial Enterprise,* he signed himself "Yours, dreamily, Mark Twain."

By the spring of 1864, with articles by Mark Twain beginning to appear regularly in California newspapers and occasionally in the East, even some old friends started calling him Mark instead of Sam, and he was using his new pen name to sign some of the letters he sent home to his family, along with regular contributions of twenty dollars to help his mother. But he was restless again. "I began to get tired of staying in one place so long," he wrote. "There was no longer satisfying variety in going down to Carson to report the proceedings of the legislature once a year, and horse-races and pumpkin shows once in three months. . . . I wanted to go somewhere. I wanted—I did not know *what* I wanted. I had the 'spring fever' and wanted a change."

In May, when a running feud with a rival newspaperman threatened to spill off the news pages and deteriorate into a duel to the death, Sam gladly took his editor's advice to leave the territory until things quieted down, and moved on to what he would call "the most cordial and sociable city in the Union": San Francisco.

> *For a few months I enjoyed what to me was an entirely new phase of existence—a butterfly idleness; nothing to do, nobody to be responsible to, and untroubled with financial uneasiness. . . . After the sagebrush and alkali deserts of [Nevada], San Francisco was Paradise to me. I lived at the best hotel, exhibited my clothes in the most conspicuous places, infested the opera. . . . I attended private parties in sumptuous evening dress, simpered and aired my graces like a born beau, and polked and schottisched with a step peculiar to myself—and the kangaroo. In a word, I kept the due state of a man worth a hundred thousand dollars (prospectively,). . . . I spent money with a free hand, and meantime watched the stock sales with an interested eye.*

Clemens had brought with him from Nevada a trunk filled with stock certificates given to him by mining officials whose activities he had covered as a reporter—a common practice in those days. His intention was to hold on to them until their prices peaked, then sell and make a killing. While he waited, he went to work for the *Morning Call* at forty dollars a week, wrote occasional pieces for a literary journal, the *Golden Era,* and began carousing with San Fran-

what I sang is of no consequence to anybody. It was only a graceful little gem from the horse opera.

At about two o'clock in the morning the pleasant party broke up and the crowd of guests distributed themselves around town to their respective homes; and after thinking the fun all over again, I went to bed at four o'clock. So, having been awake forty-eight hours, I slept forty-eight, in order to get even again, which explains the proposition I began this letter with.

Yours, dreamily, MARK TWAIN.

The first appearance in print of the pen name "Mark Twain," *Territorial Enterprise,* **February 3, 1863**

Five shares in a Nevada silver mine, given to Sam Clemens in 1863: "Stocks went on rising," he remembered, "bankers, merchants, lawyers, doctors, mechanics, laborers, even the very washerwomen and servant girls were putting up their earnings on silver stocks. . . . What a gambling carnival it was!"

San Francisco as seen from Nob Hill by the French lithographer Isador Laurent Denoy in 1860. "After the sage-brush and alkali deserts of Washoe," Twain wrote, "San Francisco was Paradise to me."

Among the assignments Mark Twain's San Francisco editors gave him were the earthquakes, large and small, that made life in San Francisco so unpredictable. No matter how often they occurred, he managed to find something fresh to say about them.

Another of Them

*The San Francisco Daily Morning Call,
June 23, 1864* At five minutes to nine o'clock last night, San Francisco was favored by another earthquake. There were three distinct shocks, two of which were very heavy, and appeared to have been done on purpose, but the third did not amount to much. Heretofore our earthquakes—as all old citizens experienced in this sort of thing will recollect—have been distinguished by a soothing kind of undulating motion, like the roll of waves on the sea, but we are happy to state that they are shaking her up from below now. The shocks last night came straight up from that direction; and it is sad to reflect, in these spiritual times, that they might possibly have been freighted with urgent messages from some of our departed friends. The suggestion is worthy a moment's serious reflection, at any rate.

The Boss Earthquake

*The San Francisco Daily Morning Call,
July 22, 1864* When we contracted to report for this newspaper, the important matter of two earthquakes a month was not considered in the salary. There shall be no mistake of that kind in the next contract, though. Last night, at twenty minutes to eleven, the regular semi-monthly earthquake, due the night before, arrived twenty-four hours behind time, but it made up for the delay in uncommon and alto-

gether unnecessary energy and enthusiasm. The first effort was so gentle as to move the inexperienced stranger to the expression of contempt and brave but very bad jokes; but the second was calculated to move him out of his boots, unless they fitted him neatly. Up in the third story of this building the sensation we experienced was as if we had been sent for and were mighty anxious to go. The house seemed to waltz from side to side with a quick motion, suggestive of sifting corn meal through a sieve; afterward it rocked grandly to and fro like a prodigious cradle, and in the meantime several persons started downstairs to see if there were anybody in the street so timid as to be frightened at a mere earthquake. The third shock was not important, as compared with the stunner that had just preceded it. That second shock drove people out of the theatres by dozens. At the Metropolitan, we are told that Franks, the comedian, had just come on the stage, (they were playing the "Ticket-of-Leave Man,") and was about to express the unbounded faith he had in May; he paused until the jarring had subsided, and then improved and added force to the text by exclaiming, "It will take more than an earthquake to shake my faith in that woman!" And in that, Franks achieved a sublime triumph over the elements, for he "brought the house down," and the earthquake couldn't. From the time the shocks commenced last night, until the windows had stopped rattling, a minute and a half had elapsed.

No Earthquake

The San Francisco Daily Morning Call,
August 23, 1864 In consequence of the warm, close atmosphere which smothered the city at two o'clock yesterday afternoon, everybody expected to be shaken out of their boots by an earthquake before night, but up to the hour of our going to press the supernatural bootjack had not arrived yet. That is just what makes it so unhealthy—the earthquakes are getting so irregular. When a community get used to a thing, they suffer when they have to go without it. However, the trouble cannot be remedied; we know of nothing that will answer as a substitute for one of those convulsions—to an unmarried man.

Earthquake

The San Francisco Daily Morning Call,
September 8, 1864 The regular semi-monthly earthquake arrived at ten minutes to ten o'clock, yesterday morning. Thirty-six hours ahead of time. It is supposed it was sent earlier, to shake up the Democratic State Convention, but if this was the case, the calculation was awkwardly made, for it fell short by about two hours. The Convention did not meet until noon. Either the earthquake or the Convention, or both combined, made the atmosphere mighty dense and sulphurous all day. If it was the Democrats alone, they do not smell good, and it certainly cannot be healthy to have them around.

cisco's leading writers: Ambrose Bierce, Joaquin Miller, and Bret Harte, whose mining-camp tales were about to gain him international fame.

September 25th, 1864. My dear Mother and Sister,

You can see by my picture that this superb climate agrees with me. And it ought, after living where I was never out of sight of snow peaks twenty-four hours during three years. Here we have neither snow nor cold weather, fires are never lighted and yet summer clothes are never worn, you wear spring clothing the year round. . . .

I am taking life easy now and I mean to keep it up for awhile. I don't work at night any more. I told the Call *folks to pay me $25 a week and let me work only in daylight. So I get up at ten every morning and quit work at five or six in the afternoon. . . . I work as I always did, by fits and starts. . . .*

I have engaged to write for the new literary paper, the Californian. *Same pay I used to receive on the* Golden Era. *One article a week, fifty dollars a month. I quit the* Era *long ago. It wasn't high-toned enough. The* Californian *circulates among the highest class*

The "regular, semi-monthly" San Francisco earthquakes Mark Twain described continued right on schedule. An artist friend of his named Edward Jump captured the chaos that accompanied the October 8, 1865, version in this lithograph, but Clemens took it in his stride: As soon as "the ground seemed to roll under me in waves," he wrote, "I knew what it was . . . and from mere reportorial instinct took out my watch and noted the time of day."

EARTH *QUAKEY* TIMES,
SAN FRANCISCO, OCT. 8, 1865.

of the community and is the best weekly literary paper in the United States. And I suppose I ought to know.

San Francisco, Twain wrote, was "Heaven on the half shell." But he took life so easily that he failed to keep track of his mining stocks, and when the Nevada boom ended, they were almost worthless. "I was an early beggar and a thorough one," he remembered. "I, the cheerful idiot that had been squandering money like water, and thought myself beyond the reach of misfortune, had not now as much as fifty dollars."

He was also having trouble with his editor at the *Morning Call.* When Twain wrote an article denouncing mob violence toward Chinese immigrants, the paper wouldn't run it. He wrote another, attacking brutality and corruption in the San Francisco police department, and when that story was also killed, sent

it for publication to his old Virginia City newspaper, the *Territorial Enterprise*, where it resulted in a libel suit.

In October of 1864, his editor quietly let him go.

For two months my sole occupation was avoiding acquaintances; for during that time I did not earn a penny, or buy an article of any kind, or pay my board. I became very adept at "slinking." I slunk from back street to back street, I slunk away from approaching faces that looked familiar, I slunk to my meals, ate them humbly and with a mute apology for every mouthful I robbed my generous land-lady of, and at midnight, after wanderings that were but slinkings away from cheerfulness and light, I slunk to my bed. I felt meaner, and lowlier and more despicable than the worms. During all this time I had but one piece of money—a silver ten cent piece—and I held to it and would not spend it on any account, lest the con-sciousness coming strong upon me that I was entirely penniless might suggest suicide.

Then, a friend named Jim Gillis invited him to visit some mining camps in the Sierra foothills. For the next three months, Clemens did a little prospecting but spent most of his time huddled inside against the winter rains, reading from Gillis's well-stocked library and making notes in a journal.

January 23rd, 1865. Rainy, stormy. Beans and dishwater for break-fast . . . dishwater & beans for dinner, & both articles warmed over for supper.
January 24th: Rained all day—meals as before.
January 25th: Same as above.
January 26th: Rain, beans & dishwater.
January 27th: Same old diet—same old weather

One day, sitting near the stove at a place called Angels Camp in Cala-veras County, he listened intently—and took a few cryptic notes—as a man named Ben Coon told an old story about how an incurable gambler who would bet on anything, even his jumping frog, was outwitted by a seemingly naive stranger who fed the frog buckshot to keep it from getting off the ground. Twain recast the simple story into a much more elaborate and comic tale and sent it east to his friend Artemus Ward.

Meanwhile, he returned to San Francisco, where he learned that the Civil War was finally over. He wanted to go home. "I am tired of being a beggar," he wrote Orion, "tired of being chained to this accursed homeless desert. I want to go back to a Christian land once more." But after more than four years away, his pride would not allow him even to consider returning home again a failure. Nothing seemed to work out

(opposite top) Sam Clemens's San Fran-cisco was an overwhelmingly masculine place. F. Gilbert's "Melodeon" block (left) included a saloon, a "segar" store, and a theater that promised "freedom from con-strained etiquette" and featured the kind of rough-and-tumble minstrel entertain-ment advertised in the upstairs windows.

(opposite bottom) Warm weekends drew hundreds of fishermen to Long Bridge in search of smelt.

for him. He was jailed for being drunk in public, put a revolver to his head, and almost pulled the trigger. "Many times I have been sorry I did not succeed," he wrote years later, "but I was never ashamed of having tried."

Just then, his luck began to change. Unbeknownst to Clemens, Artemus Ward had submitted his jumping-frog story to the *New York Saturday Press,* which had published it to rave reviews. Up and down the East Coast, all across the Midwest, other newspapers were reprinting it. "The foremost among the merry gentlemen of the California press, as far as we have been able to judge," said a writer for the *New York Round Table,* "is one who signs himself 'Mark Twain.' He is, we believe, quite a young man, and has not written a great deal. Perhaps, if he will husband his resources and not kill with overwork the mental goose that has given us these golden eggs, he may one day rank among the brightest of our wits."

In a letter to his mother, Clemens downplayed his story and the small stir it had created—calling it a "villainous backwoods sketch"—but was also careful to include a particularly admiring review. "I wish I was back there piloting up and down the river again," he assured her. "I was aware that it was only the frog that was celebrated," he recalled. "It wasn't I. I was still an obscurity."

But to his brother, Sam admitted that what had started out as a three-month trip to the West by a temporarily unemployed riverboat pilot had become something else.

> I never had but two powerful *ambitions in my life. One was to be a pilot, & the other a preacher of the gospel. I accomplished the one & failed in the other,* because *I could not supply myself with the necessary stock in trade—i.e., religion. . . . But I have had a "call" to literature, of a low order—i.e. humorous. It is nothing to be proud of, but it is my strongest suit. . . .*
>
> *It is only now, when editors of standard literary papers in the distant East give me high praise, & do not know me . . . that I really begin to believe there must be something in it.*

On March 13, 1866, Mark Twain arrived in Honolulu, the capital of what was then called the Sandwich Islands, an independent kingdom. He was thirty now, and his growing reputation had earned him a plum assignment: writing about Hawaii for the *Sacramento Union,* which hoped the rising star of Western journalism could entertain and inform its readers with a series of lively travel letters.

Twain didn't disappoint. "At noon," he wrote, "I observed a bevy of nude native young ladies bathing in the sea, and went and sat down on their clothes to keep them from being stolen. I begged them to come out,

(opposite top) Honolulu and its harbor, here photographed by Hugo Stangenwald from the tower of Kawaiaho Church about 1853, had changed little by the time Sam Clemens got there thirteen years later. "After two thousand miles of watery solitude," he wrote, "the vision was a welcome one."

(opposite bottom) Wipe-out: "I got the board placed right but missed the connection," Mark Twain wrote of his first (and only) attempt at surfing. "The board struck the shore in three quarters of a second, without any cargo, and I struck the bottom at the same time, with a couple of barrels of water in me. None but natives ever master the art of surf-bathing thoroughly." Illustration from *Roughing It* by E. F. Mullen, 1872

for the sea was rising and I was satisfied that they were running some risk. But they were not afraid, and presently went on with their sport."

It was his first glimpse of the world beyond America, and the dispatches he sent back to his California readers were filled with his fascination for the place he called "the land of happy contentment . . . the only supremely delightful place on earth." During his four-month visit he toured Oahu on horseback, inspected the sugar plantations of Maui, had an audience with King Kamehameha V, hiked down into the volcanic crater of Mount Kilauea'—and began to develop what would become a lifelong skepticism about the role of Protestant missionaries.

Near by is an interesting ruin—the meagre remains of an ancient heathen temple—a place where human sacrifices were offered up in those old bygone days . . . long, long before the missionaries braved a thousand privations to come and make [the islanders] permanently miserable by telling them how beautiful and how blissful a

FROM THE SANDWICH ISLANDS

(CORRESPONDENCE OF THE UNION.)

KEALAKEKUA Bay, July, 1866.

A Funny Scrap of History.

In my last I spoke of the old cocoanut stump, all covered with copper plates bearing inscriptions commemorating the visits of various British naval commanders to Captain Cook's death place at Kealakekua Bay. The most magniloquent of those is that left by "the Right Hon. Lord George Paulet, to whom, as the representative of Her Britannic Majesty Queen Victoria, the Sandwich Islands were ceded, February 25, 1843."

Lord George, if he is alive yet, would like to tear off that plate and destroy it, no doubt. He was fearfully snubbed by his Government, shortly afterward, for his acts as Her Majesty's representative upon the occasion to which he refers with such manifest satisfaction.

The opening of one of the Sandwich Islands dispatches to the *Sacramento Union* that made Mark Twain a household name in California in 1866

(right) The Honolulu Sailor's Home, photographed by Hugo Stangenwald. It was built by the American Seaman's Friend Society in an effort to provide a snug—and morally upright—haven for seamen as "close to the beach as possible." "Society is a queer medley in this notable missionary, whaling and governmental centre," Twain wrote. "I am now personally acquainted with seventy-two captains and ninety-six missionaries. The captains and ministers form one-half of the population; the third fourth is composed of common Kanakas and mercantile foreigners and their families, and the final fourth is made up of high officers of the Hawaiian Government. And there are just about cats enough for three apiece all around."

Kawaiaho Church, an early missionary stronghold in Honolulu. "The missionaries have Christianized and educated all the natives," Twain wrote. "All this ameliorating cultivation has at last built up in the native women a profound respect for chastity—in other people."

Sam Clemens reported to his mother and sister that he had visited the Iolani Palace in Honolulu (left) after dining with the king's Grand Chamberlain, who, "although darker than a mulatto," had "an excellent education and in manners is an accomplished gentleman."

King Kamehameha III (center) and members of the Hawaiian royal family, photographed by Hugo Stangenwald in 1852. By the time Sam Clemens landed in the Sandwich Islands, Prince Lot (top right) reigned as King Kamehameha V, and Princess Victoria Kamamalu (front row, left) had become the heir presumptive to the throne. When she died suddenly, Clemens attended her funeral and described the month-long mourning period that followed: "During all that time a great multitude of natives from the several islands . . . kept the palace grounds well crowded and had made the place a pandemonium every night with their howlings and wailings, beating of tom-toms and dancing of the (at other times) forbidden hula-hula by half-clad maidens to the music of questionable decency chanted in honor of the deceased."

The Aldrich House, photographed by Charles Weed in 1865, offered boarders the services of a "First-Class Sausagemaker." The Americanization of Hawaii was already well under way.

place heaven is, and how nearly impossible it is to get there; and showed the poor native how dreary a place perdition is and what unnecessarily liberal facilities there are for going to it . . . showed him what rapture it is to work all day long for fifty cents to buy food for the next day with, as compared with fishing for a pastime and lolling in the shade through eternal Summer, and eating of the bounty that nobody labored to provide but Nature. How sad it is to think of the multitudes who have gone to their graves in this beautiful island and never knew there was a hell!

His reports from Hawaii were a hit in California, and when he returned to San Francisco, a friend suggested he make the most of it by going into the lecture business. Twain was reluctant at first. The prospect of failing before a live audience terrified him. But he borrowed $50 to rent the Academy of Music on Pine Street, and $150 more to print advertisements that were soon showing up all over San Francisco. "Doors open at 7 o'clock," they said. "The Trouble to begin at 8."

He got to the theater early on the evening of the performance, October 2, 1866, so nervous that he hadn't eaten all day. "The house was gloomy and silent," he remembered, "its emptiness depressing. . . . I was very miserable and scared." He went backstage and sat in the darkness for an hour and a half, contemplating his impending failure. Then, on the other side of the curtain, he heard the murmur of people filing into their seats. It grew louder and louder. People began to stamp their feet and cheer. His readers were eager to see and hear him in person.

Before I well knew what I was about, I was in the middle of the stage, staring at a sea of faces, bewildered by the fierce glare of the lights, and quaking in every limb with a terror that seemed like to take my life away. The house was full, aisles and all!

The tumult in my heart and brain and legs continued a full minute before I could gain any command over myself. Then I recognized the charity and the friendliness in the faces before me, and little by little my fright melted away, and I began to talk.

He talked for a little over an hour, to a crowd that a local reviewer described as "one of the most fashionable audiences it was ever my privilege to witness." Even the state's governor was there. Everyone expected to laugh—Twain was known to the crowd

Amusements.

MAGUIRE'S ACADEMY OF MUSIC

The Sandwich Islands!

MARK TWAIN,

(Honolulu Correspondent of the Sacramento Union) will deliver a

Lecture on the Sandwich Islands,

AT THE ACADEMY OF MUSIC,

ON TUESDAY EVENING, OCTOBER 2,

In which passing mention will be made of Harris, Bishop Staley, the American Missionaries, etc. and the absurd Customs and Characteristics of the Natives duly discussed and described. The great VOLCANO OF KILAUEA will also receive proper attention.

A SPLENDID ORCHESTRA
Is in town, but has not been engaged.
ALSO,
A DEN OF FEROCIOUS WILD BEASTS
Will be on Exhibition in the next Block.
MAGNIFICENT FIREWORKS
Were in contemplation for this occasion, but the idea has been abandoned.
A GRAND TORCHLIGHT PROCESSION
May be expected; in fact, the public are privileged to expect whatever they please.

Dress Circle..............$1 | Family Circle......50 cts.
Doors open at 7 o'clock. The Trouble to begin at 8 o'clock.
Box Office open Monday, at 9 o'clock, when seats may be secured without extra charge. se28-td

primarily as a humorist—and he fulfilled their expectations. His talk was peppered with amusing asides about the native customs of the Sandwich Islanders as well as about the missionaries who were laboring to "reform" them, all delivered informally in a slow Missouri drawl, one listener said, "as if he had been addressing a few boys in a cellar." But he also surprised his audience with his vivid powers of description. "At times," the *Alta California* reported, "he would soar to the sublime, and his description of the volcano of Kilauea was as graphic and magnificent a piece of word painting as we have listened to for many a day."

The evening was a triumph. It "established his reputation as an eccentric lecturer," wrote Bret Harte. "His humor . . . is . . . of the western character of ludicrous exaggeration and audacious statement, which perhaps is more thoroughly national and American than even the Yankee delineations of [James Russell] Lowell." And it netted him $400—far more in one night than he had been paid in a month as a riverboat pilot. He quickly set off to duplicate his success across northern California and western Nevada, delivering sixteen lectures in the space of a month.

> *November 2nd, 1866.*
> *Dear Mother,*
>
> *I have lectured in San Francisco, Sacramento, Marysville, Grass Valley, Nevada [City], You Bet, Red Dog & Virginia [City]. I am going to talk in Carson, Gold Hill, Silver City, Dayton, & Washoe. . . . They offer me a full house & no expenses in Dayton—go there next.*
>
> *Sandy Baldwin says I have made the most sweeping success of any man he knows of.*
>
> > *Love to all.*
> > *Yours,*
> > *Mark*

He was an entertainer now, a performer as well as a writer. In December of 1866—after giving a sold-out farewell lecture in Congress Hall and with a new assignment to provide fifty travel letters to the *Alta California* for twenty dollars each—Mark Twain sailed away from San Francisco. The West, he believed, was no longer big enough for his talents. "Make your mark in New York, and you are a made man," he wrote. "With a New York endorsement you may travel the country over, without fear—but without it you are speculating on a dangerous issue."

(opposite) The advertisement Mark Twain wrote for his first lecture; and Maguire's Opera House—originally Maguire's Academy of Music—where he made his terrified stage debut. "All the papers were kind in the morning," he recalled. "My appetite returned; I had abundance of money. All's well that ends well."

CHAPTER FOUR

INNOCENTS ABROAD

May 26th, 1867
To the editors of the Alta California.
. . . They do not treat women with as much deference in New York as
we of the provinces think they ought. This is painfully apparent in
the street-cars. . . . The over-crowding of the cars has impelled men
to adopt the rule of hanging on to a seat when they get it, though
twenty beautiful women came in and stood in their midst. . . . When
I am with the Romans I try to do as the Romans do. I generally
succeed reasonably well. I have got so that I can sit still and let a
homely old maid stand up and nurse her poodle till she is ready to
drop, but the young and the blooming, alas! are too many for me.
I have to get up and vacate the premises when they come. Someday,
though, maybe, I shall acquire a New York fortitude and be as
shameless as any.

(opposite) **Mark Twain would take a professionally detached view of most of the Old World's treasures during the 1867 voyage of the *Quaker City*, but he was so anxious to see the Acropolis that he and three other passengers went ashore under cover of darkness and in defiance of a cholera quarantine to have a look. "I remember but little about the Parthenon," Twain wrote, but he was dazzled by the view from the hilltop: "A vision! And such a vision! Athens by moonlight!"**

(below) **In this 1866 photograph, made near New York's City Hall by E. & H. T. Anthony & Company, posters trumpet attractions at Barnum's Museum, Niblo's Garden, the Olympic Theater, and the Union Course racetrack—all familiar to Sam Clemens.**

In the thirteen years since Sam's first visit to Manhattan, the city's population had jumped 250,000 to more than 1 million. Prices for everything were too high, Sam complained: theater tickets were $1.50, a pint of roasted peanuts 20 cents; hiring a carriage for the day cost $12. "And I suppose," he added, "they would tax you to let you blow your nose anywhere within the city limits."

"The only trouble about this town," Twain wrote, "is that it is too large." Mark Twain had become an important figure in San Francisco. In New York, Sam Clemens was just another face in the crowd. "It is a splendid desert," he wrote, "a domed and steepled solitude, where the stranger is lonely in the midst of a million of his race."

A man walks his tedious miles through the same
interminable street every day, elbowing his way
through a buzzing multitude of men, yet never see-
ing a familiar face, and never seeing a strange one
for the second time. . . . Every man seems to feel
that he has got the duties of two lifetimes to accom-
plish in one, and so he rushes, rushes, rushes, and
never has time to be companionable—never has any
time at his disposal to fool away on matters which
do not involve dollars and duty and business.

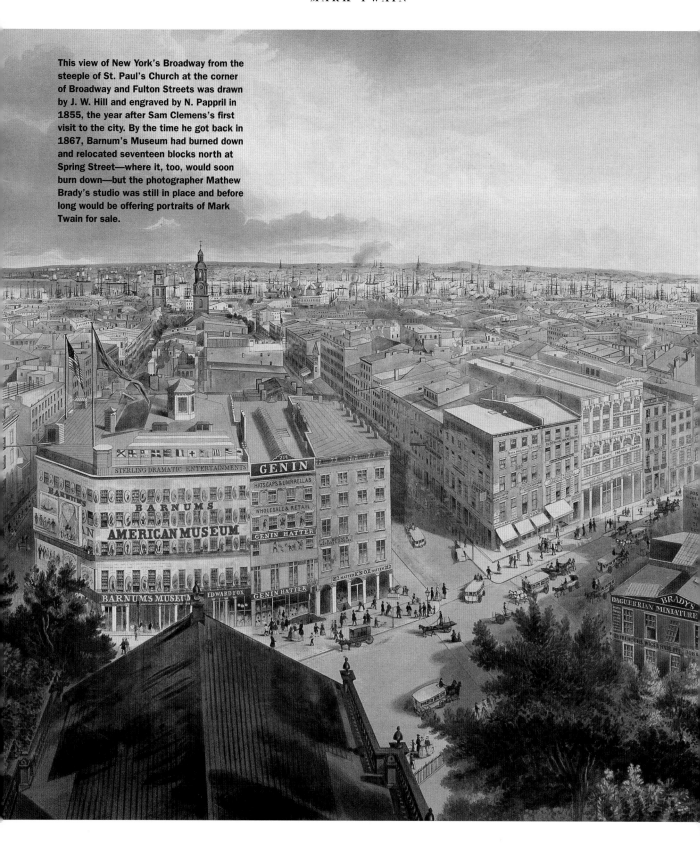

This view of New York's Broadway from the steeple of St. Paul's Church at the corner of Broadway and Fulton Streets was drawn by J. W. Hill and engraved by N. Pappril in 1855, the year after Sam Clemens's first visit to the city. By the time he got back in 1867, Barnum's Museum had burned down and relocated seventeen blocks north at Spring Street—where it, too, would soon burn down—but the photographer Mathew Brady's studio was still in place and before long would be offering portraits of Mark Twain for sale.

> *. . . There is something about this ceaseless buzz, and hurry, and*
> *bustle, that keeps a stranger in a state of unwholesome excitement*
> *all the time, and makes him restless and uneasy, and saps from him*
> *all the capacity to enjoy anything or take a strong interest in any*
> *matter whatever—something which impels him to try to do every-*
> *thing, and yet permits him to do nothing.*

Still, he doggedly gathered material for his dispatches to the *Alta California.* He attended plays and the opera, enjoyed dinner and brandy at
the Century Association, listened to the celebrated Rev. Henry Ward
Beecher preach at Brooklyn's Plymouth Church, and visited the National
Academy of Design's exhibition of Old Masters. ("I am glad the old
masters are all dead," he confided to his readers, "and I only wish they
had died sooner.") He joined the throngs at P. T. Barnum's American
Museum, too—newly rebuilt after a disastrous fire—declared it really
just "one vast peanut stand," and wondered, "why does not some philan-
thropist burn the Museum again?"

He investigated New York's dark side as well: seedy dives, a mission
dedicated to reforming prostitutes, the crowded tenements in which half
the city's residents lived in squalor. "Humiliation, hunger, persecution
and death are the wages of poverty in the mighty cities of the land,"
he wrote.

> *No man can say aught against honest poverty. The books laud it;*
> *the instructors of the people praise it; all men glorify it and say it*
> *hath its reward here and will have it hereafter. Honest poverty is a*
> *gem that even a King might feel proud to call his own, but I wish to*
> *sell out. I have sported that kind of jewelry long enough. I want*
> *some variety. I wish to become rich, so that I can instruct the people*
> *and glorify honest poverty a little, like those good, kind-hearted, fat,*
> *benevolent people do.*

During the spring of 1867, Clemens took time off for a quick trip
to his old Midwestern haunts—St. Louis, Hannibal, and Keokuk—and
in each place delivered his Sandwich Islands lecture to appreciative
audiences. Now billed as "the celebrated California humorist, and most
extraordinary delineator of human character in America or upon the
Continent of Europe," Twain was especially proud when one local newspaper reported that he had drawn a larger crowd than Ralph Waldo
Emerson.

He was achieving a measure of fame. But the fortune he had once
vowed to amass before returning home to his family still eluded him.
And seeing his brother Orion back home in Iowa again, struggling once
more to make a living, only reminded Sam of his father's financial failures. With Nevada on the verge of statehood, Orion had seemed sure to

become its first elected secretary of state until he experienced what Sam called a "spasm of virtue," declared himself a champion of temperance, and was soundly defeated by the hard-drinking electorate. Sam Clemens hurried back to New York, determined to do better.

On May 1, 1867, Mark Twain's first book was published: *The Celebrated Jumping Frog of Calaveras County, and Other Sketches*. He inscribed one copy "To My Mother—The dearest Friend I ever had, & the truest. Mark Twain" and sent it to her, along with word that James Russell Lowell himself had declared it "the finest piece of humorous writing yet produced in America." But the book sold poorly and would be out of print before long.

Likewise, his first New York lecture—at the cavernous Great Hall of the Cooper Union—won glowing reviews in the city's newspapers, but

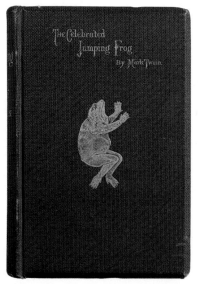

The cover of Mark Twain's first book, *The Celebrated Jumping Frog of Calaveras County, and Other Sketches*, published in 1867, and an illustration by True Williams for the version of the same tale that appeared in *Sketches Old and New*, published eight years later

lost its promoter hundreds of dollars because, in the interest of having a full house, he had handed out too many complimentary tickets.

Sam still felt isolated, drank too much, was jailed overnight again, this time for brawling.

New York, June 7.
Dear Folks—
I have just written myself clear out in letters to the Alta, and I think they are the stupidest letters that were ever written from New York. . . . I haven't anything to write [to you], except that I am so tired of staying in one place that I am in a fever to get away. . . .
I am so worthless that it seems to me I never do anything or accomplish anything that lingers in my mind as a pleasant memory. My mind is stored full of unworthy conduct toward Orion & toward

you all, & an accusing conscience gives me peace only in excitement
& restless moving from place to place. If I could say I had done one
thing for any of you that entitled me to your good opinions . . . I
know I would care little for the world's praise or blame. There is no
satisfaction in the world's praise, anyhow, & it has no worth to me
save in the way of business. I tried to gather up its compliments to
send to you, but the work was distasteful & I dropped it.

Yrs forever,
Sam

The next day, June 8, 1867, Mark Twain boarded the steamship *Quaker
City* bound for Europe.

The *Quaker City,* that carried Sam
Clemens and his pious companions on a
"great Pleasure Excursion to Europe and
the Holy Land"

With the Civil War behind them, Americans were visiting
the Old World in unprecedented numbers that summer, five
thousand departures a week by some estimates.

But the *Quaker City* represented something entirely
new: the very first full-scale pleasure cruise, a
five-month voyage to the major ports of the Mediterranean, culminating in a pilgrimage to the Holy
Land. Most of the seventy passengers aboard were
middle-class Midwesterners—prosperous, Protestant,
and so pious that not long after the ship left the pier, one
of them asked the captain if he would halt her progress in
midocean in honor of the Sabbath.

It was unlikely company for Mark Twain, but his $1,250 passage had
been paid by the *Alta California* and two New York newspapers, each
of which had promised twenty dollars per letter for regular reports on
the Holy Land tour. He was eager to see the Old World, but wary of his
fellow passengers. "There was a little difference of opinion between us,"
Twain wrote. "They thought they could have saved Sodom and Gomor-
rah, and I thought it would have been unwise to risk money upon it."

Twain liked best the late evenings in his cabin, playing cards,
drinking, smoking, and swearing with a handful of men who called
themselves the *Quaker City* Nighthawks. But he also did his best to fit
in with the other travelers. He joined the nightly readings from guide-
books about places they were to visit; played charades and shuffleboard
on deck; took part in the debating club, suggesting topics of his own,
such as "Is a tail absolutely necessary to the comfort and convenience
of a dog?" He even attended the regular prayer services, adding his
tenor voice to the choir.

And he was taken under the wing of Mary Mason Fairbanks, the
wife of a wealthy Cleveland publisher, whose attempts at guiding him
in the ways of polite society Twain appreciated. He reveled in his public persona as "the Wild Humorist of the Pacific Slope," but he also

EXCURSION

TO THE

Holy Land, Egypt, the Crimea, Greece,

AND

INTERMEDIATE POINTS OF INTEREST.

Brooklyn, February 1st, 1867.

THE undersigned will make an excursion as above during the coming season, and begs to submit to you the following programme :

A first-class steamer, to be under his own command, and capable of accommodating at least one hundred and fifty cabin passengers, will be selected, in which will be taken a select company, numbering not more than three-fourths of the ship's capacity. There is good reason to believe that this company can be easily made up in this immediate vicinity, of mutual friends and acquaintances.

The steamer will be provided with every necessary comfort, including Library and musical instruments.

An experienced physician will be on board.

Leaving New York about June 1st, a middle and pleasant route will be taken across the Atlantic, and passing through the group of Azores, St. Michael will be reached in about ten days. A day or two will be spent here, enjoying the fruit and wild scenery of these islands, and the voyage continued, and Gibraltar reached in three or four days.

A day will be spent here in looking over the wonderful subterranean fortifications, permission to visit these galleries being readily obtained.

From Gibraltar, running along the coasts of Spain and France, Marseilles will be reached in three days. Here the steamer will remain eight days, giving ample time not only to look over the city, which was founded 600 years before the Christian era, and its artificial port, the finest of the kind in the Mediterranean, but to visit Paris during the great Exhibition; and the beautiful city of Lyons, lying intermediate, from the heights of which, on a clear day, Mont Blanc and the Alps can be distinctly seen. Passengers who may wish to extend the time at Paris can do so, and, passing down through Switzerland, rejoin the steamer at Genoa.

From Marseilles to Genoa is a run of one night. Ten days will be given here in which the excursionists will have opportunity to look over this, the "magnificent City of palaces," visit the birthplace of Columbus, twelve miles off, over a beautiful road built by Napoleon I. From this point excursions may be made to Milan, Lakes Como and Maggiore, or to Milan, Verona, famous for its extraordinary fortifications, Padua, and Venice. Or if passengers desire to visit Parma, famous for Correggio's frescoes, and Bologna, they can by rail go on to Florence, and rejoin the steamer at Leghorn, thus spending about three weeks amid the cities most famous for Art in Italy.

From Genoa the run to Leghorn will be made along the coast in one night, and six days appropriated to this point in which to visit Florence; its palaces and galleries; Pisa, its Cathedral and "Leaning Tower" and Lucca and its baths and Roman Amphitheatre; Florence, the most remote, being distant by rail about sixty miles.

From Leghorn to Naples, (calling at Civiti Vecchia to land any who may prefer to go to Rome from that point,) the distance will be made in about 36 hours; the route will lay along the coast of Italy, close by Caprera, Elba, and Corsica. Arrangements have been made to take on board at Leghorn a pilot for Caprera, and, if practicable, a call will be made there to visit the home of Garibaldi.

Eight days will be spent in Naples, in which Rome, [by rail] Herculaneum, Pompeii, Vesuvius, Virgil's Tomb, and possibly the ruins of Paestum, can be visited, as well as the beautiful surroundings of Naples and its charming bay.

The next point of interest will be Palermo, the most beautiful city of Sicily, which will be reached in one night from Naples. A day will be spent here, and leaving in the evening, the course will be taken towards Athens.

Diaries.

Most of the passengers being unaccustomed to voyaging are diligently keeping diaries.

Of a lady.

First Day — The ship rolls & pitches, & Oh, I am so sick!

Second Day — We met an emigrant ship to-day full of Irish people. — From Ireland, I suppose. Our captain got on the paddle-box & shouted "Ship Yo-how!" or something like that, & the other captain shouted back through a horn & said he had been out thirty days. Then we started away, & gave the emigrant 3 cheers

privately yearned to be accepted by Eastern society. He allowed her to read some of his reports, listened to her earnest suggestions about improving them, even promised her he would try to cut back on his swearing. Although she was only seven years older than he, he called her Mother Fairbanks.

The *Quaker City* stopped at Gibraltar long enough for Sam to take a short side trip to Tangiers, then pushed on to Marseilles, where he and two friends boarded a train for a one-week visit to Paris. He reported to his readers on the international exposition, where Americans were proudly displaying the McCormick reaper and Elias Howe's sewing machine—but he also provided them with details about the saucy can-can. "I placed my hands before my face for very shame," he wrote, "but I looked through my fingers."

The tour moved on to Italy for a month—Milan, Venice, Florence, Pisa, Rome, Naples, Mount Vesuvius. Everywhere he went, Twain poked fun at the new breed of American tourist.

> *We wish to learn all the curious, outlandish ways of all the different countries, so that we can "show off" and astonish people when we get home. We wish to excite the envy of our untraveled friends with our strange foreign fashions which we can't shake off. . . . The gentle reader will never, never know what a consummate ass he can become, until he goes abroad. I speak now, of course, in the supposition that the gentle reader has not been abroad, and therefore is not already a consummate ass.*

And unlike other travel writers of the day, whose breathless descriptions of the Old World often made American readers feel that their country was somehow inferior, Twain wrote as if the United States set the standards for the world. Lake Como, he reported, was not nearly as pretty as Lake Tahoe. Mount Vesuvius was not as impressive a volcano as Mount Kilauea either, but "I was glad I visited it," he wrote, "chiefly because I shall never have to do it again."

Venice, he said, reminded him of his days on the Mississippi.

> *What a funny old city this Queen of the Adriatic is! Narrow streets, vast, gloomy marble palaces, black with the corroding damps of centuries, and all partly submerged; no dry land visible any where, and no sidewalks worth mentioning; if you want to go to church, to the theatre, or to the restaurant, you must call a gondola. . . .*
>
> *For a day or two the place looked so like an overflowed Arkansas town, because of its currentless waters laving the very doorsteps of all the houses, and the cluster of boats made fast under the windows, or skimming in and out of the alleys and by-ways, that I*

Shipboard souvenirs: (clockwise from top left) An advertising prospectus for the *Quaker City* tour; the first page of Mark Twain's journal of the voyage; a portrait of his friend and shipboard social mentor, Mary Mason Fairbanks; and Sam Clemens himself (just visible over the knee of the seated woman at left), surrounded by his fellow-passengers on deck

could not get rid of the impression that there was nothing the matter here but a spring freshet, and that the river would fall in a few weeks and leave a dirty high-water mark on the houses, and the streets full of mud and rubbish.

"Isn't this relic matter a little overdone?" he asked, after telling his readers he had been shown pieces of the True Cross in every church he'd visited, seen St. John's ashes at two different places, and gazed at enough bones of St. Denis "to duplicate him, if necessary." Then he turned his sights on Michelangelo:

I used to worship the mighty genius of Michael Angelo—that man who was great in poetry, painting, sculpture, architecture—great in everything he undertook. But I do not want Michael Angelo for breakfast—for luncheon—for dinner—for tea—for supper—for between meals. I like a change, occasionally. In Genoa, he designed every thing; in Milan he or his pupils designed every thing; . . . in Padua, Verona, Venice, Bologna, who did we ever hear of, from guides, but Michael Angelo? In Florence, he painted every thing, designed every thing, nearly, and what he did not design he used to sit on a favorite stone and look at, and they showed us the stone. In Pisa he designed every thing but the old shot-tower, and they would have attributed that to him if it had not been so awfully out of the perpendicular. . . .

I never felt so fervently thankful, so soothed, so tranquil, so filled with a blessed peace, as I did yesterday when I learned that Michael Angelo was dead.

When a number of the *Quaker City* company had their portraits taken in Istanbul, Sam Clemens (above) remained determinedly himself, and took a dim view of fellow passengers—like the man at right—who draped themselves in "the outrageous, idolatrous, extravagant, thunder-and-lightning" costumes of the Turks just for a souvenir.

The *Quaker City* was not allowed to land at Athens because of a cholera quarantine, but Clemens and some of his fellow Nighthawks slipped ashore anyway to tour the Acropolis by moonlight. They sailed on to Constantinople, then to Yalta on the Black Sea, where the arrival of a shipload of Americans was so unusual that they were granted a personal audience with Czar Alexander II and his brother, Grand Duke Michael. Twain drafted the group's welcoming remarks, and proudly reported back to his mother on his first brush with royalty: "They live right well at the Grand Duke Michael's—their breakfasts are not gorgeous but very excellent—& if Mike were to say the word I would go there & breakfast with him tomorrow. . . . My hand is in now, & if you want any more emperors feted in style, trot them out."

On September 10, the *Quaker City* reached Beirut, where Twain and seven companions decided their pilgrimage to the Holy Land would be a more memorable experience if they proceeded by pack train.

In Syria, at the headwaters of the Jordan, a camel took charge of my overcoat while the tents were being pitched, and examined it with a critical eye, all over, with as much interest as if he had an idea of getting one made like it; and then, after he was done figuring on it as an article of apparel, he began to contemplate it as an article of diet.

He put his foot on it, and lifted one of the sleeves out with his teeth, and chewed and chewed at it, gradually taking it in, and all the while opening and closing his eyes in a kind of religious ecstasy, as if he had never tasted anything as good as an overcoat before, in his life. Then he smacked his lips once or twice, and reached after the other sleeve. Next he tried the velvet collar, and smiled a smile of such contentment that it was plain to see that he regarded that as the daintiest thing about an overcoat. The tails went next, along with some percussion caps and cough candy, and some fig-paste from Constantinople.

And then my newspaper correspondence dropped out, and he took a chance in that—manuscript letters written for the home papers. But he was treading on dangerous ground now. He began to come across solid wisdom in those documents that was rather weighty on his stomach; and occasionally he would take a joke that would

The opening paragraphs of one of the newspaper dispatches from which Twain would fashion his first best-seller, *The Innocents Abroad*

(bottom right) "A sheik's house on Mount Lebanon" in what is now Lebanon, a photograph made on the *Quaker City* tour by its official cameraman, William E. James

shake him up till it loosened his teeth; it was getting to be perilous times with him, but he held his grip with good courage and hopefully, till at last he began to stumble on statements that not even a camel would swallow with impunity.

He began to gag and gasp, and his eyes to stand out, and his forelegs to spread, and in about a quarter of a minute he fell over as stiff as a carpenter's workbench, and died a death of indescribable agony. I went and pulled the manuscript out of his mouth, and found that the sensitive creature had choked to death on one of the mildest and gentlest statements of fact I ever laid before a trusting public.

In Palestine, they visited Nazareth, Bethlehem, Jericho, and scores of other places they had all read about in the Bible. Twain was incensed at the way so many tourists felt free to write their names and hometowns on the walls of ancient buildings, or chip off pieces of rock at sacred sites—though he himself picked up a stone at Solomon's Temple for his mother.

For his readers back home, he pointed out that while it took Moses forty years to cross the desert from Egypt to the Promised Land, the overland stage could have done it in thirty-six hours. And when a boatman charged eight dollars for a short sail on the Sea of Galilee, Twain asked, "Do you wonder now that Christ walked?"

But in Jerusalem, in the Church of the Holy Sepulchre, at the spot where Jesus was crucified, he gazed upon something "with a far more absorbing interest than I had ever felt in any thing earthly before."

With all its clap-trap side-shows and unseemly impostures of every kind, it is still grand, reverend, venerable—for a god died there; for fifteen hundred years its shrines have been wet with the tears of pilgrims from the earth's remotest confines; for more than two hundred, the most gallant knights that ever wielded sword wasted their lives away in a struggle to seize it and hold it sacred from infidel pollution. Even in our own day a war, that cost millions of treasure and rivers of blood, was fought because two rival nations claimed the sole right to put a new dome upon it. History is full of this old Church of the Holy Sepulchre—full of blood that was shed because of the respect and the veneration in which men held the last resting-place of the meek and lowly, the mild and gentle, Prince of Peace!

Their last stop was in Egypt, where Twain climbed the Great Pyramid of Cheops—and compared it to Holliday's Hill back in Hannibal—and where he and his fellow tourists gazed at the face of the Sphinx, "with its

Tourist sites: (clockwise from far left) the Fountain of the Virgin at Nazareth; the ruins of Baalbek in present-day Lebanon; the Great Pyramid at Giza; and the stadium at Ephesus. Clemens himself may be among the tiny figures in this last view. "We do not embellish the general desolation of a desert much," he wrote of himself and his fellow tourists at Ephesus. "We add what dignity we can to a stately ruin with our green umbrellas and jackasses, but it is little. However, we mean well." William E. James, who took the stereoscopic views on these two pages, also taught Sunday School at Brooklyn's fashionable Plymouth Church, whose celebrated pastor, Rev. Henry Ward Beecher, was originally supposed to come along. Some of James's images would be used as source material by the artists who illustrated Twain's *Innocents Abroad*.

accusing memory of the deeds of all ages, which reveals to one something of what he shall feel when he shall stand at last in the awful presence of God."

Then the *Quaker City* turned westward for what seemed to Twain an interminable voyage home:

> Friday—*Morning; dominoes. Afternoon, dominoes. Evening, promenading the deck. Afterwards, charades.*
> Saturday—*Morning, dominoes. Afternoon, dominoes. Evening, promenading the decks. Afterwards, dominoes.*
> Sunday—*Morning service, four bells. Evening service, eight bells. Monotony till midnight.—Whereupon, dominoes.*

By the time his ship arrived back in New York on November 19, Clemens was in a foul mood from five and a half months of life at close quarters with what he called "psalm-singing cattle." Touring the Holy

When Mark Twain undertook a lecture tour speaking about his *Quaker City* voyage, its eastern leg was organized by the American Lyceum Bureau, which issued this *carte de visite* advertisement that included him in a galaxy of America's most celebrated platform stars.

The Lecture Platform.

1 Rev. Talmage	24 E. C. Stanton
2 E. Yates	25 S. B. Anthony
3 "Eli Perkins"	26 E. Faithfull
4 "Josh Billings"	27 J. B. Gough
5 W. H. H. Murray	28 Kate Field
6 J. T. Fields	29 A. Livingston
7 Theo. Tilton	30 Wilkie Collins
8 John Hay	31 B. Taylor
9 Bret Harte	32 "Fat Contributor"
10 Scott Siddons	33 E. E. Hale
11 "Mark Twain"	34 Chas. Sumner
12 "P. V. Nasby"	35 J. A. Froude
13 Carl Schurz	36 R. W. Emerson
14 J. M. Bellew	37 A. E. Dickinson
15 Rev. Chapin	38 Elihu Burritt
16 Miss Cushman	39 Sidney Woollett
17 Miss Edgarton	40 Wendell Phillips
18 H. B. Stowe	41 Robt. Collyer
19 J. G. Saxe	42 H. W. Beecher
20 De Cordova	43 Prof. Tyndall
21 Geo. W. Curtis	44 MacDonald
22 Gen. Kilpatrick	45 James Parton
23 Bishop Simpson	

PUBLISHED BY THE
American Literary Bureau,
AGENCY FOR LECTURERS, READERS & SINGERS
COOPER INSTITUTE, N. Y.

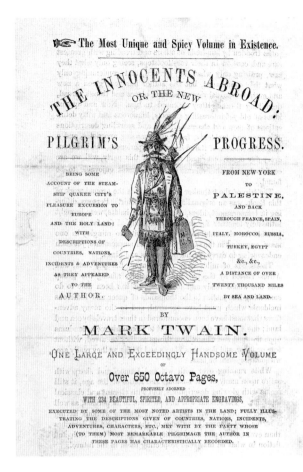

A pre-publication advertisement, intended to drum up subscribers for *The Innocents Abroad*

Land with them, he wrote one friend, had been "an awful trial to a man's religion"; the entire trip, he told the readers of the *New York Herald,* had been "a funeral without a corpse."

But his immediate concern was his own future. "Am pretty well known, now," he wrote his mother. "Intend to be better known." He took a temporary position as private secretary to Nevada senator William Stewart in Washington, D.C., filing reports on Congress for different newspapers in his spare time, moving from one boardinghouse to another, and lobbying for the postmastership of San Francisco until he learned how little it paid. He undertook a lecture tour of the West, too, and then went to work on a new book, an account of his *Quaker City* voyage to be called *The Innocents Abroad.* It was to be published by the American Publishing Company of Hartford, Connecticut, a firm that sold books only by subscription. Months before a single page was printed, an army of salesmen canvassed the country, knocking on doors and taking orders from people who rarely visited bookstores—tradesmen, small-time shopkeepers, farmers living miles from town. Subscription books needed to be richly produced, lavishly illustrated, and fat. Clemens hurled himself into writing new material to supplement his letters to the *Alta California,* better than 200,000 words in just under two months.

Meanwhile, he had begun to think about augmenting his personal life, as well. When Mary Fairbanks suggested that "a good wife would be a perpetual incentive to progress," Clemens agreed.

> *. . . & so she would. . . . I want a good wife—I want a couple of them if they are particularly good—but where is the wherewithal? It costs sixty dollars, nearly two letters [to newspapers] a week to keep me . . . but I can't turn an inkstand into an Aladdin's lamp.*
>
> *If I were settled I would quit all nonsense & swindle some poor girl into marrying me. But I wouldn't expect to be "worthy" of her. I wouldn't have a girl that I was worthy of. She wouldn't do. She wouldn't be respectable enough.*
>
> *Improvingly, yr friend*
> *Sam L. Clemens*

CHAPTER FIVE

THE BEST GIRL
IN ALL THE WORLD

*She was slender and beautiful and girlish—and she was both girl
and woman. She remained both girl and woman to the last day of
her life. Under a grave and gentle exterior burned inextinguishable
fires of sympathy, energy, devotion, enthusiasm and absolutely limitless affection. She was always frail in body, and she lived upon her
spirit, whose hopefulness and courage were indestructible.*

—*Chapters from My Autobiography*, 1906

**(opposite) Olivia Langdon photographed at
about the time Sam Clemens first saw her.
"That girl is one in a million," he wrote
Mary Fairbanks. "She is fearfully and wonderfully made."**

**(below) Sam Clemens and his future
brother-in-law, Charley Langdon, 1868**

On Friday morning, August 21, 1868, thirty-two-year-old Sam Clemens
boarded the Express Mail from Manhattan to Elmira in western New
York. When Charley Langdon, a young friend and former Nighthawk
from the *Quaker City*, had invited him to come and spend a few days
with his family, Clemens had eagerly accepted. He liked Charley, but he
was infatuated with Charley's younger sister, Olivia. He later recalled
first being impressed by her beauty when Charley showed him a miniature portrait aboard ship. And he had three times found himself in her
company in New York the previous winter—once at the hotel where
she was staying with her family, then at a lecture given by
Charles Dickens, and finally at a New Year's Day party. Now
he was hoping to get to know her better. With typical impetu-
ousness he had boarded the train for Elmira without check-
ing to see what time it got to its destination. It seemed to halt
at every whistle-stop, and at some point along the way he
jumped off long enough to send Charley a telegram: "Train
stops every fifteen minutes and stays three quarters of an
hour, figure out when it will arrive and meet me."

Charley boarded the slow-moving train at Waverly, fifteen
miles from Elmira, and found his friend in the smoking car.
Sam was wearing a bright yellow duster and a battered straw
hat—fine for traveling in the West, but not the sort of clothing worn by most visitors to Charley's parents' home. The
Langdons were, after all, Elmira's wealthiest and most prominent citizens.

Charley was worried. "You've got some other clothes,
haven't you?" he asked.

"Oh, yes," Clemens said. "I've got a fine brand-new outfit in this bag, all but a hat. It will be late when we get in and I won't see anyone tonight. You won't know me in the morning. We'll go out early and get a hat."

The next morning, wearing his new suit and with his unruly red hair now more or less hidden beneath the proper headgear, Clemens entered a world unlike any he had ever known before. The Langdons' handsome three-story home occupied an entire block; visitors had to pass through three separate automatic gates just to reach the front door. Jervis Langdon was a onetime country storekeeper who had made himself a millionaire by cornering the local coal business, and he was as forward-looking and public-spirited as he was prosperous. After the congregation of the First Presbyterian Church refused to express its written opposition to slavery in 1846, Langdon and his wife, Olivia Lewis Langdon, led a group of dissidents that established a new Independent Congregational Church, and later helped install in its pulpit Thomas Kinnicut Beecher, half-brother of Henry Ward Beecher and Harriet Beecher Stowe. Jervis Langdon helped spirit runaway slaves northward in the baggage cars of the same rail line that hauled his coal to Canada, and when Frederick Douglass passed through New York State in flight from his master, the Langdons had offered him shelter in their home. Since the Civil War, they had paid thousands of dollars toward the education of freedmen.

To Clemens, a son of the Missouri frontier who had not seen much to choose between the Union and the Confederacy in 1861, and whose

The Langdon home in Elmira, New York

Olivia's mother and father: Olivia Lewis Langdon and Jervis Langdon. Theirs, Sam Clemens wrote his mother, was "the pleasantest family I ever knew."

own father had abused and sold slaves and helped send abolitionists to prison, the Langdons were a revelation. They were affectionate toward one another, too—Sam had never seen any member of his own clan kiss another member, he remembered, unless at someone's deathbed— and they discouraged smoking, served guests nothing stronger than apple cider, and often spent their evenings singing hymns and playing cribbage.

But it was Olivia Louise Langdon—Livy, as her friends and family called her—who continued to captivate him. She was twenty-two years old that fall, lovely, highly religious, and far better educated than Sam. She read voraciously, had attended Miss Clarissa Thurston's Female Seminary and the Elmira Female College, and, even after a spinal condition confined her to bed for nearly four years, had continued her studies with private tutors and a circle of female friends. She was still delicate when Clemens began visiting, unable to move much farther than from one room to another, and she would never enjoy robust health. But her fragility only seemed to add to her appeal.

Sam declared her "the best girl in all the world, & the most sensible," in a letter to his mother. "She is only a little body, but she hasn't her peer in Christendom." He had never wanted anything so much as he now wanted to marry Livy Langdon, and not long after he got to Elmira, he got her alone long enough to tell her so. Livy gently turned him away—they had known each other for only a few days, after all. But she was intrigued by this drawling, rough-hewn Westerner, ten years her senior, who had already seen so much of the world she had only read about. She agreed that they could write to one another as brother and sister. Since they were not engaged—and to keep people at the Elmira post office from talking—she further insisted that he seal his letters in envelopes addressed to her brother Charley.

Clemens agreed to all her terms, began writing to her the very next day, and would not stop for seventeen months—184 missives, each saved and carefully numbered by Livy.

September 7th, 1868.
My Honored "Sister"—
I do not regret that I have loved you, still love & shall always love you. I accept the situation, uncomplaining, hard as it is. Of old I am acquainted with grief, disaster & disappointment, & have borne these troubles as became a man. So, also, I shall bear this last and bitterest, even though it break my heart. . . . My honored sister: Give me a little room in that great heart of yours—only the little you have promised me—& if I fail to deserve it may I remain forever the homeless vagabond I am!

When Clemens again became too ardent on paper, Livy scolded him, and when he foolishly told her he thought he'd been "quite a pleasant addition to the family circle" during his two-week stay in Elmira, she made it plain that he had in fact overstayed his welcome. Convinced he'd ruined everything, he declared himself "savage & crazy" and drank too much during a visit to his sister in St. Louis. Then he got another letter from Livy, this time including a photograph. There was still hope.

September 21
My honored Sister . . . I thank you for the happy surprise the picture brought—I thank you more than I can tell. . . . You say to me: "I shall pray for you daily." Not any words that ever were spoken to me have touched me like these . . . [and] what I have arrived at is the conviction that I would be less than a man if I went on in my old careless way while you were praying for me.

Clemens was now supporting himself on the lecture circuit with a talk about his *Quaker City* trip called "American Vandals Abroad." When he drew a Philadelphia crowd ten times the size of the one that turned out to hear the popular actress Fanny Kemble that same evening, he proudly

The sixth of the 184 love letters Sam wrote to Livy over the course of their courtship. "My letters are an ocean of love in a storm," he told his friend Joseph Twichell, "hers an ocean of love in the majestic repose of a great calm. But the waters are the same—just the same, my boy."

The parlor (above) and library of the Langdon home. The marble bust on the pillar in the parlor is a portrait of Livy. Jervis Langdon's portrait hangs above the bookshelves.

told Livy how well he'd done. In November, hoping further to impress her parents—and to see her again—he offered to speak in Elmira, and to donate the proceeds to Charley Langdon's volunteer fire department. The Langdons invited him to stay for Thanksgiving.

Clemens took the opportunity to press his suit in person. "I'll harass that girl, and harass her," he told a friend, "till she'll *have* to say yes." When, after two more tearful rejections, she finally did so—"she is no longer my sister," he exulted to Mary Fairbanks—he moved quickly to ask Jervis Langdon for her hand. The older man was stunned—he had often said he loved his invalid daughter so much that he would never be able to give her away to another—and his approval was distinctly conditional: the engagement had to be kept secret while Clemens provided him with the names of friends out west who could attest to his character.

Sam was jubilant. "Great Caesar's ghost," he wrote a friend, "if there is a church in town with a steeple high enough to make it an object— I would go out and jump over it! . . . I am so happy I want to scalp somebody." He kept up his steady barrage of letters. "[Livy] isn't demonstrative a bit (who ever supposed she would be?)," he wrote Mary Fairbanks, "but she sticks like a good girl, & answers every letter just as soon as she has read it—& lectures me like smoke, too. But I like it." Both Sam

Only "a Nigger"

*In mid-August of 1869, newly engaged and eager to impress Jervis Lang-
don, his prospective father-in-law, with his willingness to hold a steady
job, Sam Clemens began going daily to the East Swan Street offices of the
Buffalo Express. The experiment lasted only a little over two months—he
would return to the lecture circuit in November—and most of his writings
for the paper were meant to be funny. But on August 26, events in the
South elicited this very different kind of editorial, the first clear evidence
that the mind of the slave owner's son from Missouri had begun to change.*

A dispatch from Memphis mentions that, of two negroes lately sentenced to death for
murder in that vicinity, one named Woods has just confessed to having ravished a young
lady during the war, for which deed another negro was hung at the time by an avenging
mob, the evidence that doomed the guiltless wretch being a hat which Woods now relates
that he stole from its owner and left behind, for the purpose of misleading. Ah, well! Too
bad, to be sure! A little blunder in the administration of justice by Southern mob-law; but
nothing to speak of. Only "a nigger" killed by mistake—that is all. Of course, every high
toned gentleman whose chivalric impulses were so unfortunately misled in this affair, by
the cunning of the miscreant Woods, is as sorry about it as a high toned gentleman can
be expected to be sorry about the unlucky fate of "a nigger." But mistakes will happen,
even in the conduct of the best regulated and most high toned mobs, and surely there
is no good reason why Southern gentlemen should worry themselves with useless regrets,
so long as only an innocent "nigger" is hanged, or roasted or knouted to death, now and
then. What if the blunder of lynching the wrong man does happen once in four or five
cases! Is that any fair argument against the cultivation and indulgence of those fine
chivalric passions and that noble Southern spirit which will not brook the slow and cold
formalities of regular law, when outraged white womanhood appeals for vengeance?
Perish the thought so unworthy of a Southern soul! Leave it to the sentimentalism and
humanitarianism of a cold-blooded Yankee civilization! What are the lives of a few "niggers" in comparison with the preservation of the impetuous instincts of a proud and fiery
race? Keep ready the halter, therefore, oh chivalry of Memphis! Keep the lash knotted;
keep the brand and the faggots in waiting, for prompt work with the next "nigger" who
may be suspected of any damnable crime! Wreak a swift vengeance upon him, for the
satisfaction of the noble impulses that animate knightly hearts, and then leave time and
accident to discover, if they will, whether he was guilty or no.

and Livy saw it as her duty to reform her suitor. She prayed nightly for his salvation and sent him each week the full text of Henry Ward Beecher's latest sermon, which he claimed he read over and over again. He vowed to become a Christian, to stop swearing, to abandon even the "social drinking" she had reluctantly agreed to permit him. "I do not know of anything I could refuse to do if you wanted it done," he told her. "I am reasonably afraid that you'll stop me from *smoking* some day, but if ever you do, you will do it with such happy grace that I shall be swindled into the notion that I didn't *want* to smoke anymore, anyhow!" (Clemens was earnest in his desire to improve himself—"I mean to *rise*," he assured his sister—but as time went by, both his inborn skepticism and his old habits would reassert themselves. He was soon cheerfully drinking Scotch again, and eventually Livy herself would down a nightly glass of ale for its alleged medicinal effect.)

Meanwhile, the friends from whom Sam had hoped for character references did not help his cause. "They said with one accord," he remembered, "that I got drunk oftener than was necessary & that I was wild and Godless, idle, lecherous & a discontented & an unsettled rover & they could not recommend any girl of high character & social position to marry me—but as I had already said all that about myself beforehand there was nothing shocking or surprising about it to the family." Jervis Langdon had grown to like Sam, and was impressed both by his candor about his past sins and his apparent determination to reform. On February 4, 1869, he finally gave his formal blessing to the marriage. Sam slipped a plain gold ring on Livy's finger; he couldn't afford "the two-hundred dollar diamond one" he said she deserved. "My prophecy was correct," Sam wrote to his mother. "[Livy] said she never c'd or w'ld love me but she set herself the task of making a Christian of me. I said she w'd succeed, but that in the meantime she w'd dig a matrimonial pit & end by tumbling into it—& lo! The prophecy is fulfilled."

"Of course everything in the future is very uncertain," Livy wrote to a friend three months later, "as Mr. Clemens is not yet settled anywhere, but he is very tired of the wandering life that he has been leading." Jervis Langdon had made it clear that he expected anyone who married his daughter to get a steady job and settle down. He first tried to interest his future son-in-law in the family coal business: "I listened to it for an hour," Sam confided to Livy, "till the blood froze in my veins." Eventually, Langdon would loan him $25,000 with which to buy part-ownership of the *Buffalo Express*.

For nearly a year, Clemens moved back and forth between Buffalo and his fiancée's family in Elmira, carrying with him the proofs of *The Innocents Abroad* so that Livy could go over them with him, word by

Porcelain-type portrait of Livy. The case in which it was kept included a handwritten label that suggests it was made on October 29, 1869, a little over three months before Sam and its subject were married.

word. "She was my faithful, judicious and painstaking editor from that day forth," he remembered, "a stretch of more than a third of a century."

The Innocents Abroad finally appeared in July of 1869. It would sell 100,000 copies in the next two years—only Tom Paine's *Common Sense* and *Uncle Tom's Cabin* had sold more in so little time. To an old friend Clemens boasted that his book was "waltzing me out of debt so fast that I shan't owe any man a cent by this time next year. . . . We keep six steam presses and a paper mill going *night and day,* and still we can't catch up on the orders."

Literary critics in New York and Boston rarely bothered even to review subscription books, and Clemens professed not to care: he liked to say he wanted only the approval of those he called "the mighty mass of the uncultivated who are underneath." His publisher began promoting Twain as "The People's Author." "My books are water," he wrote a friend some years later; "those of the great geniuses [are] wine. Everybody drinks water." But he could not have been more pleased when William Dean Howells, associate editor of the *Atlantic Monthly,* smiled upon *The Innocents Abroad.* "Under his *nom de plume* of Mark Twain," Howells wrote, "Mr. Clemens is well known to the very large world of newspaper-readers; and this book ought to secure him better than the uncertain standing of a popular favorite. It is no business of ours to fix his rank among the humorists California has given us, but we think he is, in an entirely different way from all the others, quite worthy of the company of the best." Howells would become one of Clemens's closest friends. Twain soon started work on a new book, an account of his youthful adventures in the West, to be called *Roughing It.*

Samuel Clemens and Livy Langdon were married in the Langdon family parlor on the evening of February 2, 1870. Sam's mother did not attend, but his sister Pamela and her husband traveled all the way from St. Louis to be there, despite her fear that her clothes would be too shabby for Sam's well-to-do in-laws. The Langdons' pastor, Thomas K. Beecher, and the Rev. Joe Twichell, a freethinking Congregational minister whom Sam had befriended in Hartford, officiated jointly. Then the newlyweds, as well as the bride's family and several of the wedding

150,000 Already Sold.

AS MANY QUARRELS

Have arisen lately in families, on account of each member wishing the first reading of

Twain's "Innocents Abroad,"

we have had engraved, from a photograph, an evening scene in a family where a compromise of the difficulty was made between the parties by one of them

Reading "THE INNOCENTS" Aloud.

The cut tells its own story. It proves that Twain is entitled to the title of

The People's Author,

as no writer has ever been able so fully to interest all classes and ages. Buy the book and read it at home aloud. Your whole family will thank you. Your boys and girls will stay at home to hear you. The old folks will laugh till they cry, and in its pages you will find ample material for cheerfulness, mirth and gladness, to supply the whole family a month. Mark's drollery and bright sayings are enough to make even "the cat laugh." Furnished by publisher's agents or by addressing

AMERICAN PUBLISHING COMPANY, Hartford, Ct.

The Innocents Abroad was still a bestseller in January of 1879, six months after publication. "I never wander into any corner of the country," Clemens told his publisher Elisha Bliss, Jr., that month, "but I find that a [book] agent has been there before me, & many of that community have read the book. And on average about ten people a day come & hunt me up & tell me I'm a benefactor!! I guess that is part of the program we did not expect."

Two of Sam Clemens's warmest friends: the editor William Dean Howells (above); and the Reverend Joseph Twichell, of the Asylum Hill Congregational Church in Hartford, Connecticut

guests, boarded a private railroad car for Buffalo, where Clemens expected that he and Livy were to move into a boardinghouse arranged for them by a friend. But, he later recalled, when the wedding party reached the railroad station that evening, they "were put into several sleighs and driven all over America as it seemed to me—for apparently, we turned all the corners in the town and followed all the streets there were—I scolding freely, and characterizing that friend of mine in very uncomplimentary words for securing a boarding-house that apparently had no definite locality."

But there was a conspiracy—and although my bride knew of it I was in ignorance. Her father . . . had bought and furnished a new house for us in the fashionable street, Delaware Avenue, and had laid in a cook and housemaids and a brisk and electric young coachman . . . —and we were being driven all over that city in order that one sleighful of those people could have time to go to the house, and see that the gas was lighted all over it, and a hot supper prepared. We arrived at last and when I entered that fairy place my indignation reached the high-water mark, and without any reserve I delivered my opinion to that friend of mine for being so stupid as to put us into a boarding-house whose terms would be far out of my reach. Then Mr. Langdon brought forward a very pretty box and opened it and took from it a deed of the house. So the comedy ended very pleasantly and we sat down to supper.

The handsome brick home, staffed and completely furnished to Livy's taste, had cost her father $42,000. The coachman's uniform alone, Clemens said, was worth more than any suit of clothes he'd ever owned. In a grateful letter to his in-laws, Sam called himself "Little Sammy in Fairyland." He could not believe his luck. "Behold," he wrote to Will Bowen, an old friend from Hannibal, shortly after his wedding.

I have at the moment the only sweetheart I ever loved, & bless her old heart she is lying asleep upstairs in a bed I sleep in every night, & for four whole days she has been Mrs. Samuel L. Clemens. I am 34 & she is 24; I am young & very handsome (I make the statement with the fullest confidence, for I got it from her,) & she is much the most beautiful girl I ever saw (I said that before she was anything to me, & so it is worthy of all belief) & she is the best girl, & the sweetest, & the gentlest, & the daintiest, & the most modest & unpretentious, & the wisest in all things she should be wise in & the most ignorant in all matters it would not grace her to know, & she is sensible & quick, & loving & faithful, forgiving, full of charity—& her beautiful life is ordered by a religion that is all kindliness & unselfishness. . . . She is the most perfect gem of womankind

*that ever I saw in my life—& will stand by that remark till I die.
. . . And now my princess has come down to dinner (bless me, isn't
it cosy, nobody but us two, & three servants to wait on us & respectfully call us "Mr." and "Mrs. Clemens" instead of "Sam" &
"Livy!"). It took me many a year to work up to where I can put on
style, but now I'll do it.*

Livy called Sam "Youth" in a series of joint letters to her family. He
sometimes called her "Gravity."

*Livy gets along better and better with her housekeeping. . . . Now,
this morning she had a mackerel fricaseed with pork and oysters.*

False!

*And I tell you it was a dish to stir the very depths of one's benevo-
lence. We saved every single bit of it for the poor. . . .*

*Isn't he a funny Youth? . . . We are two as happy people as you ever
saw. Our days seem to be made up of only bright sunlight with no
shadow in them.*

Stationery from the Express Printing
Company, the Buffalo newspaper publishing firm that Sam's father-in-law
helped him purchase, signed by its new
proprietor as both "Samuel Clemens"
and "Mark Twain"

The fashionable Delaware Avenue neighborhood (opposite page), and the handsome house at Number 472 in which Sam and Livy Clemens began their marriage in Buffalo. The fully furnished house was a surprise gift from Livy's father, and in a grateful letter to his mother-in-law, the groom pronounced it "the daintiest & the most exquisite & enchanting [home] that can be found in America. . . . It is perfect. . . . It is a poem, it is music—& it speaks & sings to us all the day long."

"We are settled down & comfortable," Sam told Mrs. Fairbanks, "& the days swing by with a whir & a flash and are gone, we know not where & scarcely care. To me, passing time is a dream." As the newlyweds got to know each other, Clemens recalled later, "[Livy] poured out her prodigal affection in kisses and caresses, and in a vocabulary of endearments whose profusion was always an enlightenment to me. I was born *reserved* as to endearments of speech, and caresses, and hers broke upon me as the summer waves break on Gibraltar." And Livy's eager questions about his early life helped put him in touch with his past as nothing else in his life ever had. He wrote Will Bowen:

The fountains of my great deep are broken up, and I have rained reminiscences for four & twenty hours. The old life has swept before me like a panorama; the old days have trooped by in their old glory, again; the old faces have looked out of the mists of the past; old footsteps have sounded in my listening ears; old hands have clasped

mine, old voices have greeted me, & the songs I loved ages & ages
ago have come wailing down the centuries!

Those memories, released at the time of his marriage to Livy Langdon, would one day form the heart of a whole new kind of American literature.

The newlyweds' Buffalo idyll did not last long. On August 6, Jervis Langdon died of stomach cancer. Livy, now pregnant, suffered a nervous collapse. In September, her closest girlhood friend came to help care for her—and died of typhoid fever in the Clemenses' own bed. In November, Livy gave birth prematurely to a son. They named him Langdon, after her late father. The baby weighed just four and a half pounds at birth and would remain sickly—slow to teethe, to walk, to talk; plagued by frequent coughs and colds. Livy developed typhoid, and almost died.

"I had rather die twice over than repeat the last six months of my life," Clemens wrote his publisher in March of 1871.

Do you know that for seven months I have not had my natural rest
but have been a night and day sick-nurse to my wife?—and
still . . . yet must . . . now . . . write a damned humorous *article . . .*
promised . . . when I thought that the vials of hellfire bottled up for
my benefit must be about emptied. By the living God I don't believe
they will ever *be emptied. . . . I believe that if that baby goes on*
crying 3 more hours this way I will burst my frantic brains out and
try to get some peace.

That same month, Clemens put up for sale both his splendid house and his interest in the *Buffalo Express*, eventually selling both at a loss in his eagerness to start over again the following autumn—in Hartford, Connecticut. Clemens once wrote that "of all the beautiful towns it has been my fortune to see [Hartford] is the chief," but it was less the city's beauty that persuaded him to settle there than the fact that it had a literary neighborhood at what was then the western edge of town. Here, on some 140 shaded acres known as Nook Farm, lived a group of writers and other eminent citizens, most of whom Clemens already knew: Senator Francis Gillette, father of the future playwright and actor

Two of the most prominent citizens of Nook Farm: Isabella Beecher Hooker, whose picturesque cottage on the opposite page was the Clemenses' first home in Hartford, and her sister, Harriet Beecher Stowe, who, with her husband, Calvin, eventually became their next-door neighbor.

MARK TWAIN'S

NEW BOOK,

ROUGHING IT

Particularly adapted to Family Reading.

Designed to Amuse and Instruct.

IS A COMPANION VOLUME TO

The Innocents Abroad,

and like it is filled with descriptions of people and things seen by the author himself, with his own eyes, which differ in some respects from those of others; related in his own style, which if in no other way meritorious, is at least an original one.

It is suited to the wants of the old, the young, the rich, the poor, the sad, and the gay. "There is a time to laugh," and those who buy this book, will see clearly that the time has arrived.

To all, we say buy this book, carry it home, do good with it, read it to your family and your friends.

"And make all laugh who never laughed before,
And those who always laugh, make laugh the more."

Mark Twain in his distinctive winter garb, 1870. William Dean Howells never forgot his first glimpse of Twain. He was "wearing a sealskin coat with the fur out" when he turned up in the Boston office of the *Atlantic Monthly,* Howells wrote, "in the satisfaction of a caprice, or the love of strong effect which he was apt to indulge all his life."

Roughing It, Twain's second best-seller (top right), was originally to be titled *The Innocents at Home* to cash in on the success of the first.

Accident Insurance

Moving to Hartford brought Twain to the capital of America's insurance industry, where he served for a time as a director of the Hartford Accident Insurance Company. Even so, as this excerpt from a speech he delivered in Hartford shows, he could not help poking fun at it.

The corner of Oxford and Farmington Avenues, looking toward Nook Farm and the city of Hartford about 1884. The city's tree-lined streets delighted Sam Clemens. So did its prosperous residents: "Puritans are mighty straight-laced," he wrote, "and they won't let me smoke in the parlor, but the Almighty don't make any better people."

Certainly there is no nobler field for human effort than the insurance line of business—especially accident insurance. Ever since I have been a director in an accident-insurance company I have felt that I am a better man. Life has seemed more precious. Accidents have assumed a kindlier aspect. Distressing special providences have lost half their horror. I look upon a cripple now with affectionate interest—as an advertisement. I do not seem to care for poetry any more. I do not care for politics—even agriculture does not excite me. But to me now there is a charm about a railway collision that is unspeakable.

There is nothing more beneficent than accident insurance. I have seen an entire family lifted out of poverty and into affluence by the simple boon of a broken leg. I have had people come to me on crutches, with tears in their eyes, to bless this beneficent institution. In all my experience of life, I have seen nothing so seraphic as the look that comes into a freshly mutilated man's face when he feels in his vest pocket with his remaining hand and finds his accident ticket all right. And I have seen nothing so sad as the look that came into another splintered customer's face when he found he couldn't collect on a wooden leg.

I will remark here, by way of advertisement, that that novel charity which we have named the Hartford Accident Insurance Company is an institution which is peculiarly to be depended upon. A man is bound to prosper who gives it his custom. No man can take out a policy in it and not get crippled before the year is out.

Nook Farm neighbors: Charles Dudley Warner, who was the editor of the *Hartford Courant* as well as Sam Clemens's friend and sometime collaborator, and Warner's sister-in-law, Lilly Warner, the wife of his younger brother, George

William Gillette; the editor and novelist Charles Dudley Warner and his wife, Susan; Harriet Beecher Stowe; and her suffragist sister Isabella Beecher Hooker, whose house Mark and Livy rented till they could begin to build one of their own.

The Clemenses were happy in their new surroundings, but the move had plunged them into debt, and Sam was soon forced to set out on a grueling lecture tour to pay the bills. He wrote home to Livy every night from his hotel room to tell her how things had gone: badly at Allentown, Pennsylvania, where the "chuckle-headed Dutch" were unmoved; well at Great Barrington, Massachusetts, a few nights later; miserably at Milford, where "the very same lecture that *convulsed* Great Barrington was received with the gentlest & most well-bred smiles & rippling comfort"; and spectacularly at Boston—so spectacularly, he said, that "I wanted to talk a week."

It was not the performing that wearied him so much as the grinding struggle to get from one stop to the next—the rattling trains that often arrived late; the unheated hotel rooms and uncomfortable beds; the newspapermen who jotted down his lectures and then published them without his permission so that he had to rewrite them for fear of sounding stale; the overly effusive welcoming committees that insisted on escorting him around each little town's dreary points of interest before curtain time. He kept at it for five months while Livy, now pregnant again, struggled to keep things together at home. "I *can not* and I WILL NOT think about your being away from me this way every year," she wrote him a few days before Christmas; "it is not half living—if in order to sustain our present mode of living we are obliged to do that, then we will change our mode of living."

Sam finally returned from what he called "the most detestable lecture campaign that ever was" in mid-February 1872. Royalties from *The Innocents Abroad* had begun to lighten his financial load, and a little over a month later, on March 19, the Clemenses' second child, Olivia Susan, was born—a healthy "five-pounder," the proud father told friends, "as fat as butter, and wholly free from infelicities of any kind." He and Livy would call her Susy, and from the first she would be her father's favorite.

Then, just nine weeks later, tragedy struck again. On June 3, Lily Warner, Charles Dudley Warner's sister-in-law wrote in her journal:

A *carte de visite* portrait of Langdon, the first of the Clemens children, being cuddled by his maternal aunt, Susan Crane. His father wrote the inscription to his fellow humorist, and sometime friend, Bret Harte.

Livy in 1872, the year Susy (right) was born and Langdon died. "Seeing . . . others with their children," she wrote to a friend, "does make me so homesick for Langdon—it seems as if I could not do without him." But the grieving parents found some measure of comfort in the new baby. "Susie is bright & strong & we love her so," her father wrote, "no sacrifice seems too much to make for her."

The little Clemens boy has at last finished his weary little life. For two or three days his cold grew worse, till at last . . . it was pronounced to be diphtheria & at 9 o'clock yesterday morning he gave up his life-long struggle . . . and died quietly in his mother's arms. Of course everybody thinks what a mercy that he is at rest—but his poor devoted mother is almost heart-broken. . . . She will see it all by & by, but can't yet, & it is such a mercy they have the little baby. She is strong & well, & an uncommonly pretty little baby.

Clemens blamed himself for his son's death—he claimed he had carelessly allowed the boy to become chilled during a carriage ride—just as he had blamed himself for the death of his brothers Benjamin and Henry, just as he had once believed that thunderstorms were sent to warn him personally of his transgressions. Livy, still grieving for her father, was devastated. "I feel so often as if my path is to be lined with graves," she wrote. Her religious faith had splintered; she felt "almost perfectly cold toward God," she wrote, and no longer went regularly to church. Clemens would come to blame himself for that, too.

HARTFORD'S MARK TWAIN

JOHN BOYER

Sam Clemens was a proud product of the Missouri frontier: the world identified him with the Hannibal of his boyhood and the mighty river that flowed past it; friends and neighbors from his early life peopled much of his fiction; Missouri haunted his speech, flavored his storytelling, dictated his drawing-room manners—or lack of them. But when, after eighteen years of ceaseless wandering, it came time for Mark Twain finally to establish a home of his own, it was to Hartford, Connecticut, that he and his young wife moved in 1871. Hartford was everything Hannibal had never been—prosperous, cosmopolitan, genteel—yet it became as much a home to him as Hannibal had ever been. And it was in Hartford that he forged the closest friendship of his adult life with the Rev. Joseph Twichell, who seemed his mirror opposite in nearly every way.

Sam Clemens first visited Hartford in January 1868, just weeks after his thirty-second birthday. By then the pattern of his solitary life had already been defined by his rootlessness and world travel. Even during his childhood in Hannibal Clemens had moved from house to house. By the age of seventeen he had already lived on his own and worked in St. Louis and Philadelphia. Before he ever entered his formative profession as a steamboat pilot, his wanderings and work had taken him to Washington, D.C., New York City, and Cincinnati. And in the years immediately after his time on the Mississippi he would come to know the Nevada Territory, California, the Sandwich Islands (Hawaii), Nicaragua, North Africa, Spain, France, Italy, Greece, Russia, Turkey, Egypt, and the Holy Land.

Despite having seen much of the world and many of its greatest cities, Twain's first look at Connecticut's capital deeply impressed him. In an article for the September 6, 1868, issue of *Alta California* Twain wrote:

Of all the beautiful towns it has been my fortune to see this is the chief. It is a city of 40,000 inhabitants, and seems to be composed almost entirely of dwelling houses—not single-shaped affairs, stood on end and packed together like a "deck" of cards, but massive private hotels, scattered along the broad, straight streets, from fifty all the way up to two hundred yards apart. Each house sits in the midst of about an acre of green grass, or flower beds or ornamental shrubbery, guarded on all sides by the trimmed hedges of arbor-vitae, and by files of huge forest trees that cast a shadow like a thunder-cloud. Some of these stately dwellings are almost buried from sight in parks and forests of these noble trees. Everywhere the eye turns it is blessed with a vision of refreshing green. You do not know what beauty is if you have not been here.

Hartford was an affluent town—by the 1870s it would become the wealthiest city per capita in the nation—a hub of manufacturing and invention, the birthplace of the modern insurance industry, and a center of finance. It was a city balanced by Samuel Colt's sprawling factories on one side and an early and expansive civic park system designed by Frederick Law Olmsted on the other. And it was a growing center for book publishing: it was Clemens's first negotiations with Elisha Bliss, head of the American Publishing Company who would publish *Innocents Abroad* and several subsequent books by Mark Twain, that first drew him to the city.

But Clemens's arrival in Hartford coincided with another catalytic moment in his life—his determined courtship of Olivia Langdon of Elmira, New York. Twain's article on Hartford was published the same month in which he first proposed to Livy. Although she initially rejected his overtures, it was as though he had discovered Livy and Hartford at the same time. He wrote to her around midnight of September 7 with an urgency similar to his *Alta California* piece published just the day before. "For once, at least, in the idle years that have drifted over me, I have seen the world all beautiful, & known what it was to hope." He traveled on to St. Louis and described it to Livy as "a muddy, smoky, mean city to run about in. I am called East." For him, "East" was now synonymous with prosperity, stability, an end to his roaming, and a new life with Livy.

The young couple married in February 1870 and settled first in Buffalo, but in slightly more than a year, Clemens looked again to Hartford. By October 1871, he and Livy relocated there. The house they eventually built for themselves is widely known for its apparent idiosyncrasies, as though it were somehow emblematic of the man himself. But this young, culturally ambitious and upwardly mobile couple had settled in a sophisticated and intellectually rich neighborhood, the city's most exclusive enclave. To design their home they had hired Edward Tuckerman Potter, the architect who had just finished a major commission for the city's wealthiest patron, the widow of Sam Colt—a gentle parish church in the rural English style but complete with decorations that included the gun barrels and details of the famed "six shooter."

The Clemens house was, in fact, a thoroughly modern work, forward-looking in its style and use of materials, dynamic in its outline and elevations, delightfully irregular in its plan, and arrestingly polychromatic. It was not merely quirky; rather, it was the expression of a dedicated and cosmopolitan modernist who injected new technologies where he could and stretched the limits of historical vocabularies where he willed. With inventive and spectacular interiors designed by Louis Comfort Tiffany and Associated artists a few years later, and an owner open to progressive social ideas and struggling to find a new kind of literary voice, this house should be recognized fully for what it was—a true locus of American modernism in the largest sense of the term.

Best known of Twain's fond recollections of his Hartford home are the ones written at moments of tragedy, most memorably the moving tribute to it he penned at the time of Susy's death in 1896. Less well known, perhaps, but more fitting to the sense of youth, pride, and passion that Twain felt in September 1874, as he watched his house being built, is a passage in a letter to his beloved Livy:

Small processions of people continue to rove through the house all the time. You may look at the house or the grounds from any point of view you choose & they are simply exquisite. It is a quiet, murmurous, enchanting poem *done in the solid elements of nature. The house & and the barn do not seem to have been set up on the grassy slopes & levels by laws & plans & specifications—it seems as if they* grew up and out of *the ground & and were part of the parcel of nature's handiwork. The harmony of size, shape, color—everything—is harmonious. It is a house—and the word never had so much meaning before.*

Illustrator Walter Francis Brown's rendering of Mark Twain (with walking stick) and his traveling companion, "Mr. Harris," loosely modeled on his closest Hartford friend, Joseph Twichell, in *A Tramp Abroad*

For all his western ways, Clemens seemed to settle easily into Hartford's rarefied society. In 1873, he was asked to join the Monday Evening Club, a small group of Hartford friends who met at one another's homes to talk, have dinner, and listen to a paper presented by one of the brethren. Formed only four years earlier, its original membership of thirteen included seven ministers, including the legendary Congregationalist Reverend Horace Bushnell. In the next few years, there would be as many lawyers as there were men of the cloth, as well as leaders of industry, commerce, politics—and one humorist.

Twain gave at least thirteen Monday Evening Club papers, some with titles that would hardly seem to have been suggested by his comrades, such as "Decay of the Art of Lying," and "A Protest Against Taking the Pledge." In fact, Twain's first paper, "License of the Press," delivered before an audience that included both the owners of the *Hartford Courant* and their district's congressman, was filled with his wrathful satire and exasperated incredulity.

> *[The press] has scoffed at religion till it has made scoffing popular. It has defended official criminals, on party pretexts, until it has created a United States Senate whose members are incapable of determining what crime against law and the dignity of their own body* is, *they are so morally blind, and it has made light of dishonesty till we have as a result a Congress which contracts to work for a certain sum and then deliberately steals additional wages out of the public pocket and is pained and surprised that anybody should worry about a little thing like that.*

In later years, Clemens would recall the club with great affection. Writing from his self-imposed exile in Vienna in 1898 he imagined his comrades gathered together back in Hartford and wondered about one member in particular: "And Twichell—grandfather Twichell in these late years—hard of hearing and asleep under the disconnected mumblings of the mummies."

The Reverend Joseph Hopkins Twichell was Sam Clemens's closest adult friend, so close that Clemens once called him "first after Livy." On the surface, they seemed an unlikely pair. Twichell was a Northerner, college- and seminary-educated, and a valiant former chaplain in the Union infantry who had survived some of the most devastating battles of the Civil War before taking up his duties as pastor of the fashionable Asylum Hill Congregational Church in 1865. Clemens, on the other hand, was an untutored Southerner whose education had ended at eleven, and who had abandoned his own Confederate militia unit at the merest rumor of actual fighting.

Clemens and Twichell first met in January 1868, having been introduced by Mrs. Elisha Bliss, who, with her husband, regularly attended the young pastor's church that stood just across the street from the American Publishing Company. Just before shaking hands, Clemens was overheard saying that in light of the remarkable wealth of Twichell's parishioners his church should be renamed the "Church of the Holy Spectators." Twichell was not put off, and the two men took what seems to have been an instant liking to each other.

For all their apparent differences, Clemens and Twichell shared a lively sense of humor and a love of long ruminative walks; both were deeply engaged with the world and wide open to new ideas. (Twichell was dedicated to his ministry but never pious: Twain's

Twain and Harris endure an overenthusiastic French wagon driver (above) and dress "exceedingly comfortably" (opposite) to view a frosty sunrise in the Swiss Alps, in vignettes from *A Tramp Abroad.*

bawdy *1601: Conversations as it Was by the Social Fireside in the Time of the Tudors*, with its vivid depictions of royal flatulence, was written in large part for the private delectation of Joe Twichell.) "Send on the professional preachers," Twain once wrote, perhaps with Twichell in mind, "there are none I like better to converse with. If they're not narrow-minded and bigoted they make good company." From the first, Clemens found Twichell good company. Within weeks of their first meeting, he was writing to tell his new friend how his courtship of Livy was faring. Even after Livy's parents had given their consent, he wrote, Livy was still hesitant until he began to speak of his new Hartford friends.

> *Wednesday night—she said over & over again that she loved me but was sorry she did & hoped it would yet pass away—Thursday, I was telling her what* splendid, magnificent *fellows you & your wife were, & when my enthusiasm got the best of me & the tears sprang to my eyes, she just jumped up & said she was* glad and proud *she loved me!*

Years later, Twichell recalled how their friendship grew:

> *We were both young men, and the acquaintance so begun soon grew into a friendship which continued unbroken ever after, and went on strengthening with the flight of years. I cannot say that at that point we were wholly sympathetic in either thought or feeling. Our antecedent conditions and experience in life had been very different, and in some ways, contrasted. But while originally attracted to him by the very brightness of his mind, the incomparable charm of his talk, and his rare companionableness, I was not long in finding out that he had a big, warm and tender heart.*

The long-standing relationship between Twichell and his friend inspired several of Twain's works, including "A Literary Nightmare" (1876), "Some Rambling Notes of an Idle Excursion" (1877), *A Tramp Abroad* (1880), and "Captain Stormfield's Trip to Heaven" (begun in 1868 but not published until 1907–8 in excerpt). In each, Twichell emerges in the guise of a fictitious character. Even Twain's realization that he should begin to write about his career as a riverboat pilot emerged from a conversation with his companion during one of their many long rambles together through the hills outside of Hartford. As Twain wrote to his editor and friend William Dean Howells, "Twichell and I have had a long walk in the woods, and I got to telling him about old Mississippi days of steamboating glory and grandeur as I saw them (during 5 years) from the pilot house. He said, 'What a virgin subject to hurl into a magazine!' I hadn't thought of that before. Would you like a series of papers to run through 3 months or 6 or 9—or About 4 months, say?" The result was a series of magazine articles called "Old Times on the Mississippi," which in 1883 became part of *Life on the Mississippi*.

Twichell helped officiate at the wedding of Sam and Livy in 1870 and, with his wife, Julia—known as "Harmony" to her husband and their friends—shared with them the years in Hartford that Mark Twain called the happiest and most productive of his life. Twichell also shared with his friend the lowest moments in his life. He led the services at the funerals of three of Clemens's four children, buried Livy, and finally preached at the funeral of Mark Twain himself. In this comfortable city of armaments and actuaries, theirs was as unexpected a pairing as one might imagine—and as close a friendship as any of us might ever wish for ourselves.

CHAPTER SIX

THE GILDED AGE

Off Queenstown, Ireland.
August 29, 1872.
Livy darling, I have little or nothing to write, except that I love you
& think of you day & night, & wonder . . . what you are doing and
how [Susy] comes on. . . . Consider, my dear, that I am standing
high on the stern of the ship, looking westward with my hands to my
mouth, trumpet fashion, yelling across the tossing waste of waves,
"I LOVE YOU, LIVY DARLING!"

The brand-new Hartford residence of Mr. and Mrs. Samuel L. Clemens in the mid-1870s. The *Hartford Daily Times* declared the house "one of the oddest looking buildings in the State ever designed for a dwelling, if not in the whole country," but its owners thought it perfect. Patrick McAleer, the family coachman, holds the reins of the carriage in the foreground; he worked for the Clemenses from the day of their marriage until they left their Hartford home in 1891.

Mark Twain onstage in London, 1873. He was a hit, even though one British critic found his Missouri accent—"so characteristic of some portion of Americans"—especially grating.

Just seven weeks after Langdon's death—and with Livy still prostrated by the loss of their son—Clemens set sail for England, where he planned to lecture and collect material for a new book satirizing the British. His writings had preceded him, and—though, to his fury, some of them had been published in pirated editions that earned him nothing—he was astonished and pleased on arrival to find himself the toast of London, the most popular of all American writers. "Livy darling," he wrote home,

it was flattering at the Lord Mayor's dinner tonight to have the
. . . Lord High Chancellor of England in his vast wig and gown,
with a splendid sword-bearing lackey, following him & holding up
his train, walk me arm-in-arm through the brilliant assemblage,
& welcome me with all the enthusiasm of a girl, & tell me that
when affairs of state oppress him & he can't sleep, he always has my
books at hand & forgets his perplexities in reading
them! . . . I thought I was the humblest in that great
titled assemblage. I did not know I was a lion.

A return trip with Livy and the baby the following summer would only confirm his enthusiasm. "Rural England is too absolutely beautiful to be left out of doors," he wrote. "Ought to be under glass case." Britain's finest writers sought his company: Lewis Carroll, Robert Browning, Anthony Trollope. "I couldn't get any fun out of England," he wrote later. "She is not a good text for hilarious literature. No, there wasn't anything to satirize . . . because your conscience told you to look nearer home and you would find that very thing at your own door. A man

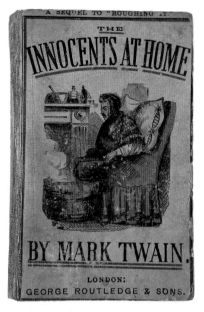

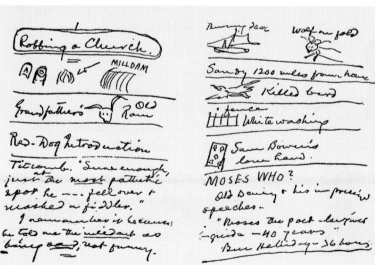

Twain's first visit to Britain in 1872, where British editions of his writings (above) were soon selling briskly, went so well that he returned the following summer, bringing with him Susy, Livy, and one of her girlhood friends, Clara Spaulding. They were photographed (top left) in Edinburgh at the home of Sam's friend the physician and essayist Dr. John Brown. The lecture notes at the bottom of the page date from later in Twain's life but were similar to those he had begun to use onstage by the early 1870s.

with a hump-backed uncle mustn't make fun of another man's cross-eyed aunt."

When Twain returned home from his first trip to Britain, it was his own country, not England, that he set out to satirize. One evening in January of 1873, while Sam and Livy were dining at Nook Farm with the Warners, the men teased the women about the inferior quality of the popular novels they were reading. The wives challenged their husbands to do better. Clemens and Warner agreed to try. The result would be *The Gilded Age*, a caustic all-out assault on the scandal and corruption and frenzied speculation that gripped the country during the administration of Ulysses S. Grant. Its central character is Eschol Sellers, a self-styled "Colonel" from Tennessee who never stops believing that great riches are just around the corner. His real-life model was an amiable cousin of Sam's named James Lampton, who, Twain wrote, "floated all his days in a tinted mist of magnificent dreams, and died at last without seeing one of them realized." Lampton's favorite phrase, "There's millions in it," became Eschol Sellers's, and Twain liked writing about him so much that he went on to write a successful play in which Sellers was featured and years later would bring him back yet again as the hero of another novel, *The American Claimant.*

"Some men worship rank," Twain would write later, "some worship heroes, some worship power, some worship God, and over these ideals they dispute and cannot unite—but they all worship money." Mark Twain gave the Gilded Age its name, but Sam Clemens personified it. Sometimes, he admitted later to a friend, "*I* feel like Colonel Sellers." No one loved money and the comfort and luxury it could buy more

The Gilded Age, the satirical novel advertised at bottom left, was meant in part to lampoon the corruption that flourished in Washington under President Ulysses S. Grant, here savaged in an 1880 cartoon by Joseph Keppler when there was talk of a third term for the former general.

than he did. No one was more constantly on the lookout for schemes that would make him wealthier than he already was. And no one would prove more keen on showing off his new prosperity. In 1873, he and Livy bought a five-acre plot on Farmington Avenue, hired a fashionable architect named Edward Tuckerman Potter, and instructed him to build them a house unlike any other in town—or anywhere else. "Mr. Clemens," Livy wrote, "seems to glory in his sense of possession." No expense was to be spared: three floors, nineteen rooms, five baths, turrets, balconies—anything that would set their home apart.

As construction began, the neighbors could not quite understand what sort of home the Clemens family was building. "[Readers] will agree with us in the opinion that it is one of the oddest looking buildings in the State ever designed for a dwelling, if not in the whole country," said the *Hartford Daily Times.* "The novelty displayed in the architecture of the building, the oddity of its internal arrangement, and the fame of its owner, will conspire to make it a house of note for a long time to come." That was exactly what Sam Clemens wanted to hear.

As work on their Hartford house went forward in the spring of 1874, the Clemens family moved to Quarry Farm, the home of Livy's adopted sister, Susan Langdon Crane, just outside Elmira. Livy was pregnant with the fourth member of the family: Clara Clemens was born in June. She weighed seven and a half pounds at birth; her father called her "the Great American Giantess."

The family would spend some twenty summers at Quarry Farm. It was a children's paradise, with at least a dozen resident cats and a constantly shifting cast of cousins for the girls to play with. And Clemens's sister-in-law soon surprised him with a hilltop pavilion where he could write in peace. "It is the loveliest study you ever saw," he reported to William Dean Howells:

(opposite top) Twain at work in the study where he would write most of *The Adventures of Tom Sawyer* and *Adventures of Huckleberry Finn*, and (bottom) the farmhouse in which he and his family spent twenty happy summers. "Mr. Clemens was never so good and loveable as he is now," Livy wrote from here, "we never were so happy together it seems to me—He is *perfectly brim full* of work, says he never worked with such perfect ease and happiness in his life. It is splendid to see him so heartily love his work, he begrudges every moment's interruption."

(left) Clemens's Quarry Farm study and its spectacular view of Elmira and its surroundings. "We are perched on a hilltop that overlooks a little world of green valleys, shining rivers, sumptuous forests and billowy uplands veiled in the haze of distance," he wrote. "We have no neighbors. It is the quietest of all quiet places, and we are hermits that eschew caves and live in the sun."

octagonal with a peaked roof, each face filled with a spacious window, . . . perched in complete isolation on the top of an elevation that commands leagues of valley and city and retreating ranges of distant blue hills. It is a cozy nest and just room in it for a sofa, table, and three or four chairs, and when the storms sweep down the remote valley and the lightning flashes behind the hills beyond and the rain beats upon the roof over my head—imagine the luxury of it.

Clemens loved it from the first. He'd set out to work right after his breakfast of steak and coffee, his daughter Clara would one day remember, with a sheaf of papers under his arm and "a little caper of delight." He spent five days a week there in splendid

A TRUE STORY

The Clemens family spent summer after summer at Quarry Farm, just outside Elmira, New York, surrounded by the family of Livy's adopted sister, Susan Langdon Crane. But Sam Clemens sought out other company at Quarry Farm as well, just as he had when a boy in Hannibal. John T. Lewis was a tenant farmer, a free-born African-American from Maryland, and an elder in his Dunkard Baptist church, who earned Clemens's undying gratitude for saving the lives of several members of the Langdon family by stopping their runaway carriage. Twain would later use Lewis as one of the models for Jim in *Adventures of Huckleberry Finn*.

Mary Ann Cord—"Aunty" Cord to the Clemens family; Aunt Rachel in the story Twain would write about her—was the Quarry Farm cook, who joined Livy, Susan, and the girls on the porch each afternoon to hear Twain read aloud what he had written that day. Late one afternoon, Twain recalled, she was pressed into telling a story of her own.

It was summer time and twilight. We were sitting on the porch of the farm-house, on the summit of the hill, and "Aunt Rachel" was sitting respectfully below our level, on the steps—for she was our servant, and colored. . . . She was sixty years old . . . a cheerful, hearty soul, and it was no more trouble for her to laugh than it is for a bird to sing. . . . I said: "Aunt Rachel, how is it that you've lived sixty years and never had any trouble?" . . .

"Misto Clemens, is you in 'arnest?" . . .

"Why, I thought—that is, I meant—why, you can't have had any trouble. I've never heard you sigh, and never seen your eye when there wasn't a laugh in it." . . .

"Has I had any trouble? Misto Clemens, I's gwyne to tell you, den I leave it to you. I was bawn down mongst de slaves."

She had been born in Virginia, where she married and gave birth to seven children. Then, in 1852, her family was torn apart.

"An' dey sole my ole man, an' took him away, an' dey began to sell my chil'en and take dem away, an' I begin to cry, an' de man say 'Shet up yo' blubberins,' an' hit me on de mouf wid his han.' An' when de las' one was gone but my little Henry, I grab him clost up to my breas', so, an' I ris up an' says, 'You shan't take him away,' I says; 'I'll kill de man dat tetches him!' . . . But my little Henry whisper an' say, 'I gwyne to run away, and den I work an' buy yo' freedom.' O, bless de chile, he always so good! . . . But dey got him—dey got him, de men did—but I took and tear de cloes mos' off of 'em an' beat 'em over de head wid my chain; an' dey give it to me, too, but I didn't mine dat."

Cord lost touch with her husband and all her children. Years later, during the Civil War, she was living in North Carolina when black troops fighting for the Union occupied her owner's plantation and asked her to bring them breakfast.

"I was a-stoopin' down by de stove . . . an' I'd jist got de pan o' hot biscuits in my han' an' was 'bout to raise up, when I see a black face come aroun' under mine, an' de eyes a-lookin' up into mine . . . an' I jist stopped right dah, an' never budged! Jist gazed an' gazed, . . . an' de pan begin to tremble, an' all of a sudden I knowed! De pan drop' on de flo' an' I grab his lef' han' an' shove back his sleeve . . . an' den I goes for his forehead an' push de

The Quarry Farm cook, Mary Ann Cord (left), was part of a sizeable staff that looked after the Clemens and Crane families at Quarry Farm. Sam Clemens himself wrote the caption for the photograph above in 1874: "The group represents the vine-clad carriageway in front of the farm-house. On the left is Megalopis (Susy) sitting in the lap of her German nurse-maid. I am sitting behind them. Mrs. Crane is in the center. Mr. [Theodore] Crane is sitting next to her. Then Mrs. Clemens and the new baby [Clara]. Her Irish nurse stands at her back. Then comes the table waitress, a young negro girl, born free. Next to her is Auntie Cord (a fragment of whose biography I have just sent to a magazine). She is the cook; was in slavery more than forty years; and the self-satisfied wench, the last of the group, is the little baby's American nurse-maid. In the middle distance . . . my mother-in-law's coachman . . . has taken a position unsolicited to help out the picture. No, that is not true. He was waiting there a minute or two before the photographer came. In the extreme background, under the archway, you glimpse my study."

hair back so, an' 'Boy!' I says, 'if you ain't my Henry, what is you doin' wid dis welt on yo' wris' an' dat sk-yar on yo' forehead! De Lord God ob Heaven be praise,' I got my own agin!'

"Oh, no, Mister Clemens, I ain't had no trouble. An' no joy!"

Twain was so moved by Mary Ann Cord's story he wrote it down precisely as she had told it. He was already a master of vernacular storytelling, but black dialect had heretofore been used in American literature almost entirely for crude comic effect. This was something altogether different, and when he sent the story off to William Dean

Howells, he was careful to include a note warning: "It has no humor in it. . . . You can pay as lightly as you choose . . . if you want it for it is rather out of my line." Titled "A True Story, Repeated Word for Word as I Heard It," it made his first appearance in the *Atlantic Monthly.* That same month, Twain published in the *New York Times* another story, "Sociable Jimmy," mostly told in the voice of a garrulous black child who was, he wrote, *"the most artless, sociable and exhaustless talker I ever came across."*

In the heart of his wife's family, Mark Twain was discovering new ways of looking at the world, and developing new voices in which to tell about it.

isolation, his hand racing across the page, the air thick with smoke from the forty Wheeling "long nine" cigars he smoked every day—so strong, one friend liked to say, "they kill at thirty yards." Here, words seemed to come to Clemens as they came nowhere else, and in the summer of 1874 he was summoning them up from eight hundred miles away and thirty years before—from the Hannibal of his boyhood, when, he wrote, "all the summer world was bright and fresh" and "the sun rose upon a tranquil world, and beamed down . . . like a benediction."

The Adventures of Tom Sawyer, finished the following summer but not published until 1876, was "simply a hymn," Clemens wrote, "put into prose to give it a worldly air." It was a celebration of a small-town American boyhood before the Civil War in which the hero chafes under the "captivity and fetters" of school, falls in love, witnesses a murder and outwits the murderer, finds a hidden treasure, manages to eavesdrop on his own funeral, and tricks his friends into painting his aunt Polly's fence.

> *Tom resumed his whitewashing and answered carelessly: . . .*
>
> *"Like it? Well, I don't see why I oughtn't to like it. Does a boy get a chance to whitewash a fence every day?"*
>
> *That put the thing in a new light. Ben stopped nibbling his apple. Tom swept his brush daintily back and forth—stepped back to note the effect—added a touch here and there— . . . Ben watching every move and getting more and more interested, more and more absorbed. Presently he said:*
>
> *"Say, Tom, let me whitewash a little."*

The book's protagonist was more or less based on Clemens himself. Becky Thatcher, the beautiful girl Tom worshiped from afar, was inspired by his boyhood neighbor

Mark Twain is thought to have begun *The Adventures of Tom Sawyer* in Hartford in 1873 and, as the notes scrawled at the top of the first page suggest (above), he originally planned to follow his hero into old age. Published three years later, the book would become Twain's most popular work. True Williams, whose drawing of Tom talking a gullible friend into whitewashing a fence appears at the left, was only the first artist drawn to its themes. Perhaps the best-loved illustrations were those of Norman Rockwell, published in 1936 (opposite page). Clockwise from top left: Aunt Polly doses Tom with castor oil; Tom endures "the most merciless flaying that even [the schoolmaster] Mr. Dobbins had ever administered"; and (at right) the worldly Huck Finn savors his pipe while Tom and his friend Joe Harper reel from their first encounter with tobacco.

Laura Hawkins. Tom's raffish friend Huckleberry Finn was modeled on the town drunk's son, Tom Blankenship.

"The story is a wonderful study of the boy-mind which inhabits a world quite distinct from that in which he is bodily present with his elders," Howells wrote after reading the manuscript, "and in this lies his great charm and its universality, for boy nature . . . is the same everywhere." It would become the most popular of all Twain's books, and its success would encourage him to return again and again to the scenes of his youth, beginning with a series of magazine articles drawing upon his steamboat years that eventually became the first half of another book, *Life on the Mississippi*. After reading the first installment, Howells told him: "The piece about the Mississippi is capital. It almost made the water in our ice-pitcher muddy."

Clemens's past now seemed an inexhaustible source of inspiration for him. "When the tank runs dry," he wrote, "you've only to leave it alone and it will fill up again in time." During the 1870s and early 1880s, it almost always would.

In September of 1874, the Clemens family moved into their new, still unfinished house in Hartford. "I have been bullyragged all day by the builder," Sam wrote to his mother-in-law,

> *by his foreman, by the architect, by the tapestry devil who is to upholster the furniture, by the idiot who is putting down the carpets, by the scoundrel who is setting up the billiard table (and has left the balls in New York), by the wildcat who is sodding the ground and finishing the driveway . . . by a book agent whose body is in the backyard and the coroner notified. Just think of this going on the whole day long, and I am a man who loathes details with all my heart! But I haven't lost my temper, and I've made Livy lie down* most *of the time; could anybody make her lie down* all *the time?*

Despite his complaints, the house was everything Clemens had hoped for. There were balconies with splendid views of the surrounding countryside and an elongated porch for summer afternoons; a master bedroom for him and Livy, dominated by what he called "the most comfortable bedstead that ever was, with space enough in it for a family, and carved angels enough to bring peace to the sleepers, and pleasant dreams." Clemens and Livy liked the wooden cherubs so much that they slept with their heads at the foot of the bed so they could see them better; the girls loved their parents' bed, too, Clara recalled, and relished being at least slightly ill because then they were allowed to spend the day beneath its blankets, dressing and undressing the angels as if they were oversize dolls.

Susy, the eldest child, was given a room of her own. Clara shared the nursery with a third daughter, Jean, born in 1880, and the three girls soon took over as their schoolroom what had been originally designed as their father's study. To accommodate them—and to get away from the noise they made—he moved his desk upstairs to the big third-floor billiard room, where he could smoke and write and entertain his friends without fear of being disturbed.

Some, recalling Sam Clemens's youthful years on the Mississippi, imagined that his house, with its tur-

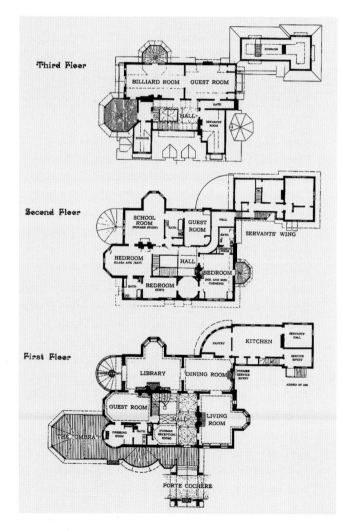

rets and balconies, was all meant somehow to evoke a steamboat. There isn't a hint of it in any of the correspondence having to do with the house's construction, but Clemens grew to like the analogy: one of his favorite parts of the house was the shady octagonal balcony just off the billiard room. Here he had a hammock strung, from which he liked to look down into the green tops of his trees or admire the clouds mirrored in the stream that wandered off through the meadows below; he called his retreat his "Texas deck."

It eventually took seven servants to run the household, headed by Livy's Irish-American maid, Katy Leary, and the African-American butler, George Griffin, who turned up to wash the windows not long after the Clemenses moved in and stayed with the family throughout their time in Hartford. He was a shrewd and resourceful man, a deacon of his church, and especially adept at inventing tactful ways of turning away visitors who arrived unannounced, expecting to be ushered right in to see Mark Twain.

The family often gathered in the crowded, friendly library. There, with a fountain gently splashing in the adjacent glassed-in conservatory, they sometimes played at big-game hunting: Clemens was the elephant, scrambling on all fours among the oriental carpets with one or another

Edward Tuckerman Potter (above) was an innovative and fanciful architect whose plans for the Clemens house (left) delighted his clients. At right, on a warm summer afternoon in 1875, Mr. and Mrs. Sam Clemens and Susy enjoy the deeply shaded porch, with two of Sam's friends from the *Quaker City* tour, Dr. and Mrs. Abraham Reeves.

small huntress on his back. "George was the lion," he wrote, "also the tiger, but preferably the tiger because as a lion his roaring was over-robust and embarrassed the hunt by scaring Susy." Clemens read aloud to the girls here, too, and was often asked to make up a brand-new bed-time story for them, beginning with the cat at one end of the mantelpiece and then incorporating every item in turn until he reached the other end and the watercolor portrait of a young girl his daughters had named Emmeline.

The children required me to construct a romance—always impromptu—not a moment's preparation permitted—and into that romance I had to get all that bric-a-brac and the . . . pictures. I had to start always with the cat and finish with Emmeline. I was never allowed the refreshment of a change, end for end. It was not permissible to introduce a bric-a-brac ornament into the story out of its place in the procession.

These bric-a-bracs were never allowed a peaceful day, a reposeful day, a restful Sabbath. . . . They knew no existence but a monotonous career of violence and bloodshed. In the course of time the bric-

The Clemens house in midwinter, 1882. Not infrequently, Sam's daughter Clara recalled, "we awoke to find the many trees behind our house one mass of dazzling ice. Each branch and twig glistened with beauty and absorbed the attention of the entire family."

a-brac and the pictures showed wear. It was because they had had
so many and such tumultuous adventures in their romantic career.

Livy with Susy and Clara, about 1880

Christmas was the high point of the family's year. A ten-foot-tall fir filled the alcove in the library. Evergreens festooned the doors and windows and all eighteen mantelpieces. The doors to the guest room were kept locked. Behind them, Livy wrapped and tagged a mountain of packages and prepared the fifty Christmas baskets of food and wine she and the girls distributed by sleigh on Christmas Eve. Clemens once called these elaborate preparations "the infernal Christmas suicide," but he loved it all. Sometimes he dressed up as St. Nicholas, stomping around among his delighted girls in the schoolroom—its lamps discreetly lowered to add to the illusion—demanding to be thanked in advance in case they didn't like what he had brought. They almost always did. Their parents stayed up most of the night making sure of that—once, an upright piano was somehow spirited up the staircase and into the schoolroom to astonish Clara, then six.

In 1881, Clemens decided his house was still not large or grand enough, and had its first floor redone by Louis Comfort Tiffany, with a polished marble floor in the entrance hall, ornate brasswork specially made in India, and a stained-glass window created by the master decorator himself. When William Dean Howells brought his small son to visit soon thereafter, the boy was awestruck. "Why, they've even got their *soap* painted," he told his father when he saw a cake of pink soap on the bathroom sink; and when he spotted George Griffin preparing to serve breakfast the next morning, he hurried back to wake his father: "Better get up, Papa. The *slave* is setting the table!" Howells himself was impressed. "The Clemenses are wholesouled hosts," he wrote to his wife, "with inextinguishable money and a palace of a house."

For all the luxury that now surrounded Livy Clemens, life as "Mrs. Mark Twain" was never easy. She remained physically frail, subject to a host of ailments that kept her in bed, and she was often left alone for months at a time to care for the girls, supervise the servants, and oversee every detail of the house and garden. She also had to cope with the constant flood of casual visitors. The Nook Farm colonists did not lock their doors, wandering in and out of one another's homes as mood and weather suited. This was not an unmixed blessing. The Clemenses' neighbor Harriet Beecher Stowe grew increasingly vague and restless in her old age, and Livy and the girls were sometimes startled late at night to hear

Your Loving Santa Claus

No parents ever worked harder—or with more success—to make their children's Christmases memorable than Sam and Livy Clemens. This letter was addressed to their oldest daughter in 1875, but since she was not yet four when it was written, many of its fancies must have been meant for her mother.

Santa Claus, Whom People Sometimes Call The Man in the Moon:
My dear Susy Clemens:

   I have received and read all the letters which you and your little sister have written me by the hand of your mother and your nurses; I have also read those which you little people have written me with your own hands—for although you did not use any characters that are in grown people's alphabet, you used the characters that all children in all lands on earth and in the twinkling stars use; and as all my subjects in the moon are children and use no character but that, you will easily understand that I can read your and your baby sister's jagged and fantastic marks without any trouble at all. But I had trouble with those letters which you dictated through your mother and the nurses, for I am a foreigner and cannot read English writing well. You will find that I made no mistakes about the things which you and the baby ordered in your own letters—I went down your chimney at midnight when you were asleep and delivered them all myself—and kissed both of you, too, because you are good children, well-trained, nice-mannered, and about the most obedient little people I ever saw. But in the letters which you dictated there were some words which I could not make out for certain, and one or two orders which I could not fill because we ran out of stock. Our last lot of kitchen-furniture for dolls has just gone to a very poor little child in the North Star away up in the cold country above the Big Dipper. Your mama can show you that star and you will say: "little Snow Flake" (for that is the child's name) "I'm glad you got that furniture, for you need it more than I." That is, you must write that, with your own hand, and Snow Flake will write you an answer. If you only spoke it she wouldn't hear you. Make your letter light and thin, for the distance is great and the postage very heavy.

   There was a word or two in your mama's letter which I couldn't be certain of. I took it to be "trunk full of doll's clothes." Is that it? I will call at your kitchen door about nine o'clock this morning to inquire. But I must not see anybody and I must

The library fireplace in the restored Twain house: The elaborately carved mantel was salvaged from a Scottish castle. Just below it is a brass plate that reads, "The ornament of a house is the friends that frequent it."

not speak to anybody but you. When the kitchen doorbell rings George must be blindfolded and sent to open the door. Then he must go back to the dining-room or the china closet and take the cook with him. You must tell George he must walk on tiptoe and not speak—otherwise he will die some day. Then you must go up to the nursery and stand on a chair or the nurse's bed and put your ear to the speaking-tube that leads down to the kitchen and when I whistle through it you must speak in the tube and say, "Welcome, Santa Claus!" Then I will ask whether it was a trunk you ordered or not. If you say it was, I shall ask you what color you want the trunk to be. Your mama will help you to name a nice color and then you must tell me every single thing in detail which you want the trunk to contain. Then when I say "Goodbye and Merry Christmas to my little Susy Clemens," you must say "Goodbye, good old Santa Claus, I thank you very much and please tell that little Snow Flake I will look at her star tonight and she must look down here—I will be right in the West bay-window; and every fine night I will look at her star and say, 'I know somebody up there and like her, too.' " Then you must go down into the library and make George close all the doors that open into the main hall, and everybody must keep still for a little while. I will go to the moon and get those things and in a few minutes I will come down the chimney that belongs to the fireplace that is in the hall—if it is a trunk you want—because I couldn't get such a thing as a trunk down the nursery chimney, you know.

People may talk if they want, until they hear my footsteps in the hall. Then you tell them to keep quiet a little while till I go back up the chimney. Maybe you will not hear my footsteps at all—so you may go now and then and peep through the dining room doors, and by and by you will see that thing which you want, right under the piano in the drawing-room—for I shall put it there. If I should leave any snow in the hall, you must tell George to sweep it into the fireplace, for I haven't time to do such things. George must not use a broom, but a rag—else he will die some day. You must watch George and not let him run into danger. If my boot should leave a stain on the marble, George must not holy-stone it away. Leave it there always in memory of my visit; and whenever you look at it or show it to anybody you must let it remind you to be a good little girl. Whenever you are naughty and somebody points to that mark which your good old Santa Claus's boot made on the marble, what will you say, little Sweetheart?

Goodbye for a few minutes, till I come down to the world and ring the kitchen door-bell.

Your loving Santa Claus
Palace of St. Nicholas in the Moon, Christmas Morning

The entrance hall (above), designed by Louis Comfort Tiffany; the nursery table set for a dolls' tea party; and the conservatory in which, William Dean Howells recalled, guests sometimes breakfasted while the coachman, Patrick McAleer, "sprinkled the pretty bower, which poured out its responsive perfume in the delicate accents of its varied blossoms."

The Clemenses' bed and one of the carved angels their daughters especially loved

old songs sung in a dry, almost disembodied voice drifting up out of the darkened parlor into which their aged neighbor had ghosted to sit at the piano. Mrs. Stowe was also fond of flowers and liked to surprise Livy with bouquets of them, often torn up by the roots from the Clemenses' own greenhouse when the gardener wasn't looking. Livy hung scissors there for a time in the hope that her visitor would at least snip the blossoms rather than destroy the plants, but the bright-eyed old lady's horticultural fervor could rarely be controlled.

It also fell to Livy to pay the bills and keep the accounts and to ask her mother for loans when—as continually happened—her husband's airy extravagance got them into financial trouble. "I get a little homesick to see you once in a while," she once wrote her mother; "tonight I should like to put my head in your lap and cry just a little bit, I want to be somebody's baby. . . . I have . . . servants to manage, I have a glorious husband to try and be a woman for, but sometimes I would like to lie down and give it all up—I feel so incompetent for everything. I come so very far short . . . yet I think I do try earnestly every day."

When Clemens was home, he expected everything to revolve around him. His moods shifted from minute to minute, and his temper was volcanic. One Sunday morning, neighbors on their way to church watched in astonishment as one by one he hurled his shirts out a second-floor window because he had found one with a missing button. He himself wondered at what he once called the "periodical and sudden changes of mood in me, from deep melancholy to half-insane tempests and cyclones of humor."

The drawing room features the same marble bust of Livy that had once graced her parents' parlor in Elmira.

His daughters all adored him, but even their adoration was alloyed with fear. "He was a constant surprise in his varied moods which dropped unheralded upon him," Clara remembered, "creating day and night for those about him." She and her sisters loved to be with their father, she added, and his sudden rages were rarely aimed at them, but they preferred, even as little girls, to visit him in pairs—the prospect of witnessing one of his lunges from joy to anger and back again was too unsettling for any one of them to endure alone.

Some thought the Clemens marriage a mismatch. The woman's-rights orator Anna Dickinson, a longtime friend of the Langdon family, wrote that she could never understand how Olivia, "as frail in body as she is clear of mind & loving of soul, ever married the vulgar boor to whom she gave herself—I hear him all about the country at wine suppers . . . dirty, smoking, drinking." But there is no evidence that the Clemenses were ever unhappy with each other. "Livy my darling," Sam had written from England one evening in 1874:

I love to be writing about arriving [home]. . . . And I love to picture myself ringing the bell at midnight—then a pause of a second or two—then the turning of the bolt, & "Who is it?"—then ever so many kisses . . . then I drinking my cocktail & undressing & you standing by—then to bed and—everything happy & jolly as it should be. I do love & honor you, my darling.

They would continue to love and honor each other all their lives.

CHAPTER SEVEN

TRUTH

You don't know about me without you have read a book by the name of The Adventures of Tom Sawyer; *but that ain't no matter. That book was made by Mr. Mark Twain, and he told the truth, mainly. There was things which he stretched, but mainly he told the truth.*
— *Adventures of Huckleberry Finn*, 1885

At Quarry Farm in the summer of 1876, Twain had begun another book drawn in large part from memories of his own boyhood, a sequel to *The Adventures of Tom Sawyer* but centered this time on Tom's friend, Huckleberry Finn. Beginning with *The Celebrated Jumping Frog of Calaveras County*, he had made a specialty of writing short pieces told by vernacular narrators, but this was something new: a full-scale novel told in the authentic voice of a semiliterate small-town American boy. It began, like its predecessor, as a lighthearted adventure story for children, but the resemblance ended soon thereafter.

Events in the wider world that summer seem to have influenced that decision. As Clemens worked away in his hilltop pavilion, the United States was celebrating its centennial summer—a century of freedom —but it was also witnessing the denial of freedom to those African- Americans who had been liberated from slavery just eleven years earlier. Reconstruction was coming to its bitter end. The white North, now preoccupied with its own political and economic problems, no longer seemed interested in the plight of four million freedmen; and one by one, the states of the former Confederacy were reestablishing white Democratic rule. White mobs and terrorist night riders like the members of the Ku Klux Klan kept former slaves from enjoying the rights of full citizenship that the Fourteenth and Fifteenth Amendments were supposed to have guaranteed to them. Black Southerners were being abandoned.

Adventures of Huckleberry Finn would reflect Mark Twain's feelings about all of it. Tom Sawyer's St. Petersburg—Twain's fictional version of Hannibal—had been a sunny place in which what he once called the "bald, grotesque and unwar- rantable usurpation" of slavery that had been such a presence in Sam Clemens's own boyhood had remained mostly out of sight. In *Huckleberry Finn*, slavery—and race—were brought front and center. Huck's father had been merely shiftless and alcoholic in *Tom Sawyer*. Now he became a violent, potentially murderous thief whose

(opposite) **Mark Twain muses for the cam- era, about 1884.**

(below) **"The end. Yours Truly, Huck Finn,"** the final illustration by E. W. Kemble for the first edition of *Adventures of Huckle- berry Finn*, **1885**

sense of his own worth rests solely on his supposed superiority to African-Americans. The sight of a well-dressed, well-educated free black visitor from Ohio—"a mulatter, most as white as a white man"—is nearly more than he can bear.

> *He had the whitest shirt on you ever see . . . and the shiniest hat; and there ain't a man in that town that's got as fine clothes as what he had; and he had a gold watch and chain, and a silver-headed cane—the awfulest old gray-headed nabob in the State. And what do you think? They said he was a p'fessor in a college, and could talk all kinds of languages, and knowed everything. And that ain't the wust. They said he could vote when he was at home. Well, that let me out. Thinks I, what is the country a-coming to? It was 'lection day, and I was just about to go and vote myself if I warn't too drunk to get there; but when they told me there was a State in this country where they'd let that nigger vote, I drawed out. I says I'll never vote agin. . . . And to see the cool way of that nigger—why, he wouldn't a give me the road if I hadn't shoved him out o' the way.*

The plot is a deceptively simple story about two runaways: Huck, a white boy fleeing civilization, and Jim, a black man running away from slavery. Together they drift down the Mississippi on a raft, encountering all manner of people and places—and getting to know each other.

> *This . . . night we run between seven and eight hours, with a current that was making over four mile an hour. We catched fish and talked, and we took a swim now and then to keep off sleepiness. It was kind of solemn, drifting down the big, still river, laying on our backs, looking up at the stars, and we didn't ever feel like talking loud, and it warn't often that we laughed—only a little kind of a low chuckle.*

Huck's experiences with Jim turn upside down everything he has been taught about black people and white, slavery and freedom, good and evil.

Preliminary notes for *Adventures of Huckleberry Finn*

The Hardest-Working Creature in the World

Mark Twain's A Tramp Abroad, *published in 1880, dealt mostly with what he, his family, and his friend Joseph Twichell saw and did during a long visit to Europe the previous year, but he also found within it room for this disquisition on the lowly ant.*

It seems to me that in the matter of intellect the ant must be a strangely over-rated bird. During many summers, now, I have watched him, when I ought to have been in better business, and I have not yet come across a living ant that seemed to have any more sense than a dead one. I refer to the ordinary ant, of course; I have had no experience of those wonderful Swiss and African ones which vote, keep drilled armies, hold slaves, and dispute about religion. Those particular ants may be all that the naturalist paints them, but I am persuaded that the average ant is a sham. I admit his industry, of course; he is the hardest-working creature in the world—when anybody is looking—but his leather-headedness is the point I make against him. He goes out foraging, he makes a capture, and then what does he do? Go home? No—he goes anywhere but home. He doesn't know where home is. His home may be only three feet away—no matter, he can't find it. He makes his capture, as I have said; it is generally something which can be of no sort of use to himself or anybody else; it is usually seven times bigger than it ought to be; he hunts out the awkwardest place to take hold of it; he lifts it bodily up in the air by main force, and starts; not toward home, but in the opposite direction; not calmly and wisely, but with a frantic haste which is wasteful of his strength; he fetches up against a pebble, and instead of going around it, he climbs over it backward dragging his booty after him, tumbles down on the other side, jumps up in a passion, kicks the dust off his clothes, moistens his hands, grabs his property viciously, yanks it this way, then that, shoves it ahead of him a moment, turns tail and lugs it after him another moment, gets madder and madder, then presently hoists it into the air and goes tearing away in an entirely new direction; comes to a weed; it never occurs to him to go around it; no, he must climb it; and he does climb it, dragging his worthless property to the top—which is as bright a thing to do as it would be for me to carry a sack of flour from Heidelberg to Paris by way of Strasburg steeple; when he gets up there he finds that that is not the place; takes a cursory glance at the scenery and either climbs down again or tumbles down, and starts off once more—as usual, in a new direction. At the end of half an hour, he fetches up within six inches of the place he started from and lays his burden down; meantime he has been over all the ground for two yards around, and climbed all the weeds and pebbles he came across. Now he wipes the sweat from his brow, strokes his limbs, and then marches aimlessly off, in as violent a hurry as ever. He traverses a good deal of zig-zag country, and by and by stumbles on his same booty again. He does not remember to have ever seen it before; he looks around to see which is not the way home, grabs his bundle and starts; he goes through the same adventures he had before; finally stops to rest, and a friend comes along. Evidently the friend remarks that a last year's grasshopper leg is a very noble acquisition, and inquires where he got it. Evidently the proprietor does not remember exactly where he did get it, but thinks he got it "around here somewhere." Evidently the friend contracts to help him freight it home. Then, with a judgment peculiarly antic (pun not intentional), they take hold of opposite ends of that grasshopper leg and begin to tug with all their might in opposite directions. Presently they take a rest and confer together. They decide that something is wrong, they can't make out what. Then they go at it again, just as before. Same result. Mutual recriminations follow. Evidently each accuses the other of being an obstructionist. They warm up, and the dispute ends in a fight. They lock themselves together and chew each other's jaws for a while; then they roll and tumble on the ground till one loses a horn or a leg and has to haul off for repairs. They make up and go to work again in the same old insane way, but the crippled ant is at a disadvantage; tug as he may, the other one drags off the booty and him at the end of it. Instead of giving up, he hangs on, and gets his shins bruised against every obstruction that comes in the way. By and by, when that grasshopper leg has been dragged all over the same old ground once more, it is finally dumped at about the spot where it originally lay, the two perspiring ants inspect it thoughtfully and decide that dried grasshopper legs are a poor sort of property after all, and then each starts off in a different direction to see if he can't find an old nail or something else that is heavy enough to afford entertainment and at the same time valueless enough to make an ant want to own it.

*Jim talked out loud. . . . He was saying how the first thing he would
do when he got to a free State, he would go to saving up money and
never spend a single cent, and when he got enough he would buy his
wife . . . and then they would both work to buy the two children, and
if their master wouldn't sell them, they'd get an Ab'litionist to go
and steal them.*

*It most froze me to hear such talk. . . . Here was this nigger,
which I had as good as helped to run away, coming right out flat-
footed and saying he would steal his children—children that
belonged to a man I didn't even know; a man that hadn't ever done
me no harm.*

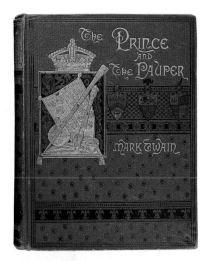

At summer's end, with his characters still drifting southward on the
Mississippi, Twain shelved the manuscript. "I like it only tolerably
well, as far as I have got," he told Howells after writing four hundred
manuscript pages, "and may possibly pigeonhole it or burn the manuscript when it is done." He couldn't quite see where the story—or the
country—was to go from there.

Over the next seven years Twain would often put *Huckleberry Finn* aside
for other things. He wrote *1601*, a ribald Elizabethan sketch intended
only for the private amusement of his friend Joe Twichell. He took his
family to Europe for a stay of seventeen months—in part, simply to
reduce the expenses of his household and to get away from the admirers
who never seemed to stop knocking at his Hartford door—and from it
produced a new book of travel writing called *A Tramp Abroad*.

The Prince and the Pauper, **1881; and
an illustration for it by Frank Merrill.
The book was dedicated to "those good-
mannered and agreeable children, Susie
and Clara Clemens."**

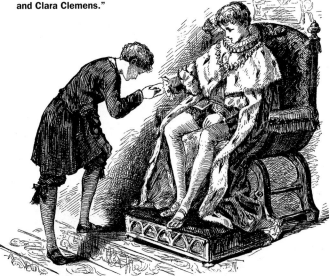

And in 1881 he made a bid for the kind of literary respectability that had always been denied
him, by publishing a children's book set in Tudor
England, called *The Prince and the Pauper*. It
was a genteel tale, well plotted and meticulously
researched, but told with little of the vigor or wit
or directness that had characterized his work so
far. Livy and the girls loved it. To them, it was
proof that he was more than a mere "humorist."
"It is unquestionably the best book he has ever
written," wrote Susy. "It troubles me to have so
few people know, I mean *really* know him. They
think of Mark Twain as a humorist *joking* at
everything. That is the way people picture papa,
I wanted papa to write a book that would reveal
something of his kind sympathetic nature. . . .
The book is full of lovely charming ideas and oh,
the language, it is perfect!" Conventional critics

loved the language, too; it was "pure," they said, "refined," "ennobling." "I like this book better than *Tom Sawyer*," Clemens told a friend, "because I haven't put any *fun* in it. . . . You know a body always enjoys seeing himself attempting something out of his line."

Then, in April of 1882, Mark Twain returned to the great river that had been the scene of his first adventures, traveling by steamboat the length of the Mississippi from St. Louis to New Orleans and all the way north again to Minnesota, gathering material for the second half of the volume that would become *Life on the Mississippi*. He relished getting together with his old friends and delighted in the soft spring landscape, but found the river's course had changed so much since his time in the pilothouse that it "was as brand new to me as if it had been built yesterday & built while I was absent"; trying to get his bearings was "like a man pointing out to me a place in the sky where a cloud had been. I can't reproduce the cloud." Railroads had long since robbed his beloved steamboats of much of their business: "In [the] old days the boats lay singly with their noses against the wharf, wedged in, stern out in the river, like sardines in a box"; now, he noted, there was plenty of room for them to tie up end to end. He was saddened to see tumbledown villages, "miserable cabins," and deserted plantations over-looked by the exploding American economy that followed the Civil War, and he was frankly con-temptuous of the romantic nostalgia for slavery days that helped to hold the whole region back. Two former slaves working as laundresses aboard a steamboat who chatted about old times in his hearing seemed to him to have it right: the sight of an espe-cially handsome old plantation house only reminded one that "many a poor nigger has been killed there, just for nuffin', & flung into that river thar' & that's the last of 'em." And when one said she'd like to see a return to slavery days "just for a minute, just to see how it would seem," the other was adamant: "I don't want 'em back again even for a minute," she said. "It was mighty rough times on the niggers."

Back at Quarry Farm the following summer, his first-hand impressions of the troubled South still fresh in his mind, Clemens returned with new eagerness to *Adventures of Huckleberry Finn*. "I haven't piled up MS so in years as I have done since we came here . . . three weeks ago," he wrote Howells.

Traveling on the Continent in 1878 and weary of European hotel fare, Twain got up this list of the American dishes he most longed for.

Susy, Jean, Livy, and Clara Clemens, about 1883

Why, it's like old times to step straight into the study, damp from the breakfast table, & sail right in & sail right on, the whole day long, without thought of running short of stuff or words. I wrote 4000 words today & I touch 3000 & upwards pretty often, & don't fall below 2600 on any working day. And when I get fagged out, I lie abed a couple of days & read & smoke, and then go at it again for 6 or 7 days. . . . am away along in a big one that I half-finished two or three years ago. I expect to complete it in a month or six weeks or two months more. And I shall like it, whether anybody else does or not.

The simple boy's story became a morality tale in which, Twain later wrote, "a sound heart & a deformed conscience come into collision & conscience suffers defeat." The novel reaches its moral climax in Chapter 31. Through all of their adventures, Huck has grown closer and closer to Jim. Early one morning Huck hears him weeping,

sitting there with his head down betwixt his knees, moaning and mourning to himself. I didn't take notice nor let on. I knowed what it was about. He was thinking about his wife and his children, way up yonder, and he was low and homesick; because he hadn't ever been away from home before in his life; and I do believe he cared

119

just as much for his people as white folks does for their'n. It don't seem natural, but I reckon it's so. He was often moaning and mourning that way nights, when he judged I was asleep, and saying, "Po' little 'Lizabeth! po' little Johnny! it's mighty hard; I spec' I ain't ever gwyne to see you no mo', no mo'!" He was a mighty good nigger, Jim was.

Huck is soon faced with what he sees as a terrible choice. He has come to love Jim, but everything he has been taught also suggests that he has committed a grievous sin in helping him escape. "The more I studied about this," Huck says, "the more my conscience went to grinding me. . . . My wickedness was being watched all the time from up there in heaven, whilst I was stealing a poor old woman's nigger that hadn't ever done me no harm."

Finally, Huck writes out a letter to Jim's owner, telling her where her runaway property can be found. He feels good about doing this at first, and marvels at "how near I come to being lost and going to hell." But then he hesitates.

[I] got to thinking over our trip down the river and I see Jim before me all the time: in the day and in the night-time, sometimes moonlight, sometimes storms, and we a-floating along, talking and singing and laughing. But somehow I couldn't seem to strike no places to harden me against him, but only the other kind. I'd see him standing my watch on top of his'n, 'stead of calling me, so I could go on sleeping; and see how glad he was when I come back out of the fog . . . and such-like times; and would always call me honey . . . and do everything he could think of for me, and how good he always was; and at last I struck the time . . . [when he said] I was the best friend old Jim ever had in the world, and the only one he's got now; and then I happened to look around and see that paper.

It was a close place. I took it up, and held it in my hand. I was a-trembling because I'd got to decide, forever, betwixt two things, and I knowed it. I studied a minute, sort of holding my breath, and then says to myself:

"All right, then, I'll go to hell"—and tore it up.

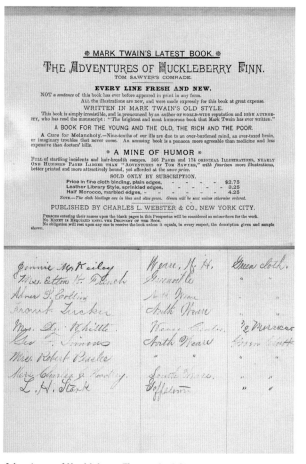

Adventures of Huckleberry Finn marked Clemens's debut as a publisher. The prospectus above was carried by subscription agents working for his firm, Charles L. Webster & Company; customers signed up for one of three kinds of binding. The call for more book agents below appeared in newspapers.

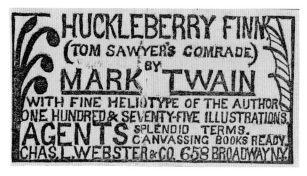

More adventures follow, and in the last few chapters Jim finds himself in chains again for a time, precisely as the former slaves Clemens had seen on his Southern journey were finding themselves trapped in new kinds of bondage.

In 1884, eager to see his new book in print—and certain as always that publishers and magazine editors were either inept or out to cheat him—Clemens decided to form his own company to publish it. It would be named after the young nephew-by-marriage, Charles L. Webster, who was already Clemens's "business manager," responsible for everything from defending his copyrights and looking after his far-flung investments to finding a good plumber for the Hartford house. Now in charge of day-to-day affairs at the new company, he would be responsible for increasing Mark Twain's book profits as well.

Twain worried that the language in which he had told his tale was too unrefined for the book to do well and, as always, counted on Livy to comb through the manuscript, searching out anything she thought might offend readers. "Clara and I would be sitting with Mama while she was looking the manuscript over," Susy recalled, "and I remember . . . with what pangs of regret we used to see her turn down the leaves of the pages which meant that some delightfully terrible part must be scratched out. We thought the book would be almost ruined without it

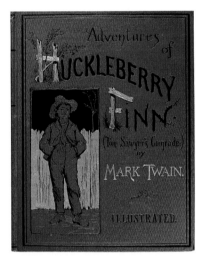

The cover of the first edition of *Adventures of Huckleberry Finn* and (below) two illustrations by Norman Rockwell for a 1940 edition show Huck with his drunken father and with Jim, the runaway slave

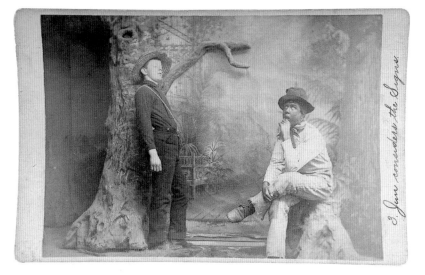

(left) Two rare cabinet cards depicting scenes from an unauthorized stage production of *Huckleberry Finn* made sometime during the late 1880s. Jim is played by a white actor in blackface.

(below) The ban on *Huckleberry Finn* in which Twain saw a rare business opportunity, as reported in the *Boston Evening Transcript*, March 17, 1885

For the true life of a nation, as of an individual, consists not in the multitude of possessions, but in righteousness and peace, in intelligence and education, in the love of truth and justice, in the fulfilment of the destiny which God has assigned to her in the world.

"HUCKLEBERRY FINN" BARRED OUT. The Concord (Mass.) Public Library committee has decided to exclude Mark Twain's latest book from the library. One member of the committee says that, while he does not wish to call it immoral, he thinks it contains but little humor, and that of a very coarse type. He regards it as the veriest trash. The librarian and the other members of the committee entertain similar views, characterizing it as rough, coarse and inelegant, dealing with a series of experiences not elevating, the whole book being more suited to the slums than to intelligent, respectable people.

TOWN MEETINGS YESTERDAY.

NATICK. The annual town election in Natick yesterday was a close contest between the license and temperance parties, which resulted in the election of a mixed ticket of town officials, but is so close that the result at 10.30 had not been announced. The following-named are known to be elected: Town clerk, George L. Sleeper; treasurer, Edward Clark; school committee. G. D

but we gradually came to feel as mamma did." The editor of *The Century* magazine, in which it was first serialized, went through it, too, excising references to nakedness and dead cats, even changing "in a sweat" to "in a hurry."

But when *Adventures of Huckleberry Finn* was published by Twain's company in February of 1885, *Life* magazine still denounced its "blood-curdling humor" and "coarse and dreary fun" as unsuitable for children. Louisa May Alcott was appalled, too: "If Mr. Clemens cannot think of something better to tell our pure-minded lads and lasses, he had best stop writing for them. It is time that this influential pseudonym should cease to carry into homes and libraries unworthy productions. The trouble with Mr. Clemens is that he has no reliable sense of propriety."

Most critics failed to review *Huckleberry Finn* at all, and when the Concord, Massachusetts, public library banned it from its shelves, Clemens professed to be delighted. "The Committee of the Public Library of Concord, Mass., has given us a rattling tip-top puff," he told Charley Webster, "which will go into every paper in the country. They have expelled Huck from their library as 'trash and suitable only for the slums.' That will sell 25,000 copies for us sure."

In the early 1880s, Clemens had been a frequent visitor to the office of Ulysses S. Grant at Number Two Wall Street. In *The Gilded Age*, he had savagely caricatured the scandal-ridden Washington over which Grant had presided as president, but he had nothing but admiration for the

Charles L. Webster, the harassed nephew-by-marriage who was at least nominally in charge of Twain's publishing company, and the firm's best-selling author, ex-president Ulysses S. Grant, working on the galleys of his memoir during the last weeks of his life

general himself. "He was a very great man and superlatively good," Clemens remembered, and they had become friends after Grant left the White House.

Then, in the spring of 1884, it was discovered that Grant's trusted business partner, Ferdinand Ward, had swindled their banking firm out of all its assets. Ward went to prison for his crimes—and Clemens threatened to horsewhip him when he got out—but Grant was ruined. Humiliated, and desperate to provide for his family, he was persuaded to write his memoirs and tentatively took the first offer he got for their publication. Clemens quickly doubled that offer and talked Grant into signing on with his own firm. He was sure, he told Charley Webster, that he could sell at least 300,000 two-volume sets and that Grant's royalties would amount to nearly half a million dollars, "the largest single check," he promised, "ever paid an author in the world's history."

Then Grant developed cancer of the throat. Though he lost his ability to stand or talk, he did not retreat from the task, just as he had refused to retreat during the Civil War. "General Grant wrought heroically with his pen while his disease made its steady inroads upon his life," Clemens recalled. "Toward the last he was not able to speak, but used a pencil and small slips of paper when he needed to say anything. I went to see him once toward the end, and he asked me with his pencil . . . if there was a prospect that his book would make something for his family. I said that . . . the subscriptions and the money were coming in fast. . . . He expressed his gratification, with his pencil."

Grant corrected the last page proofs on July 10, 1885. Thirteen days later, he died. As Clemens watched the five-hour funeral procession pass up Broadway from the offices of his publishing company on Union Square, orders for the general's *Memoirs* were pouring in, and the book was already at the printer's. The future of Charles L. Webster & Company—and Mark Twain—never seemed brighter.

Sam Clemens turned fifty that fall, and tributes poured in from all over the world. He was the most famous writer in America—and the richest, rich enough for his family to live like millionaires. And he had just invested in another business he felt would make him even wealthier, a marvelous machine that promised to revolutionize the printing business—"very much the best investment I ever made," he boasted to a friend.

There was every sign that he had put his hardscrabble boyhood and his wandering youth far behind him. "I am frightened," he wrote, "at the proportions of my prosperity. It seems to me that whatever I touch turns to gold." But not even in his wildest dreams—or his worst nightmares—could he have foreseen all that was about to happen to him and to his family.

By 1886, Mark Twain had reached a level of celebrity no other American author had ever approached. This short biography was given away with every pack of Duke Cigarettes. It was part of a series of "Histories of Poor Boys who have become rich" that included P. T. Barnum and Buffalo Bill Cody.

Plymouth Rock and the Pilgrims

Asked to address the First Annual Dinner of the Philadelphia Chapter of the New England Society—an organization dedicated to preserving the memory of the first Puritan settlers—on December 22, 1881, Mark Twain gave his listeners more than they'd bargained for.

My first American ancestor, gentlemen, was an Indian—an early Indian. Your ancestors skinned him alive, and I am an orphan. Not one drop of my blood flows in that Indian's veins today. I stand here, lone and forlorn, without an ancestor. They skinned him! I do not object to that, if they needed his fur; but alive, gentlemen—alive! They skinned him alive—and before company! That is what rankles. Think how he must have felt; for he was a sensitive person and easily embarrassed. If he had been a bird, it would have been all right, and no violence done to his feelings, because he would have been considered "dressed." But he was not a bird, gentlemen, he was a man, and probably one of the most undressed men that ever was. I ask you to put yourselves in his place. I ask it as a favor; I ask it as a tardy act of justice; I ask it in the interest of fidelity to the traditions of your ancestors; I ask it that the world may contemplate, with vision unobstructed by disguising swallow-tails and white cravats, the spectacle which the true New England Society ought to present. Cease to come to these annual orgies in this hollow modern mockery—the surplusage of raiment. Come in character; come in the summer grace, come in the unadorned simplicity, come in the free and joyous costume which your sainted ancestors provided for mine.

Later ancestors of mine were the Quakers William Robinson, Marmaduke Stevenson, *et al*. Your tribe chased them out of the country for their religion's sake; promised them death if they came back; for your ancestors had forsaken the homes they loved, and braved the perils of the sea, the implacable climate, and the savage wilderness, to acquire that highest and most precious of boons, freedom for every man on this broad continent to worship according to the dictates of his own conscience—and they were not going to allow a lot of pestiferous Quakers to interfere with it. Your ancestors broke forever the chains of political slavery, and gave the vote to every man in this wide land, excluding none!—none except those who did not belong to the orthodox church. Your ancestors—yes, they were a hard lot; but, nevertheless, they gave us religious liberty to worship as they required us to worship, and political liberty to vote as the church required; and so I the bereft one, I the forlorn one, am here to do my best to help you celebrate them right. . . .

O my friends, hear me and reform! I seek your good, not mine. You have heard the speeches. Disband these New England societies—nurseries of a system of steadily augmenting laudation and hosannaing, which, if persisted in uncurbed, may some day in the remote future beguile you into prevaricating and bragging. Oh, stop, stop, while you are still temperate in your appreciation of your ancestors! Hear me, I beseech you; get up an auction and sell Plymouth Rock! The Pilgrims were a simple and ignorant race. They never had seen any good rocks before, or at least any that were not watched, and so they were excusable for hopping ashore in frantic delight and clapping an iron fence around this one. But you, gentlemen, are educated; you are enlightened; you know that in the rich land of your nativity, opulent New England, overflowing with rocks, this one isn't worth, at the outside, more than thirty-five cents. Therefore, sell it, before it is injured by exposure, or at least throw it open to the patent-medicine advertisements, and let it earn its taxes.

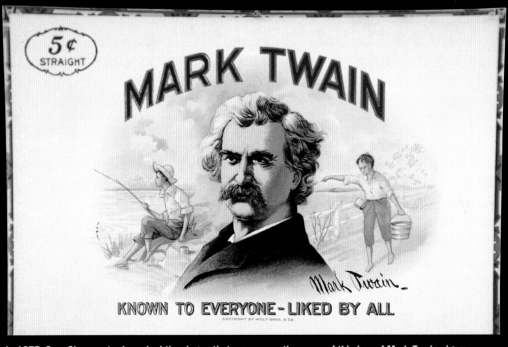

In 1877, Sam Clemens trademarked the slogan that appears on the cover of this box of Mark Twain cigars.

(opposite) Twain onstage, drawn by Joseph Keppler for the December 16, 1885, issue of *Puck*

OFFICE OF "PUCK." 23 WARREN ST. NEW YORK.

MAYER, MERKEL & OTTMANN. LITH. 21–23 WARREN ST. N.Y.

"MARK TWAIN,"
America's Best Humorist.

THE SIX-LETTER WORD

JOCELYN CHADWICK

Nigger: a vile, hateful, demeaning term that occupies a unique place in American history, culture, and language. For African-Americans, it is so much more than a simple word; throughout our history it has been a degrading label, a dirty name, an identity, and a negative judgment inflicted on those whose only offense is an unalterable difference in color. A search for the origins of the word must begin with the unique legacy of America's "peculiar institution," slavery. First used by the slave master and overseers, *nigger* was a description of their personal property—people seen not as distinct human beings, but as little more than valuable livestock.

Now, almost a century and a half after slavery was abolished, this six-letter word continues to haunt us. *Nigger:* just the sound of it leaves many African-Americans with painful questions about who they are, how they are seen, how they are judged, and what place they can comfortably occupy in America today. And its repeated use in Mark Twain's greatest work, *Adventures of Huckleberry Finn*, continues to prompt calls for banning the book from schools and libraries around the nation.

Twain himself, in writing this novel, was acutely aware that he was producing a controversial and challenging work, one that would compel readers of his time to confront an issue they would rather not have faced: race and racism. Many writers tried during the nineteenth century to bring this issue to the consciousness and conscience of America, but none did it better than the Southerner who had gone through his own awakening—his own evolution—in the important dialogue about race.

A Northerner could not have written *Huckleberry Finn;* it took someone who understood slavery and its culture firsthand to render it in such a way as to be believable. It would take a Southern writer—a Southern writer whose perspective had shifted. And it

would take a writer with a genius for narrative—a writer like Mark Twain.

Twain's technique is to draw us in with a story. He gives us these seemingly simple sentences, by these seemingly simple people whom we end up trusting, until we say, "Okay, I'll bite. I'll listen to the story." And before we know it, we're into Chapter 6, with Pap Finn confronting an African-American freeman on Main Street. In his own words, Pap Finn—the town drunk, the racist's racist, who can't read or write and who doesn't want his son to read or write—describes a college-educated black professor as nothing but a "nigger." From that moment on, Twain puts the issue of race in our faces and challenges us to think.

The novel proceeds with a parallel plot: the private conversations and developing friendship between Jim and Huck Finn, the runaway slave and the adolescent white boy, juxtaposed against the demands of their daily life as they descend farther and farther down the Mississippi. It's only when they decide to go ashore or when "civilization" intrudes upon them that they find significant trouble.

The book's pivotal moment is when Huck awakens to hear Jim "moaning and mourning." Jim's been crying for his family, and Huck says some of the most significant words I've ever read in fiction: "I do believe he cared just as much for his people as white folks does their'n. It don't seem natural, but I reckon it's so." Jim's a man. Jim's a person. He's not three-fifths a person, he's not invisible; he's a father, he's a husband, he's a real individual. And Huck, at that moment, is not making a racist statement. He's unlearning—literally—everything society has taught him. We can hear him making those connections in his head: "I've been taught that they don't care about family; that you can separate them, you can sell them, you can do anything you want to them. And yet here's this man crying day after day, talking about his poor little Elizabeth and poor little Johnny. He must care about his family."

Twain allows us to observe the evolution and maturation of Huck as an emerging individual who at the novel's conclusion no longer sees Jim as an invisible *thing:* a nigger—a commodity to be bought and sold. More important, we come to know Jim as a man who balances himself between the world of the nigger-slave stereotype and that of the concerned family man who has his own distinctive voice—a voice that will be heard when *he* deems it necessary. (It should be noted that Twain here expressed something that had previously gone unstated in fiction about the Southern African-American slave, and that is his *need* for two voices—the voice of survival within a white slave culture and the voice of the individual: Jim, the father and the man.) As Langston Hughes said, this was the first time Americans had a realistic depiction of an unlettered slave clinging to the hope of freedom.

Throughout the book, Twain demythologizes the culture that bred slavery, stripping it of any romanticism. He even reintroduces Tom Sawyer at the end to provide a contrast to Huck and Jim, because we need to know what lessons Huck has learned and how well he has learned them. Tom Sawyer represents the blithely racist society in which Jim and Huck will have to survive; and he represents an attitude, Twain believed, that still existed long after the Civil War and the Emancipation Proclamation. In that society, *nigger* remained an acceptable term.

Initially, *Huckleberry Finn* found censorship among Northern whites who felt that Huck was simply too rough and his language too unrefined. Among Southern whites, Twain was labeled a traitor. Most African-Americans, from Frederick Douglass to the NAACP in the early twentieth century, considered the novel a positive affirmation of a slave asserting his right to freedom by the means he deemed necessary.

But by the 1950s the novel was controversial again, particularly because of the repetitive use of the racial slur *nigger.* Today, some whites and African-Americans (including at least one chapter of the NAACP) want *Huckleberry Finn* banned from school libraries and classrooms. Others have suggested that parts of the novel be rewritten so that the very aspects that generate its social impact would be excised or compromised. Increasing numbers of white and African-American teachers have become nervous about teaching the book, even if they believe it legitimately belongs in their courses.

I tell them that *Huckleberry Finn* needs to be read—not in spite of its language and the nervousness it so often engenders, but precisely *because* of those things. Twain obliges readers of all colors to gaze into the imperfect mirror of race relations and prejudice in America. He makes me ask myself, What do I know about my own culture, my own background? Those slaves in my family, how did they endure? How did they come to grips with the whites who were in my family? Twain makes me engage in dialogues with young people about race. He makes them say things to me that they might not ask of their parents or their teachers.

Twain keeps before us the idea that we can never feel so comfortable or ambivalent about people that we allow racism to creep in. He reminds us that if we are ever going to come to the table to discuss the issue of race and its significance to how we view one another, we must be willing to wrestle with the troubling images, the symbols, the suffering, and the provocative conversations contained in this novel. No other piece of literature of its time allows the reader to peer into the nature of racism and the nature of equality at the same time. And no other novel so clearly renders the American paradox about the issue: our wanting to see and yet not see race, to talk and yet not talk about race, to think that race is no longer an issue while knowing that it is, in fact, unavoidable.

When I talk with students and teachers about *Huckleberry Finn,* I urge them to allow the work to speak for itself. As readers, we must allow Jim and Huck to use their own voices, state their own views, and act as they would normally. We must experience the other characters of color in the novel, both free and slave, and we must digest the white characters who firmly believe in the institution of slavery. We

Sam Clemens and his friend and frequent companion at Quarry Farm John T. Lewis, photographed during the author's last visit to Elmira, in 1903. Lewis is thought to have been one of the models for Jim in *Adventures of Huckleberry Finn*.

must expose ourselves to the duplicity of Tom Sawyer: his pretending to be Huck and Jim's friend while in reality being a product of the South. In order to recognize the novel's scope, we must listen closely to Jim's redefinition of freedom as well as to the South's refusal to reconstruct, in spite of the Emancipation Proclamation. We must suffer with Jim and Huck. We must let Jim spark and awaken our conscience just as he does Huck's, so that we, too, can come to understand him as a man. We must experience with Huck his tremendous tension over whether to turn in the runaway slave, and his final decision to save Jim and therefore "go to hell"—to become, in essence, a Southern abolitionist.

This is not a novel of comfort. It is a novel that forces us to think and reflect. With the exception of the writings of William Faulkner and Toni Morrison, no other work of American literature addresses race with such unrelenting candor. Do we still need *Adventures of Huckleberry Finn* when we have Morrison and Faulkner—who also, I might add, use racial slurs? Yes, we do.

Encountering any racial epithet is painful. Seeing *nigger* in print, and hearing it, are both painful. But I don't think there's supposed to be an inoculation against the pain of racial slurs. I think that they're supposed to be painful; they're supposed to hurt. You're not ever supposed to become anesthetized. I tell students that a racial slur is a racial slur, regardless of who uses it. That Twain decided to use it should not be lost on any of his readers. But he is not sanctioning the use of the slur; quite the opposite. In this novel, as in some of his later works, Twain desires us to see people as people and not as things or chattel. Part of Twain's legacy is that he refuses to allow us to be indifferent to the pain of man's inhumanity to man. He wants us to be uncomfortable, because only then will it matter.

Adventures of Huckleberry Finn lays out before us a terrible truth, a truth we cannot escape. It reminds us of the trail of blood that surrounded Huck and Jim in the culture of slavery, and it reminds us of the blood and suffering that was yet to come—all focused on race and racism. That history is summarized by the six-letter word *nigger.*

On a Sunday evening in June of 1964, the silence of early summer in Mississippi was shattered by a series of sharp, angry sounds that ended the lives of three young men. Within moments, Andrew Goodman, Mickey Schwerner, and James Chaney lay dying in a swamp just outside a small town ironically named Philadelphia, after the "City of Brotherly Love," and the conscience of America was about to change forever. Their deaths marked a moment in our history no less significant than the fury that pitted brother against brother on another hot summer day in a place called Gettysburg. The very last words James Chaney heard were "Die, nigger, die."

The word symbolized the issue that has literally ripped this country apart and that still significantly divides us. But by forcing us to peer into the darkness and suffering of our past, great literature can help us confront the issue more openly today—and perhaps ultimately unite us.

Coming to grips with Mark Twain's greatest novel means coming to grips with who we are—looking at ourselves in the mirror, warts and all. To remove *Adventures of Huckleberry Finn* from America's libraries and America's classrooms would be to remove the American voice. You simply can't have an American literature and not have *Adventures of Huckleberry Finn* on the shelf.

America still needs to read Twain's novel and feel the sting of the six-letter word. And it still needs to get to know Huck and Jim, and learn from a backwoods boy and a runaway slave the fervent hope eloquently reasserted by the Rev. Dr. Martin Luther King, Jr., a hundred years later: that we can become a nation that judges a person by the content of his character rather than by the color of his skin.

CHAPTER EIGHT

A CONNECTICUT YANKEE

I am a border-ruffian from the State of Missouri. I am a Connecticut Yankee by adoption. In me, you have Missouri morals, Connecticut culture; this . . . is the combination which makes the perfect man.
—"Plymouth Rock and the Pilgrims," 1881

In 1885, when she was just thirteen years old, Susy Clemens took it upon herself to write a biography of her father. Every night in her bedroom, she would add a little more to it—details about her father and their family and the life they were all leading together in the magnificent house he had built for them on Farmington Avenue.

We are a very happy family. We consist of Papa, Mamma, Jean, Clara and me. It is Papa I am writing about, and I shall have no trouble in not knowing what to say about him, as he is a very striking character.

Papa's appearance has been described many times, but very incorrectly. He has beautiful gray hair, not any too thick or any too long, but just right; a Roman nose, which greatly improves the beauty of his features; kind blue eyes and a small mustache. He has a wonderfully shaped head and profile. He has a very good figure— in short, he is an extraordinarily fine looking man. All his features are perfect, except that he hasn't extraordinary teeth. . . .

He is a very good man and a very funny one. He has got a temper, but we all of us have in this family. He is the loveliest man I ever saw or ever hope to see.

"He is known to the public as a humorist," she continued, "but he has much more in him that is earnest than that is humorous. . . . He is as much of a Philosopher as anything I think. . . . In a great many such directions he has greater ability than in the gifts which have made him famous."

Susy tried to keep her work a secret, but her mother soon discovered it and privately shared it with Clemens. "I had had compliments before," he wrote later, "but none that touched me like this; none that could approach it for value in my eyes."

Everything about his life in Hartford assured Clemens that at last he had achieved the kind of success and could provide his wife and chil-

(opposite) The Clemens family on the porch of their Hartford home, 1884: (left to right): Clara, Sam, Jean, Livy, and Susy

(below) Susy at seventeen, dressed as "Music" in *The Love Chase*, a two-act play she herself wrote and performed in 1889

133

dren with the security and comfort that had always eluded his own father. "If there is one [person] who is more thoroughly and unceasingly happy than I am," he wrote a friend, "I defy the world to produce him."

In his mind, the house itself grew to symbolize his newfound sense of happiness and contentment:

> To us our house was not unsentient matter—it had a heart and soul and eyes to see us with, and approvals and solicitudes and deep sympathies; it was of us, and we were in its confidence, and lived in its grace and in the peace of its benediction. We never came home from an absence that its face did not light up and speak out its eloquent welcome—and we could not enter it unmoved.

At a time when the average annual wage in the United States was less than $500, Twain was spending $30,000 a year simply on household expenses. There were private tutors for the three children, daily visits from a barber for Clemens himself.

He shone at dinner. An *orchestrelle,* an imported music box the size of a sea chest, provided continuous music: the "Wedding March" from *Lohengrin,* the "Pilgrim Chorus" from *Tannhäuser,* and eight other favorites. The family cook served up the rich dishes of that day: canvasback duck, filets of beef, cherubs molded in pink or green ice cream. But the guests—among them William Tecumseh Sherman, Edwin Booth, Matthew Arnold, and the journalist and explorer Henry M. Stanley— came primarily to see and hear their famous host perform, and he was happy to oblige, prowling the long room between courses, puffing a black cigar and waving his napkin for emphasis as he told long stories that so convulsed the butler, George Griffin, that he sometimes had to retreat into the pantry to recover. The stories pleased his daughters, too, who often sat on the staircase to listen. They learned to measure the progress of the dinner by the story their father was telling, Clara remembered: "Father is telling the beggar story; they must have reached the meat course."

Clemens's antics sometimes embarrassed his wife, who would later reprimand him for his offenses. The children, he wrote, had a name for this: "dusting off papa."

> At last I had an inspiration. . . . We set to work to arrange a system of signals to be delivered by [Livy] to me during dinner; signals which would indicate definitely which particular crime I was now engaged in, so that I could change to another. . . .
>
> Livy would look down the table and say, in a voice full of interest, if not of counterfeited apprehension, "What did you do with the blue card that was on the dressing table—". I knew what was happening—that I was talking the lady on the right to death and never

Hand-painted program for a family production of *The Prince and the Pauper,* presented in the conservatory of the Clemenses' Hartford house on January 13, 1886; and a scene from the play (below), in which Clara played Lady Jane Grey and her neighbor, Daisy Warner, portrayed Tom Canty. "I have seen nothing prettier or more moving than the acting of these little creatures," Twain recalled. "The fire they put into it was real, not a fiction of the stage."

paying any attention to the one on my left . . . so I would at once go to talking vigorously to the lady on my left. . . .

A red card . . . meant, "Oh, are you going to sit there all the evening and never say anything? Do wake up and talk." So I woke up and drowned the table with talk. We had a number of cards, of different colors, each meaning a definite thing. . . .

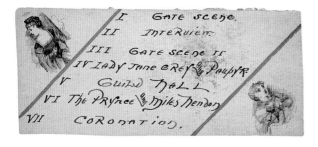

The children got a screen arranged so that they could be behind it during the dinner. . . . If Mrs. Clemens happened to be so busy . . . talking with her elbow neighbor that she overlooked something that I was doing, she was sure to get a low-voiced hint from behind that screen in these words: "Blue card, mamma"; or "Red card, mamma"—"Green card, mamma"—so that I was under double and triple guard. What the mother didn't notice the children detected for her.

It headed off crime after crime all through the dinner, and I always came out at the end successful, triumphant, with large praises owing me, and I got them on the spot.

After dinner, Clemens sometimes sat at the piano, performing the spirituals he had learned from Uncle Dan'l and the other slaves he'd known as a boy, swaying on the bench as he sang, his eyes fixed on the chandelier. "Rise and Shine and Give God the Glory, Glory" was a favorite; so was "Swing Low, Sweet Chariot." "His fingers stretched straight out over the keys," Clara recalled, "so that each time a chord was struck it seemed as if a miracle had happened."

The children were encouraged to be performers, too. One winter evening, they put on an elaborate homegrown production of *The Prince and the Pauper* for some two hundred friends. The backdrop was a curtain hung over the arched entrance to the conservatory. Livy had written the script and helped make the costumes. Susy played the prince; neighbors' children were given supporting roles. When one small member of the cast fell ill at the last minute, Clemens himself eagerly stood in, managing to spill a pitcher of water and devising other bits of business to keep the audience laughing—and its attention firmly focused on him. "I was born modest," he once wrote, "but it didn't last."

In 1886, Twain began work on a new novel, a fanciful tale about a New Englander who finds himself transported back to medieval England. He called it *A Connecticut Yankee in King Arthur's Court*—and meant to satirize both the ancient institutions still dominating the Old World and the brash, inventive, go-ahead spirit fueling the New. Its protagonist, Hank Morgan, is a factory foreman and inveterate tinkerer from Hartford who believes that a "country without a patent office [is] just a crab and [can't] travel any way but sideways or backward." When Morgan miraculously shows up in sixth-century England, his Yankee ingenuity soon makes him King Arthur's court wizard, and he sets out to modernize everything. He introduces the Knights of the Round Table to the bicycle and talks them into renting out their armor as advertising space. He tries to undermine Merlin the magician and the priests of the established church, both of whom Morgan considers representatives of superstitions standing in the way of human progress; but in the end, Morgan employs the impersonal mechanized weapons of modern war to destroy society instead of reforming it.

Most critics disliked the book, and it did not sell well. Clemens professed not to care. "It's my swan song," he said, "my retirement from literature permanently." He was sure he had found an easier way to get rich, now saw himself as a shrewd

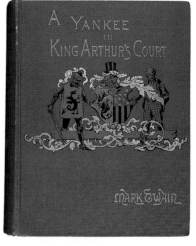

The cover of the first edition of *A Connecticut Yankee in King Arthur's Court*, 1889, and its frontispiece by Dan Beard, in which the protagonist, Hank Morgan, comes face to face with one of the special dangers presented by the sixth century

THE GREATEST BOOK OF THE AGE!

PUBLISHED·SIMULTANEOUSLY IN SIX LANGUAGES.

LIFE OF POPE LEO XIII.

From an Authentic Memoir Furnished by His Order.

WRITTEN WITH THE ENCOURAGEMENT, APPROBATION, AND BLESSING OF

HIS HOLINESS THE POPE,

BY BERNARD O'REILLY, D.D., L.D. (LAVAL)

ELEGANTLY AND
PROFUSELY
ILLUSTRATED.

EVERY CATHOLIC
IN THE LAND SHOULD
POSSESS THIS VOLUME,
AS IT IS ISSUED
WITH THE
APPROBATION
AND
BLESSING
OF
THE POPE,
AS A SOUVENIR OF HIS
GOLDEN JUBILEE
YEAR, 1887

TWO
MAGNIFICENT
CHROMOS
PRINTED IN TEN
COLORS.

TWO
ELEGANT,
STEEL PLATES.

TWENTY-TWO
OTHER FINE FULL-PAGE
ILLUSTRATIONS.

BEWARE OF
IMITATIONS.

SOLD ONLY
BY SUBSCRIPTION.

LEO XIII. ON HIS THRONE IN HIS PRIVATE AUDIENCE-ROOM.

A SIX-DOLLAR BOOK FOR $3.75. PLAIN EDITION $3.00.

THESE EXTREMELY LOW PRICES HAVE BEEN FIXED UPON TO ENABLE

Every One to Own a Book Blessed by the Sovereign Pontiff.

IN ONE VOLUME, ROYAL OCTAVO, OF ABOUT 600 PAGES.

COPYRIGHT, 1886, BY BERNARD O'REILLY.

WEBSTER & CO.'S ANNOUNCEMENT OF THE "LIFE OF THE POPE"

When this officially sanctioned biography of Pope Leo XII that Sam Clemens commissioned from Father Bernard O'Reilly was finally published in 1887 it turned a small profit but failed to match its publisher's extravagant hopes for it.

businessman rather than merely an author. On the strength of the sales of Grant's *Memoirs*, his publishing company had expanded its operations and, at Clemens's urging, signed up other celebrated subjects to write their autobiographies: Union generals Sherman, George McClellan, and Phil Sheridan and the widow of George Armstrong Custer. The king of Hawaii was commissioned to produce a collection of Hawaiian legends. Clemens also acquired an authorized life of Pope Leo XIII, advertising it as "the Greatest Book of the Age" and insisting that it be translated into six languages because he was sure every Catholic on earth would want a copy.

He bought and sold stocks, too, more often losing money than making it. "I must speculate in something, such being my nature," he explained to Howells. It was the age of invention, and Clemens was caught up in it. He bought a typewriter—and claimed to be the first author ever to submit a typewritten manuscript. But his initial enthusiasm for the device quickly vanished as he struggled to master its keyboard; it was ruining his morals, he said, because it made him "*want* to swear." And he installed a telephone in his mansion—the very first one in a private home in Hartford. Clemens was proud to own it, despite its frustrating unreliability. On good days, he noted in a chart he kept nearby as a weekly report to the telephone company, artillery might be audible over the phone line; on other days, thunder might be heard; but on bad days, not even the sound of artillery *and* thunder could make it through.

He impulsively invested $25,000 each in a steam generator, a steam pulley, a marine telegraph; twice that amount in an engraving process called Kaolotype. None of them paid off. He patented three of his own inventions, too: an automatically self-adjusting vest strap, a history game meant for improving the memory, and "Mark Twain's Patent Self-Pasting Scrapbook," the only one ever to make him any money. Profits didn't seem to matter:

What is it that confers the noblest delight? What is it which swells a man's breast with pride above that which any other experience can bring to him? Discovery! . . . To give birth to an idea . . . to invent a new hinge, to find the way to make the lightnings carry your messages. . . . These are the things which confer a pleasure compared

A TIME-SAVING, PROFANITY-BREEDING . . . INVENTION

Clemens's fascination with the profusion of new mechanical inventions was perhaps best symbolized by the telephone he installed in his Hartford house. He boasted that he was the first person in New England to have one for private use—and once expanded that claim to encompass the entire world. He loved having the ability to read the morning's newspaper and immediately call the Western Union office to fire off a telegram to an editor, and he envisioned a time when people would be able to talk to each other across the continent.

But the phone also infuriated him, as his maid Katy Leary explained in her memoir:

> It made Mr. Clemens so mad—"just to hear the damned thing ring," he said. Yes, that telephone used to make Mr. Clemens wild, because he would hear all right, but he couldn't give his message out good. It wasn't very good service them days, and he used to fight the telephone girls all the time. He'd say: "Why, damn it, are you all asleep down there? If you don't give me better service you can send somebody right up here now and pull this thing out. I won't have this damned thing in the house—it's a nuisance!"
>
> One day he tried to call up Mrs. Dr. Taft. He could not hear plainly and thought he was talking to central. "Send down here and take this d— thing out of here," he said; "I'm tired of it." He was mad, and using a good deal of bad language. All at once he heard Mrs. Dr. Taft say, "Oh, Mr. Clemens, good morning." He said, "Why, Mrs. Taft, I have

> just come to the telephone. George, our butler, was here before me and I heard him swearing as I came up. I shall have to talk to him about it."

Further fueling his indignation was the fact that he had been given an early opportunity to invest in Alexander Graham Bell's company but had passed it up, unsure that the everyday public would ever embrace the new device. With all that as a backdrop, Clemens finally issued this Christmas message:

> It is my heart-warm and world-embracing Christmas hope and aspiration that all of us,

Report

for the week ending . . . . . .

of the condition of the telephone

at 351 Farmington Avenue,

Hartford, Conn.

Explanation of the Signs.

+ Artillery can be heard.

++ Thunder can be heard.

+++ Artillery & thunder combined can be heard.

++++ All combinations fail.

S	M	T	W	T	F	S
A.M.	A.M.	A.M.	A.M.	A.M.	A.M.	A.M.
P.M.	P.M.	P.M.	P.M.	P.M.	P.M.	P.M.

Remarks.

Mark Twain's 1879 notes on the "condition of the telephone" (opposite) and the third-floor billiard room in Hartford in which he tried to write despite the distractions of his household

the high, the low, the rich, the poor, the admired, the despised, the loved . . . the hated, the civilized, the savage . . . may eventually be gathered together in a heaven of everlasting rest and peace and bliss, except the inventor of the telephone.

Later in life, Clemens would note how the telephone had spread to even the smallest of villages. But he never lost his sense that it was a mixed blessing. The telephone, he wrote, "is a time-saving, profanity-breeding, useful invention, and in America is [now] to be found in all houses except parsonages."

*with which other pleasures are tame and common-
place, other ecstasies cheap and trivial.*

But of all the inventions that captured his imagination, nothing compared to the typesetting compositor
being developed by a Hartford-based machinist
named James W. Paige. With eighteen thousand separate parts, Paige claimed, it would be able to set type
as quickly as six men and promised to revolutionize
the newspaper and book-printing industries. Only
a former typesetter like himself, Clemens told his
friends, could fully appreciate its marvelous properties. It could do everything a human could do, he
bragged, except drink, swear, and go on strike. And
its inventor, he believed, was no less remarkable:
"James W. Paige . . . is a dreamer, a visionary. In all
the ages he has no peer. Indeed, there is none that
even approaches him. His imagination runs utterly
away with him. He is a poet, a most great and genuine
poet, whose sublime creations are written in steel.
He is the Shakespeare of mechanical invention."

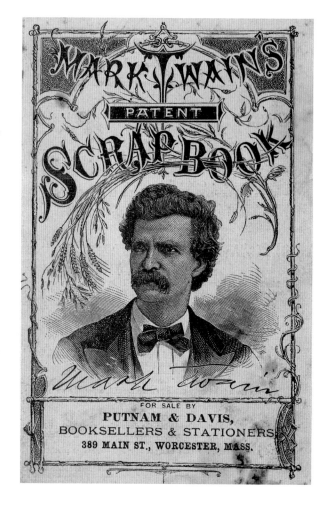

Clemens had seen an early prototype of Paige's
compositor in 1880 and immediately invested $2,000.
By 1885, he had bought half-ownership for $30,000
more and was busily filling his notebooks with calcu-
lations about how much money a newspaper could
save with a single machine, how many machines each
major paper would want, and finally how many machines would be
required to fill the whole world's needs. "Why, he thought he could buy
all New York," the Clemenses' maid Katy Leary remembered. "He was
asking how much it would take to buy all the railroads in New York, and
all the newspapers, too—buy everything in New York on account of the
typesetting machine. He thought he'd make millions and own the world,
because he had such faith in it. That was Mr. Clemens' way."

Sam Clemens now believed himself on the verge of becoming a multi-
millionaire. His business successes, especially the Paige compositor,
would free him at last from ever having to return to the lecture circuit.
From now on, the only writing he intended to do would be for the love
of it, not for the money; "it is to be my holiday amusement," he told a
friend, "for six days every summer the rest of my life."

Meanwhile, some of his business ventures began to sour. None of the
new books his company published—not even the life of the pope—came
close to matching the success of Grant's recollections. A bookkeeper

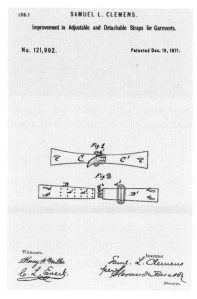

THE TYPE WRITER.

12, KENT GARDENS, EALING, W.
28th January, 1876.

THE REMINGTON SEWING MACHINE COMPANY.

GENTLEMEN : I have much pleasure in testifying to the usefulness of your little Machine the Type-Writer. I find that a beginner of average quickness can at first trial print a letter slowly with it ; a week's practice renders him familiar with the manipulation, even to altering letters or introducing stops where omitted, and a month's practice enables him to beat the pen with it in rapidity of execution, while the legibility of its productions is superior to that of any caligraphy.

Yours faithfully,
R. H. WALLACE DUNLOP.

WHAT "MARK TWAIN" SAYS ABOUT IT.
HARTFORD, March 19, 1875.

GENTLEMEN : Please do not use my name in any way Please do not even divulge the fact that I own a machine. I have entirely stopped using the Type-Writer, for the reason that I never could write a letter with it to anybody without receiving a request by return mail that I would not only describe the machine, but state what progress I had made in the use of it, etc., etc. I don't like to write letters, and so I don't want people to know I own this curiosity-breeding little joke.

Yours truly,
SAML. L. CLEMENS.

Twain's qualified endorsement of the typewriter; and (top right) the Paige compositor, the repository of his financial hopes for fifteen years

(opposite) Advertising folder meant to sell Twain's self-pasting scrapbook, which he believed to be a "great humanizing and civilized invention. . . . The only rational scrapbook the world has ever seen"; and (below) the patent drawing for one of his less profitable notions, an "improvement in adjustable and detachable straps for garments" that its inventor was never able to persuade anyone to manufacture

embezzled $25,000. Clemens gave a $5,000 advance to Henry Ward Beecher for his memoirs, only to have him drop dead three weeks later; the loss to Christendom was great, Clemens said, but the loss to Charles L. Webster & Co. was greater. Harried by his employer's constant meddling in the company, Charles Webster was driven to physical and emotional collapse and was forced to resign his post as head of the firm; he died a few years later, before reaching the age of forty.

Whatever meager profits the book company did manage to earn from time to time, Clemens diverted to Paige and his typesetting machine, now requiring infusions of $3,000 to $5,000 a month. "Paige was all the time thinking up something new that he would invent before it would be perfect, and Mr. Clemens had to give him money all the time," said Katy Leary. "Of course, Paige was always promising and expecting it would be all ready next month, and then poor Mr. Clemens, he'd have to send more money, and the next month it wasn't ready and that's the way it went."

By December of 1887, Twain could afford to send his sister Pamela's family just fifteen dollars for Christmas; he was feeling "a little crowded" because of the typesetter, he wrote her. But his belief in the machine's prospects remained high. A patent had now been applied for—275 sheets of drawings and 123 pages of specifications had been

THE SHAME IS OURS

In 1885, the same year he published *Adventures of Huckleberry Finn,* Clemens made a visit to Yale University, where he met a young man named Warner T. McGuinn, one of the school's first black law students. McGuinn was a brilliant scholar, but having trouble making ends meet: he boarded with the college's carpenter and held three part-time jobs just to get by.

When Clemens learned of McGuinn's difficulties, he wrote to the administration, offering to pay the young man's expenses. "I do not believe I would very cheerfully help a white student . . . but I do not feel so about the other color," Clemens said. "We have ground the manhood out of them, & the shame is ours, not theirs, & we should pay for it."

With Clemens's help, McGuinn was able to quit his jobs and concentrate on his studies. He graduated from Yale Law School in 1887 at the top of his class and became a respected lawyer in Baltimore, a member of the city council, and eventually a director of the local chapter of the National Association for the Advancement of Colored People (NAACP).

In 1917, McGuinn would win a major court victory, overturning a Baltimore law that had enforced segregated housing in the city. And he, in turn, became a mentor to a young lawyer in an adjoining office named Thurgood Marshall, who would one day become the first African-American to serve on the United States Supreme Court and who always remembered McGuinn as "one of the greatest lawyers who ever lived."

Warner T. McGuinn (second from right, second row from the top), the recipient of Sam Clemens's generosity, with other local leaders attending a conference on public education for black children in Baltimore, 1900

Pages from Sam Clemens's notebook, detailing the number of Paige compositors he had convinced himself each of the world's major cities would require

required—and in early tests the Paige compositor was seen to set type three times faster than its main competitor, the Mergenthaler Linotype. The Linotype's chief investors offered to give Clemens stock in their company and much-needed capital for Paige's typesetter in exchange for part ownership; that way, they said, whichever machine eventually prevailed, everyone would profit. Clemens turned them down. Confident that the Paige device was superior, he wanted all the profits for himself and instead borrowed against his personal savings to keep Paige going. "The other day the children were projecting a purchase," he told a friend, "Livy and I to furnish the money—a dollar and a half. Jean discouraged the idea. She said, 'We haven't got any money. . . . Remember the machine isn't done.' "

Throughout 1888, Paige kept promising that his machine was almost perfected; that with just a few more adjustments—and some additional cash from Clemens—everything would be ready at last. Clemens continued to believe it, too. "All the other wonderful inventions of the human brain sink pretty nearly into commonplaces contrasted with this awful mechanical miracle," he wrote his brother Orion. "Telephones, telegraphs, locomotives, cotton-gins, sewing machines, Babbage calculators, Jacquard looms, perfecting presses, all mere toys, simplicities! The Paige Compositor marches alone and far in the land of human inventions."

EUREKA! Saturday, January 5, 1889—12.20 p.m. At this moment I have seen a line of moveable type spaced and justified by machinery! This is the first time in the history of the world that this amazing thing has ever been done.

Monday, January 7—4:45 p.m. The first proper name ever set by this new keyboard was William Shakespeare. I set it at the above hour; and I perceive, now that I see the name written, that I either mis-spelled it then or I've mis-spelled it now.

But Paige himself was still not satisfied, insisted on further refinements. Clemens reluctantly agreed to let him disassemble the machine and go back to work. Christmas of 1889 arrived. Paige still wasn't finished. Against the warnings of his advisers, Clemens borrowed $160,000 more to keep the inventor at work—and sent his brother, sister, and mother only $5 each for Christmas, along with an apology: "The machine still has a grip on our purse." Six months later, as a letter to an old Nevada friend attests, it still retained its grip on his imagination.

June 22, 1890.

I have been sitting by the machine 2 and ½ hours this afternoon and my admiration of it towers higher than ever. There is no sort of mistake about it, it is the Big Bonanza. . . .

The machine is totally without a rival. . . . I claim yet, as I have always claimed, that the machine's market . . . is today worth $150,000,000, without saying anything about the doubling and trebling of this sum that will follow within the life of the patents.

Now here is a queer fact: I am one of the wealthiest grandees in America—one of the Vanderbilt gang, in fact—and yet if you asked me to lend you a couple of dollars I should have to ask you to take my note instead.

In October of 1890, Clemens's mother died at eighty-eight in Keokuk and was buried in the family plot in Hannibal. A month later, Livy's mother died in Elmira. The family's finances continued to deteriorate. "Merry Christmas to you!" he wrote in a brief December note to an associate, "and I wish to God I could have one myself before I die."

The following February, when a group of rich Nevada investors Clemens had wined and dined in hopes of obtaining fresh cash for the typesetter backed off at the last minute, he declared himself finished with Paige's device. "I've shook the machine and never wish to see it or hear it mentioned again," he told Orion. "It is superb, it is perfect, it can do ten men's work. It is worth billions; and when the pig-headed lunatic, its inventor, dies, it will instantly be capitalized and make the Clemens children rich."

Sam Clemens and his family would once again have to rely on the writings of Mark Twain. He threw himself into his work, finishing a new novel, *The American Claimant*, in a matter of months despite a bout of rheumatism that shot excruciating pains up his arm with every stroke of his pen. He tried to dictate his thoughts onto a wax cylinder but gave it up, eventually managed to teach himself to write with his left hand in order to keep pumping out material.

Livy's frail health was failing, too. She contracted her own case of rheumatism, and developed what doctors called a "heart disturbance." They recommended rest and treatment for her in Europe, far from the financial chaos and constant social and housekeeping obligations of Hartford.

(opposite) Sam Clemens visits the laboratory of the electrical wizard Nikola Tesla in 1904. Despite all his investments in inventions that went nowhere, he never lost his enthusiasm for new technology.

Jane Lampton Clemens, Sam's mother, photographed in New York on her seventy-ninth birthday, in 1882. With her are her daughter, Pamela Clemens Moffett (right), Pamela's daughter, Annie Moffett Webster, and Mrs. Webster's daughter, Jean—holding a doll made for her by Susy and Clara Clemens.

Sam was initially reluctant to go. "Travel has no longer any charm for me," he wrote Howells. "I have seen all the foreign countries I want to see except heaven and hell—and I have only a vague curiosity as concerns one of those." But a temporary removal to Europe could provide him with travel-writing assignments. And if they closed the Hartford house, whose expenses he admitted to Howells continued to be "ghastly," it could actually save them money.

By late spring of 1891, Katy Leary had packed their clothes into twenty-five trunks, and they were ready to go. None of them, Clara recalled, was happy about it:

Pulling up anchor and sailing away from our beloved Hartford was a sorrowful episode. We adored our home and friends. We had to leave so much treasured beauty behind that we could not look forward with any pleasure to life abroad. We all regarded this break . . . as something resembling a tragedy. We had showered love on the home itself—the library; the conservatory sweet with the perfume of flowers; the bright bedrooms; and outside, the trees, the tender eyebrights, the river reflecting clouds and sky. These were our

The Clemens clan spent the summer of 1890 in the Catskills near Tannersville, New York. There (above), Sam played charades with Susy. "No one could ever be quite so ridiculous as Father was," Clara recalled. "We were trying to enact the story of Hero and Leander. [Father] played the part of the impassioned lover obliged to swim across the Hellespont to snatch a kiss from his sweetheart on the other side of the foaming water. For this scene Father wore a bathing-suit, a straw hat tied under his chin with a big bow, and a hot-water bottle slung around his chest." In more placid moments he took his ease (second from right, opposite) among the other members of the Onteora Club, a largely literary group that included the essayist and drama critic Brander Matthews (center, holding his hat) and Mary Mapes Dodge (sixth from the left), editor of *St. Nicholas* magazine, the nation's best-loved publication for children.

friends. They belonged to us; and we to them. How could we part? . . .

We passed from room to room with leaden hearts, looked back and lingered—lingered. . . . We scanned the faces of friends, servants, pets. We spoke that heart-breaking word "Good-by," and, tear-blinded, passed . . . through the front door.

Shortly before they left for Europe, someone wrote Clemens, asking where he found the material for his books. "When pretending to portray life," he answered, "I confine myself to life with which I am familiar." Then he listed all the lives he had known: boyhood on the Mississippi, printer's apprentice and riverboat pilot, Confederate soldier, prospector and newspaper reporter, lecturer and publisher—and now a failure at a business venture, he wrote, whose story "would make a large book in which a million men would see themselves in a mirror . . . and after would cast dust upon their heads, cursing and blaspheming."

"I have been an author for twenty years," he added, "and an ass for fifty-five."

CHAPTER NINE

NEVER QUITE SANE
IN THE NIGHT

*In my age as in my youth, night brings me many a deep remorse.
I realize that from the cradle up I have been like the rest of the
race—never quite sane in the night.*
        —*Chapters from My Autobiography*, 1907

The Clemens family spent the summer and fall of 1891 in France, Switzerland, and Germany. They took a boat trip down the Rhone; visited Aix-les-Bains and Marienbad, where Sam and Livy tried mud baths for their rheumatism; and spent more than a week at the Wagner Festival in Bayreuth.

Livy and the girls enjoyed their immersion in European culture. Clemens claimed that he did not. "I feel strongly out of place here," he wrote in one of his dispatches. "Sometimes I feel like the one sane person in the community of the mad; sometimes I feel like the one blind man where all others see." And he detested opera: the "banging and slamming and booming and crashing" of Wagner's *Lohengrin,* he said, brought back "the memory of the time that I had my teeth fixed. . . . Nothing can make a Wagner opera absolutely perfect and satisfactory to the untutored but to leave out the vocal parts. I wish I could see a Wagner opera done in pantomime once."

They spent the winter in Berlin. Twain's arm still ached whenever he tried to write, and worries about his precarious finances still dogged him. "I have never felt so desperate in my life," he admitted to a business associate, "for I haven't got a penny to my name." But Europeans had been reading his novels in translation for years, and wherever he went, he was hailed as both a great writer and a fascinating American celebrity. People recognized him on the streets of Berlin, gawked at him when his family appeared in public. "Why papa," his youngest daughter, Jean, said one morning, "if it keeps going on like this, pretty soon there won't be anybody for you to get acquainted with but God."

On February 20, Twain was invited to a private dinner with Kaiser Wilhelm II, who told him that of all his works *Life on the Mississippi* was unquestionably the finest. That same evening, when he returned to his hotel, Twain was pulled aside by the hotel porter, who pointed into his tiny room. There sat the complete German translations of Twain's work.

(opposite) **Sam Clemens, 1890**

(below) **German edition of** *Life on the Mississippi*, **1892**

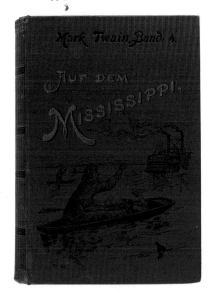

"That one there," the porter said, gesturing toward the Mississippi book, "is the best one you ever wrote."

Susy (left), gowned for a ceremony at Bryn Mawr in 1890; and Clara at sixteen that same year

The Clemenses moved on. After a summer in France—a country, Twain wrote, that "has neither winter nor summer nor morals"—they settled in Florence, where they rented a huge house, the Villa Viviani, on a hill overlooking the city. "In Florence it was possible to live like princes on limited means," Clara recalled. But the villa "was a good example of the kind of European-furnished house that Father detested. He called the front hall . . . the skating-rink, because it was of huge dimensions and had a slippery floor. In fact the whole house was so large that a lot of time was wasted looking for different members of the family. Finally, Father made the law that we should all assemble in the skating-rink every hour or two, if only for a moment."

It was growing harder and harder for Samuel Clemens to make the laws for his family. There were new strains now within what he had called its "charmed circle," tensions which his complicated personality only intensified. Life in Hartford and at Quarry Farm had always revolved around him: the highlight of each day had been the late-afternoon gathering at which Livy and his admiring daughters listened to whatever it was he had written since morning. His had always been an unusually close-knit clan; he had labored hard to keep it that way—never even allowing his girls to attend school with other children—and he seemed strangely oblivious to the price they had paid for being at the mercy of his moods.

"Yesterday," he had confessed to Howells six years earlier, "a thunder-stroke fell upon me out of the most unsuspected of skies. . . . I found that all their lives my children have been afraid of me! have stood all their days in uneasy dread of my sharp tongue & uncertain temper. The accusing instances stretch back to their babyhood, & are burnt into their memories: & I never suspected." Since that belated discovery, things had only grown more difficult. Susy, high-strung and sensitive and always her father's most-prized child, had spent a single difficult year at Bryn Mawr before her parents pulled her out again for the trip to Europe. She was at once admiring of her father and embarrassed by him: when he'd spoken at her college and launched into the surefire story of the "Golden Arm" he'd learned as a boy from his uncle's slave "Uncle Dan'l," she fled the room in mortification, convinced that it was unsuitable for a sophisticated crowd, that her classmates would dismiss him as a mere "humorist." She was nineteen when they got to Florence and quickly bored by what she called her family's "perfectly quiet eventless life"; above all, she told Clara, she was *heartily* tired of . . . the long lonely evening[s] when we read *again* by way of a *change*." She was made miserable by an infatuation with a dashing but married Italian count; tried singing lessons, only to be told that while she had a lovely soprano voice, she did not have the lung power to perform well from the stage; and complained to Clara of having to live constantly within range of her father's "storms."

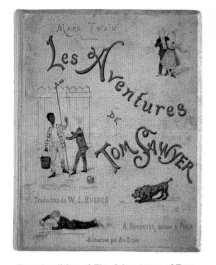

French edition of *The Adventures of Tom Sawyer*, 1884

(right) Envelope of a letter that pursued Sam Clemens on his peripatetic travels from Paris to Florence and, finally, to Frankfurt in the summer of 1892

View of Florence, where the Clemens family spent ten months in 1892 and '93, painted by Andreas Marko. "Livy is progressing admirably," Clemens wrote. "This is just the place for her. This care-free life at Florentine villa is an ideal existence. The weather is divine, the outside aspects lovely, the days and nights tranquil and reposeful, the seclusion from the world and its worries as satisfactory as a dream. Late in the afternoon friends come out from the city and drink tea in the open air and tell what is happening in the world; and when the great sun sinks down upon Florence and the daily miracle begins they hold their breath and look. It is not a time for talk."

Clara was a curious amalgam of her parents. Serious and sensitive like her mother, but headstrong and self-dramatizing like her father, she resolved to pursue an independent career in music and moved to Berlin, out from under her father's gaze, to study with a celebrated pianist. When Clara reported that she had found herself the sole woman in a room otherwise filled with German officers, her father was outraged and accused her of bringing both her family and her country into "disrepute." When she returned to Florence for a visit and a young officer with whom she'd danced repeatedly came to call while her mother was out of town, her father locked her in her bedroom for several days. He could not bear to have his girls grow up.

Clemens may have disliked the villa in Florence, but he was dazzled by the panorama that could be seen from its windows each afternoon over tea. "No view that I am acquainted with in the world is at all comparable to this for delicacy, charm, exquisiteness, dainty coloring and bewildering rapidity of change," he told his sister-in-law. "It keeps a person drunk with pleasure all the time. Sometimes Florence ceases to be substantial and becomes just a faint soft dream with domes and towers of air, and one is persuaded that he might blow it away with a puff of his breath." Best of all, Florence seemed to be "just the place" for Livy. Her health steadily improved. Two doctors assured her that her ailment was not heart disease and she would soon be well again. That alone, Clemens wrote Orion, "was worth going to Europe to find out."

Clemens was feeling better, too. His arm no longer hurt, and he had been writing steadily again, 1,800 pages in five months: a book called *Tom Sawyer Abroad;* a short story about a young clerk who suddenly finds himself in possession of a million-pound bank note; and another novel, *Pudd'nhead Wilson,* an assault on the idiocy of defining people by race, in which a slave mother named Roxy—"as white as anybody, but the one sixteenth of her which was black outvoted the other fifteen parts and made her a Negro . . . and salable as such"—switches her own still lighter-skinned infant—"thirty-one parts white, and [therefore] by a fiction of law and custom a Negro"—with her master's offspring.

"Work is the darlingest recreation in this world," he wrote, "and whomsoever Nature has fitted to love it, is armed against care and sorrow." He could command large fees for his work now—$800 for a story for *Cosmopolitan* magazine, several thousand to let another periodical serialize *Pudd'nhead Wilson*—but they did little to erase the steadily mounting debts at his publishing company, which now owed its creditors $200,000, including $60,000 borrowed from Livy's inheritance.

If he wanted to restore his wife and children to the comfortable life they had once led, Clemens decided, the publishing company had to

First edition of *Pudd'nhead Wilson*, 1894; and an advertisement for it by the American Publishing Company, to which Sam Clemens had been forced to turn after his own firm went bankrupt

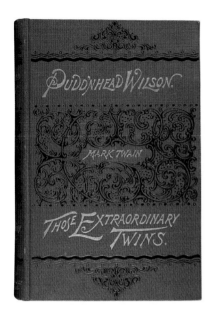

start making profits again. And another old dream came back to him: if only Paige's compositor could finally be manufactured and sold, Clemens's remaining share in it could still make him fabulously wealthy.

In March of 1893, leaving Livy and the girls in Europe, he sailed for America to attend to both businesses. Over the next year and a half, he would make eight such transatlantic crossings, shuttling between the family he loved and the increasingly desperate financial dealings he was counting on to bring them all together again in the house they cherished.

Livy darling.

Oh, I hate business, and so these days do drag along most wearily. I miss you, and I often wish we lived out of the world where one might never more hear of business or worry about money.

Youth darling: If you want to know what a lonely place is, just stay in it when you have gone away from it and see how you miss yourself. This long separation is depressing and it seems as if nothing could be worth it. . . . If failure comes we shall not be cast down and you must not allow yourself to be.

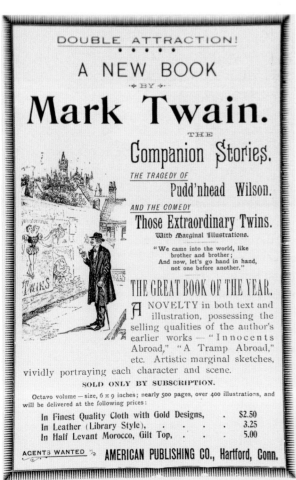

Clemens tried desperately to find investors to help bail out his publishing firm. The steel magnate Andrew Carnegie, an admirer, was approached for $100,000. He declined, passing on to Twain his investment maxim: "Put all your eggs in one basket—and watch that basket."

Paige, as usual, remained optimistic. His marvelous machine was nearly ready for testing by newspapers, he promised; all it needed was a few more improvements. Twain excitedly reported the news back to Livy in Florence: "What a talker he is! He could persuade a fish to come out and take a walk with him. When he is present I always believe him; I can't help it."

Livy sought to remain hopeful, too. "Youth darling: Your letters rec'd this morning made me just about wild with pleasurable excitement. It does not seem credible that we are really again to have money to *spend*. . . . It is astonishing to think that perhaps there is not yet a very long time for us to keep this economy."

Then the Panic of 1893 hit. The stock market crashed, and with it the great economic boom that had begun with the end of the Civil War came to an abrupt end. All across the country, businesses and factories closed. More than seventy railroads slipped into receivership. Two and a half million men were thrown out of work.

The publishing company's creditors now demanded their money; fresh investors and low-interest loans were harder than ever to come by. Clemens paced the floor at night, made notes on the edges of his manuscripts totaling up his debts and expenses. Moving from hotel rooms to friends' homes, he caught a series of colds and developed a cough so severe it caused a hernia. Orion Clemens reported more bad news. Two newspapers, a law firm, and a magazine had all turned him down for jobs. At age sixty-eight, he was more reliant than ever on his younger brother's money. His latest string of setbacks reminded Sam once more of their father's constant financial failures. "The billows of hell have been rolling over me," he wrote Livy. "A body forgets pretty much everything, these days, except his visions of the poorhouse."

It was at that dark moment that Clemens met the man he would later call "not only the best friend I ever had, but . . . the best man I have ever known." In many respects, Henry Huttleston Rogers represented everything Twain had so ferociously attacked in his writings about the Gilded Age and the corrupting power of Big Money. Rogers had helped found Standard Oil and now was the vice president and director of its vast trust, whose tentacles reached into coal, steel, railroads, and financial markets. He proudly listed his occupation as "capitalist," was personally worth more than $100 million, and had a well-earned reputation for ruthlessness. "We are not in business for our health," he once told a government commission investigating the trust, "but are out for the dollars."

"He's a pirate all right," Clemens said of Rogers, "but he owns up to it and enjoys being a pirate. That's the reason I like him."

Rogers, in turn, loved Twain's books well enough to read them aloud to his children, and when he learned of what had befallen his favorite author, he offered to help. He quickly approved a loan of $8,000 to provide the publishing company with some breathing room, then agreed to look into all of Clemens's business affairs—including the compositor— to see if they could be made profitable.

Henry Huttleston Rogers, known to his many enemies in business as "Hell Hound" Rogers, proved an invaluable friend and financial counselor to Sam Clemens and his family.

Meanwhile, he told Clemens, "you stop walking the floor." Sam telegraphed the good news to Livy. Once again, she offered encouragement.

December 17th, 1893.
Youth My Darling,
Your dispatch reached me last night and greatly rejoiced my heart because it does look as if perhaps you were going to be able to come here some day. . . . It also seems as if perhaps you were beginning to see your way through financially. How is Webster & Co. situated now? Are they working out of debt?

Yours always, Livy

But even Henry Rogers could not easily untangle Clemens's finances. In April of 1894 he convinced Clemens that the only option for Charles Webster & Company was voluntary bankruptcy. Sam's immediate concern was how Livy would respond to the news. "I seem to see you grieving and ashamed and dreading to look people in the face," he wrote her. "There is temporary defeat," he added, "but no dishonor, and we will march again."

With the Atlantic between them, Livy continued to be supportive. But a letter to her sister Susan revealed just how hard the blow of bankruptcy was to her:

The hideous news of Webster & Co.'s failure reached me by cable on Thursday, and Friday morning Galignani's Messenger *had a squib about it. Of course I knew it was likely to come, but I had a great hope that it would be in some way averted. Mr. Rogers was so sure there was no way out but failure that I suppose it was true. But I have a perfect* horror *and heart-sickness over it. I cannot get away from the feeling that business failure means disgrace. I suppose it will always mean that to me. . . .*

Sue, if you were to see me you would see that I have grown old very fast during this last year. I have wrinkled.

Most of the time I want to lie down and cry. Everything seems to me so impossible . . . and I feel that my life is an absolute and irretrievable failure. Perhaps I am thankless, but I so often feel that I should like to give it up and die.

The Clemenses were humiliated, but Rogers worked hard to make sure that bankruptcy did not completely ruin them. He insisted that since the Hartford house had been built with Livy's inheritance, it did not have to be auctioned off to pay her husband's debts. And since she had also loaned the publishing firm $60,000, he declared her a preferred creditor, thereby retaining the invaluable copyrights on her husband's works.

There even seemed to be a glimmer of hope. Rogers had persuaded the *Chicago Herald* to test Paige's compositor—and if it performed as

MARK TWAIN'S FAILURE.
Talk of the Street—Some Rumors Set Right.
The announcement in yesterday's "Courant" of the assignment of Mark Twain's publishing house of Charles L. Webster & Co., caused a great deal of talk about town, yesterday. The expressions of sympathy and regret are universal, for Mr. Clemens, as a citizen of Hartford, has made a host of friends here, and his hospitality has been proverbial.

So many idle and unfounded stories were in circulation that it seems proper to say, by authority, that the beautiful family residence of the Clemenses on Farmington avenue, in this city, is and always has been the property of Mrs. Clemens. The land was bought and the house built out of the private fortune which has her own inheritance

The *Hartford Courant* story from which the Clemenses' friends and neighbors learned of what had befallen the family, April 20, 1894

well under real work conditions as it had in Paige's shop, the Clemens family might be wealthy once more.

The test began in October of 1894. Twain was back in Europe when Rogers reported that the compositor was setting type with amazing speed, and included a copy of the newspaper partly set by the machine. The possibility of success at long last, Clemens wrote, "affects me like Columbus sighting land," and Livy began to talk once again of returning to their home in Hartford. They'd been away three long years.

Then, in late December, came another report from Rogers: the machine kept breaking down. "It was the nearest approach to a human being in the wonderful things it could do of any machine I have ever known," Clemens remembered. "But that was just the trouble; it was too much of a human being and not enough of a machine." The newspaper owners considered it impractical, Rogers advised; it could never be sold commercially.

The news, Twain wrote back, "hit me like a thunderclap [and] knocked every rag of sense out of my head." During the last fourteen years of dreaming of the riches it could bring, the Paige compositor had disappointed him many times, he admitted in a letter to Rogers,

> but I couldn't shake off the confidence of a lifetime in my luck. All my life I have stumbled upon lucky chances of large size, and whenever they were wasted it was because of my own stupidity and carelessness. [Now I need] to teach myself to endure a way of life which I was familiar with during the first half of my life but whose sordidness and hatefulness and humiliation long ago faded out of my memory and feeling.

Two months later, in February 1895, the Clemenses marked their twenty-fifth wedding anniversary. Feeling a total failure, Sam pulled out a silver five-franc coin and presented it to Livy. "It is our silver wedding day," he said, "and so I give you a present."

That March, he shuttled back to the United States once more to deal with the financial wreckage and stopped briefly at the family home in Hartford, to make preparations for renting it out. Privately, he doubted his family could ever afford to live there again, but in a letter to Livy back in Europe, he could not bring himself to admit it to her and the girls:

> Livy darling, when I arrived in town I did not want to go near the house, and I didn't want to go any-

Poster for the magazine serialization of *Joan of Arc* in *Harper's* magazine, April 1896. At Twain's insistence, the story appeared anonymously because he feared readers would not take it seriously if they knew it was his work.

where or see anybody. I said to myself, "If I may be spared it I will never live in Hartford again."

But as soon as I entered this front door I was seized with a furious desire to have us all in this house again and right away, and never go outside the grounds any more forever—certainly never again to Europe.

How ugly, tasteless, repulsive, are all the domestic interiors I have ever seen in Europe compared with the perfect taste of this ground floor, with its delicious dream of harmonious color, and its all-pervading spirit of peace and serenity and deep contentment. You did it all, and it speaks of you and praises you eloquently and unceasingly. It is the loveliest home that ever was. I had no faintest idea of what it was like. . . .

I had wholly forgotten its olden aspect. And so, when I stepped in at the front door and was suddenly confronted by all its richness and beauty . . . it almost took my breath away. . . .

It seemed as if I had burst awake out of a hellish dream, and had never been away, and that you would come drifting down out of those dainty upper regions with all the little children tagging after you.

**Livy Clemens in 1895. "If failure comes,"
she wrote her husband, she and the children would not "be cast down and you
must not allow yourself to be."**

During this time of financial chaos, Twain had somehow managed to keep working on a new novel, *Personal Recollections of Joan of Arc*. Now, back in Paris with the family, he threw himself into finishing it—even though, he told Rogers, it was the hardest writing he had ever done. The book was not meant to be humorous, and partly because of that, Livy and the girls, who continued to believe the public never appreciated Twain's more serious side, considered it his greatest work. Susy wrote that it

> *promises to be his loveliest book. Perhaps even more sweet and beautiful than* The Prince and the Pauper. *The character of Joan is pure and perfect to a miraculous degree. Hearing the M.S. read aloud is an uplifting and revealing hour to us all. Many of Joan's words and sayings are historically correct and Papa cries when he reads them. In fact he almost always fills up when reading any speech of hers.*

Years later, Twain would also contend that *Joan of Arc* was his best book. After all, he would remember, his descriptions of St. Joan had been based in large part on his beloved Susy.

CHAPTER TEN

FOLLOWING THE EQUATOR

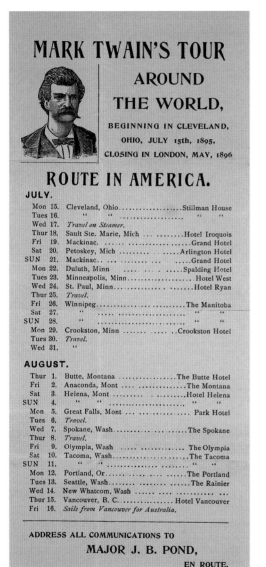

MARK TWAIN'S TOUR
AROUND
THE WORLD,
BEGINNING IN CLEVELAND,
OHIO, JULY 15th, 1895,
CLOSING IN LONDON, MAY, 1896.

ROUTE IN AMERICA.

JULY.

Mon 15.	Cleveland, Ohio	Stillman House
Tues 16.	" "	" "
Wed 17.	*Travel on Steamer.*	
Thur 18.	Sault Ste. Marie, Mich	Hotel Iroquois
Fri 19.	Mackinac.	Grand Hotel
Sat 20.	Petoskey, Mich	Arlington Hotel
SUN 21.	Mackinac.	Grand Hotel
Mon 22.	Duluth, Minn	Spalding Hotel
Tues 23.	Minneapolis, Minn	Hotel West
Wed 24.	St. Paul, Minn	Hotel Ryan
Thur 25.	*Travel.*	
Fri 26.	Winnipeg	The Manitoba
Sat 27.	"	" "
SUN 28.	"	" "
Mon 29.	Crookston, Minn	Crookston Hotel
Tues 30.	*Travel.*	
Wed 31.	"	

AUGUST.

Thur 1.	Butte, Montana	The Butte Hotel
Fri 2.	Anaconda, Mont	The Montana
Sat 3.	Helena, Mont	Hotel Helena
SUN 4.	" "	" "
Mon 5.	Great Falls, Mont	Park Hotel
Tues 6.	*Travel.*	
Wed 7.	Spokane, Wash	The Spokane
Thur 8.	*Travel.*	
Fri 9.	Olympia, Wash	The Olympia
Sat 10.	Tacoma, Wash	The Tacoma
SUN 11.	" "	" "
Mon 12.	Portland, Or	The Portland
Tues 13.	Seattle, Wash	The Rainier
Wed 14.	New Whatcom, Wash	
Thur 15.	Vancouver, B. C.	Hotel Vancouver
Fri 16.	*Sails from Vancouver for Australia.*	

ADDRESS ALL COMMUNICATIONS TO
MAJOR J. B. POND,
EN ROUTE.

Mark Twain in the cab of a Great Northern Railroad locomotive specially engaged to get him from Tacoma, Washington, to Portland, Oregon, as part of the hectic 1895 lecture tour advertised above

APRIL 1.
This is the day upon which we are reminded of what we are on the other three hundred and sixty-four.
—*Pudd'nhead Wilson*, 1894

In the spring of 1895, Sam Clemens was nearly sixty years old and bankrupt. Livy's pride—and Henry Rogers's concern for his reputation—had persuaded him publicly to promise to pay his creditors in full, even though he was not legally required to do so. There was only one way for him to make money quickly, and it was something he had sworn to himself and his family he would never do again: return to the lecture circuit. "I've *got* to mount the platform or starve," he told Rogers.

"My sisters and I were aghast at the prospect," wrote Clara Clemens. For Susy, the thought of her father returning to the platform as the "mere humorist" Mark Twain was particularly galling: "How I hate that name! I should like never to hear it again! My father should not be satisfied with it! He should not be known by it! He should show himself the great writer that he is, not merely a funny man. Funny! That's all the people see in him—a maker of funny speeches!"

It was a "heart-torturing idea" and a "hellish struggle," Clemens admitted, but in late April he signed a contract for the most ambitious lecture tour of his life, one that would begin with a cross-country progress across North America and eventually take him around the world—nearly 150 appearances on five continents.

Concerned about her husband's spirits and his health, and dreading another prolonged separation, Livy insisted on coming along. So did Clara. Susy, citing her fear of seasickness and determined to build up her strength in order to become a singer, preferred to remain in the United States, at the home of her aunt Susan Crane. Jean, thought too delicate for lengthy travel, was to stay with her and attend school in Elmira. Livy assured them both that they

Colonel James Burton Pond, whose Kodak camera captured the informal images on these and the following three pages, managed the first leg of Mark Twain's grueling around-the-world tour in 1895 and kept an informal journal of their travels. Above, Sam broods aboard the Great Lakes steamer *Northland* on his way to Cleveland, the first stop on the tour. Above right, Livy urges him to put on his overcoat. "He is nervous and weak," Pond wrote, suffering from fatigue, tension, and "a massive carbuncle . . . but he is nursed and cared for by his tender, affectionate wife, whose soothing influence on him seems instantaneous."

(opposite top) By the time this photograph of a smiling Livy with Pond's wife, Martha, was taken aboard a train heading for Manitoba sometime in late July, the party seemed considerably more relaxed. But Clemens could still be testy. When their party reached the Crookston, Minnesota, depot (opposite bottom) ready to board the four a.m. train for Great Falls, Montana, only to find it would be an hour and a half late, he was furious. "He had contracted with Pond to travel," Pond recalled his saying, "and not to stand shivering around depots at this inhuman hour waiting for trains that were never known to arrive." Livy asked if he weren't being "a little unreasonable. 'No. I am not unreasonable. I insist on Pond keeping his contract by traveling me on this truck.' So I wheeled him about the station . . . and Clara got a snap shot of the act, which Mark said would provide documentary evidence of my having kept the agreement."

Out for a stroll in Great Falls, Montana, on July 31 (above), Mark came upon a cluster of shanties occupied by Norwegian immigrants. "He caught a pair of kittens in his arms," Pond noted, "greatly to the discomfort of their owner, a little girl. He tried to make friends with the child, and buy the kitties, but she began to cry and beg that her pets might be liberated. He soon captured her with a pretty story, and finally consented to let them go." At Fort Missoula, Montana (left), on August 6, Twain and an officer watched the men of the 27th U.S. (Colored) regiment drill in his honor. "The band played quite a program," Pond wrote, "and we all declared it one of the finest military bands in America."

On August 8, the Clemens party was aboard the SS *Flyer*, about to set sail from Seattle to Tacoma, Washington. "Mark sat on the deck," Pond wrote, "watching its baggage-smashers removing our trunks from the baggage car. . . . He exclaimed, 'Oh! how I do wish one of those trunks were filled with dynamite and that all the baggage-destroyers were gathered about it, and I just far enough off to see them hurled into Kingdom Come!'" In Olympia, Washington, the travelers stayed at the Olympia Hotel, where, Pond noted, "Mark had his breakfast in his room and declared that it was nice to have a quiet breakfast and not be interrupted."

NOTICE
ALL STOWAWAYS WILL
BE PROSECUTED AT HONOLULU,
AND RETURNED TO THIS PORT.
BY ORDER.

Clemens, Clara, and Livy (above) set sail for Hawaii aboard the SS *Warrimoo* (left) on August 23, 1895. "Mrs. Clemens is disappointed in the ship," Pond wrote. "The whole thing looks discouraging, and our hearts are almost broken for the poor woman. She tells me she is going to brave it through, for she must do it. It is for her children."

would all be together again in a year, and that after a successful tour "we shall be able to settle down in our home" once more.

"Pray for me," a nervous Clemens wrote to Henry Rogers as he set off on the first leg of the tour—a grueling succession of twenty-two cities, from Cleveland to Vancouver, in less than a month. The days were long and the rail travel was tiresome, and Twain was nearly crippled by a painful carbuncle on his left thigh. But he carried with him in his baggage some three thousand "manila cheroots" with which to ease the tension, and the crowds were enthusiastic everywhere he appeared. "It is constant unceasing adulation of Papa," Clara wrote Susy; audiences seemed to know much of his work by heart. He was a masterful performer now, employing his deadpan drawl—his late mother had called it "Sammy's slow talk"—and patented pauses. "For one audience the pause will be short," he said, "for another a little longer, for another a shade longer still. . . . I . . . play with the pause as other children play with a toy." His talks were pretty nearly surefire, too: "The Jumping Frog," "The Awful German Language," "The Decay of the Art of Lying." "There is but one Mark Twain," said the *Seattle Post-Intelligencer,* and his talks "are strange medleys of humor and philosophy which have . . . the sound of a great literary improvisation."

By the time he was ready to sail across the Pacific, Twain had sent $5,000 back to Henry Rogers as the first payment toward retiring his debt. Based on the success so far, Twain told reporters, he was confident that "if I live I can pay off the last debt within four years, after which, at the age of sixty-four, I can make a fresh and unencumbered start in life."

Lecturing is gymnastics, chest-expander, medicine, mind-healer, blues-destroyer, all in one. I am twice as well as I was when I started out. I have gained nine pounds in twenty-eight days, and expect to weigh 600 before January. I haven't had a blue day in all the twenty-eight. My wife and daughter are accumulating health and strength and flesh nearly as fast as I am. When we reach home, two years hence, we think we can exhibit as freaks.

They docked first at Hawaii, but to Clemens's disappointment a quarantine prevented them from going ashore to visit the islands he had enjoyed so much as a young man. Then it was on to Fiji and finally the British colonies of Australia and New Zealand. Livy wrote:

Susy darling, dearest child:

Tuesday night we were at Horsham, a small town that has an Agricultural College. I think Papa never talked to a more enthusiastic audience than that night. They were entirely uproarious, taking

A Lecture on Morals

Mark Twain began his round-the-world lecture tour in Cleveland, where (much to Clemens's dismay) a reporter wrote down one of his stories word for word and printed it in the paper. It was quickly reprinted in the New York Times *on July 23, 1895, under the headline: "Mark Twain Begins His Tour; He Is Carrying a Lecture on Morals Around the World."*

The first time that I ever stole a watermelon . . . I carried that watermelon to a secluded bower in the lumber yard, and broke it open and it was green. I began to reflect, and I said to myself, I have done wrong; it was wrong in me to steal that watermelon—that kind of watermelon. And I said to myself: Now what would a right-minded and right-intentioned boy do, who found that he had done wrong—stolen a watermelon like this. What would he do, must he do? Do right; make restitution. He must restore that property to its owner; and I resolved to do that, and the moment I made that good resolution I felt that electrical moral uplight which becomes a victory over wrongdoing.

I was spiritually strengthened and refreshed, and carried that watermelon back to that wagon and gave it to the farmer—restored it to him, and I told him he ought to be ashamed of himself going around working off green watermelons in that way on people who had confidence in him, and I told him in my perfectly frank manner it was wrong. . . .

He was ashamed; he said he would never do it again, and I believe that I did that man a good turn, as well as one for myself. He did reform; I was severe with him a little, but that was all. I restored the watermelon and made him give me a ripe one. I morally helped him, and have no doubt that I helped myself the same time, for that was a lesson which remained with me for my perfection. Ever since that day to this I never stole another one—like that.

"Bourke Street, Melbourne," painted by Tom Roberts a few years before Mark Twain lectured in that city. Twain called Melbourne a "juvenile city of sixty years and half a million inhabitants . . . a stately city architecturally as well as in magnitude. It has an elaborate system of cable-car service; it has museums, and colleges, and schools, and public gardens, and electricity, and gas, and libraries, and theaters, and mining centers, and wool centers . . . and as many churches and banks as can make a living."

a point almost before he had reached it. The house was packed, people sitting on the stage and standing around the sides of the hall. The town has only 3,000 inhabitants but many came from neighboring towns. One man came 75 miles and went immediately back after the lecture, giving him a trip of 150 miles. . . . A young fellow who sat next to me . . . began to pound his sides as if troubled with stitches in them and turning to me said, "Well if it is all as funny as this I shall die!"

Twain's carbuncle reappeared, confining him to bed for a week at one point, but he soldiered on, night after night speaking to sold-out audiences, sending more money back to Rogers in the States, and constantly jotting down notes for the travel book he intended to write.

[All across Australia] there were little villages, with neat stations well placarded with showy advertisements—mainly of . . . brands of sheep-dip. . . . It is a stuff like tar, and is dabbed on to places where the shearer clips a piece out of the sheep. It bars out the flies, and has healing properties, and a nip to it which makes the sheep skip. . . . It is not good to eat. That is, it is not good to eat except when mixed with railroad coffee. It improves railroad coffee. Without it railroad coffee is too vague. But with it, it is quite assertive and enthusiastic. By itself, railroad coffee is too passive; but sheep-dip makes it wake up and get down to business.

After celebrating his sixtieth birthday—and suffering from a third carbuncle—Twain and his entourage sailed on to Ceylon, then India, "the most extraordinary country," he wrote, "that the sun visits on his round." For nearly three months he crisscrossed the subcontinent, from Bombay to Rawalpindi to Darjeeling and Calcutta, speaking to large and adoring crowds. "In addition to almost every prominent [British] citizen of Bombay," wrote a reporter for the *Times of India,*

was the comparatively large number of Parsee, Mahomedan, and Hindoo ladies and gentlemen who were no whit behind their European friends in the manifestation of their appreciation of the unflagging humor of the lecturer. It is a rugged and even something of a romantic figure that Mark Twain presents upon the stage, with his masses of curly hair, now nearly white, his keen, kindly eyes looking out from great shaggy brows, and his strangely magnetic smile. . . . The hour and a-half during which he spoke (almost without a break) seemed little more than ten minutes, and yet it was perhaps the most delightful hour and a-half's speaking that had ever been heard by any member of that large audience.

A RAMBLE WITH MARK TWAIN.

HIS VIEWS ON MEN AND THINGS.

He was standing at the bar of the Australia Hotel. Two friends were with him, and if one might judge from appearances, they were all three drinking whisky "cocktails." Mark Twain, as he subsequently confided to the writer, drinks whisky hot without any sugar in it. He once found out that whisky with sugar in it disagreed with him. So, instead of abandoning the whisky, as some dull people might have done, he "swore off" the sugar and the lemon, and thus made the discovery that in itself whisky is one of the most harmless, as well as one of the most agreeable, of beverages. He took a sip of the "cocktail," put the glass down on the bar, and went on with his story. The listeners seemed mightily amused. What it was all about is more than ayone beyond ear-shot would venture to imagine. Mark Twain's hands were moving up and down like two ships at sea, and this was happening by way of illustration to a narrative spoken with ex-

An account of Sam Clemens offstage from the *Sydney Daily Telegraph*, September 17, 1895

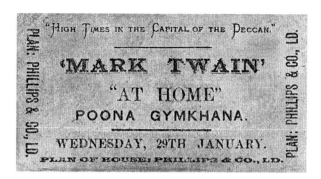

"High Times in the Capital of the Deccan."

'MARK TWAIN'
"AT HOME"
POONA GYMKHANA.

WEDNESDAY, 29TH JANUARY.

PLAN OF HOUSE: PHILLIPS & CO., LD.

PLAN: PHILLIPS & CO., LD.

FIRST APPEARANCE IN CALCUTTA
OF THE
GREATEST HUMORIST OF THE AGE,
The Author of " The Innocents Abroad."
MARK TWAIN,
MARK TWAIN,
MARK TWAIN,
MARK TWAIN,
WHO,
Next Monday afternoon, at 5-30
IN THE
THEATRE ROYAL,
WILL GIVE HIS
First Mark Twain " At Homes,"
First Mark Twain " At Homes,"
First Mark Twain " At Homes,"
Illustrated with Humorous
LIFE AND CHARACTER SKETCHES

ADMISSION—Reserved Seats, Rs. 4; Boxes,
Rs. 20; Dress Circle, Rs. 3; Pit, Re. 2. Plans and
Tickets at T. E. Bevan and Co.'s.
R. S. SMYTHE,
WEDNESDAY AFTERNOON, AT 5-30,
Mr. Clemens will give his
Second Mark Twain " At Home "
(AN ENTIRELY DIFFERENT ENTERTAINMENT.)
THURSDAY AFTERNOON, AT 5-30,
The Author of " The Jumping Frog " will make his
LAST APPEARANCE IN CALCUTTA,
WHEN HE WILL PRESENT HIS
Third Mark Twain " At Home."

While in India, Mark Twain spoke before the members of the Poona Gymkhana Club (top) and at Calcutta's Theatre Royal, and visited the lofty hill station of Darjeeling (right), from where, he said, he was told he could see into three countries—"Thibet is one of them, Nepaul another, and I think Herzegovina was the other."

The Taj Mahal was lovely, Twain said, though not quite as lovely as the trees in Hartford when covered by a winter ice storm—"Nature's supremest achievement in the domain of the superb and beautiful." The Himalayas were "the loftiest land I had ever seen, by 12,000 feet or more," he wrote, but "I think that mountains that are as high as that are disagreeable." Nonetheless, he took a boyish joy in careening down a mountain slope on a railroad handcar, calling it "the most enjoyable day I have spent in the earth."

In the holy city of Benares, Clemens spent an afternoon with a Hindu holy man who had reportedly reached perfection after innumerable reincarnations. Clemens gave him a copy of *Huckleberry Finn*, saying, "I thought it might rest him up a little to mix it in along with his meditations." And he watched nine corpses being cremated on the bank of the sacred Ganges. "I should not wish to see any more of it," he said, "unless I might select the parties."

And he was especially intrigued by India's wildlife: tigers and cobras, and the monkeys that fearlessly invaded homes through open windows. In Jaipur, two of them came into his room one morning. One groomed its hair with his brush, he claimed; the other picked up his humorous notes

"The city of Benares," Twain wrote, "is in effect just a big church, a religious hive, whose every cell is a temple, a shrine or a mosque, and whose every conceivable earthly and heavenly good is procurable under one roof, so to speak—a sort of Army and Navy Store, theologically stocked. . . .

"We made the usual trip up and down the river; made it two or three times, and could have made it with increasing interest and enjoyment many times more. . . . I think one would not get tired of the bathers, nor their costumes, nor of their ingenuities in getting out of them and into them again without exposing too much bronze, nor of their devotional gesticulations and absorbed bead-tellings.

"But I should get tired of seeing them wash their mouths with that dreadful water and drink it."

View from the River Ganges of the Burning Ghats, watercolor by Edward Lear in 1873, and Hindu pilgrims (above) bathing in the river

and began crying over them. "I did not mind the one with the hair-brush," he wrote later, "but the conduct of the other one hurt me; it hurts me yet." He rode an elephant there, too: "I could easily learn to prefer an elephant to any other vehicle, partly because of that immunity from collisions, and partly because of the fine view one has from up there, and partly because of the dignity one feels in that high place, and partly because one can look in at the windows and see what is going on privately among the family."

From India, the Clemenses sailed to South Africa for two months of performances in Pretoria, Johannesburg, Cape Town, and half a dozen other cities. Sam toured the huge Kimberley diamond pit and marveled at the gold mines that were yielding up $45 million a year. "I had been a gold miner myself, in my day," Twain wrote, "and knew substantially everything that those people knew about it, except how to make money at it."

Everywhere in Africa, European colonial powers were brazenly extending their empires. Taking someone else's land was nothing new in the world, Twain noted, but this modern imperialism cloaked itself in a hypocritical self-righteousness that he found particularly disgraceful. "Christian governments," he wrote, "are as frank to-day, as open and above-board, in discussing projects for raiding each other's clothes-lines as ever they were before the Golden Rule came smiling into this inhospitable world and couldn't get a night's lodging anywhere."

Even more troubling was the treatment of native peoples he had witnessed throughout his tour, from Australia to India to Africa, treatment that awakened in Sam Clemens powerful and disturbing memories of the way slaves had been mistreated during his Missouri boyhood. It made him angry and ashamed of his own race.

In many countries we have chained the savage and starved him to death; . . . in many countries we have burned the savage at the stake; . . . in more than one country we have hunted the savage and his little children and their mother with dogs and guns through the woods and swamps for an afternoon's sport, and filled the region with happy laughter over their sprawling and stumbling flight, and their wild supplications for mercy; . . . in many countries we have taken the savage's land from him, and made him our slave, and lashed him every day, and broken his pride, and made death his only friend, and overworked him till he dropped in his tracks. . . .

There are many humorous things in the world; among them the white man's notion that he is less savage than the other savages.

On July 15, 1896—one year and one day since starting out on the tour—Clemens, Livy, and Clara set sail from South Africa for England.

After seeing Sam, Livy, and Clara off on their tour, Colonel Pond and his wife traveled to Quarry Farm, where he took this photograph on September 15, 1895. It includes (left to right) Susan Crane, Mrs. Pond and her son, Bim, and Susy Clemens. "I am living in a kind of haze and do not fully take in the misfortune of this separation," Susy had written Clara from the farm that summer. "I say 'Is it a dream? Have they really gone and have I entered upon this strange long desolate year without them?' Generally, I cannot believe it but sometimes a ghastly wave of realization surges over me and then . . . !—it is a mistake to separate from the people we love and whom we belong to. I do not really love anybody but you dear three, and of course nobody else loves me." This is among the last photographs ever made of Susy Clemens.

He was exhausted. He felt as if the trip had lasted a thousand years, not twelve months, he said, and the prospect of more appearances in England, then yet another lecture tour, made him feel that much worse. "I got horribly tired of the platform toward the last," he wrote to Henry Rogers from the ship. "I hope I have trodden it for the last time; that bread-and-butter stress will never crowd me onto it again."

But the tour had been a triumph, netting nearly $35,000 toward his debts, providing him with enough material for yet another travel book, to be called *Following the Equator,* and extending his fame to every corner of the globe. Emerging from bankruptcy might not take him the four years he had estimated at the start of the long journey.

Better yet, in England the family would at last be reunited. Upon arrival in Southampton, Sam, Livy, and Clara cabled to the States for Jean and Susy to prepare to sail from New York. Then a letter arrived from Hartford saying that their departure had been postponed because Susy had fallen ill with a fever.

A brief telegram followed: Susy's recovery would be long, it said, but certain. Alarmed, Livy left England for the United States on the next steamer, taking Clara with her. Twain stayed behind, to begin work on his new book and to find more suitable lodgings for the family when Livy and the girls returned.

Three days later, on August 18, alone in their rented house in Guildford, he received another telegram from the States. Susy was dead.

Later he would gather the grim details. Susy had been spending the summer in Hartford, staying with the Clemenses' friends the Warners but going to the family's old home to play the piano and practice her singing. Neighbors sometimes gathered outside the open windows to enjoy the music. Then she had developed a mysterious fever. At first, she refused to see a physician, convinced that a spiritual healer would restore her health. Finally, Katy Leary had taken charge, overruling the reluctant patient and calling in a doctor—who diagnosed spinal meningitis. For two weeks, increasingly delirious as her fever spiraled, Susy wandered through the house of her childhood. She found a gown of Livy's hanging in a closet and, believing it was her mother and that she had died, kissed it and cried. She watched the traffic passing on Farmington Avenue, too, and sang out: "Up go the trolley cars for Mark Twain's daughter. Down go the trolley cars for Mark Twain's daughter."

These sheets of paper and forty-three others covered with Susy's last delirious writings were carefully preserved after her death by her grief-stricken parents.

The infection spread deeper into her brain. She lost her sight, then lapsed into a coma. When she died, she was only twenty-four years old.

Once again, Sam Clemens took the blame for tragedy upon himself. The strain of the bankruptcy and the tour that had pulled the family apart had been his doing, and he was sure that, together, they had killed his beloved daughter. Meanwhile, Livy was on a ship, halfway across the Atlantic, still unaware of what had happened. Sam poured out his heart to her in a stream of letters to be delivered to her after her arrival in New York.

August 19th, 1896.

. . . Oh, my heart-broken darling—no, not heart-broken yet, for you still do not know—but what tidings are in store for you! What a bitter world, what a shameful world it is. . . . I love you, my darling—I wish you could have been spared this unutterable sorrow.

I have spent the day alone—thinking; sometimes bitter thoughts, sometimes only sad ones. Reproaching myself for laying the foundation of all our troubles. . . . Reproaching myself for a million things whereby I have brought misfortune and sorrow to this family.

It rains all day—no, it drizzles, and is sombre and dark. I would not have it otherwise. I could not welcome the sun today.

Be comforted, my darling—we shall have our release in time. Be comforted, remembering how much hardship, grief, pain, she is spared; and that her heart can never be broken, now, for the loss of a child. . . .

I seem to see her in her coffin—I do not know in which room. In the library, I hope; for there she and [Clara] and I mostly played when we were children together and happy. I wish there were five of the coffins, side by side and out of my heart of hearts I wish it. How lovely is death; and how niggardly it is doled out.

She died in our own house—not in another's; died where every little thing was familiar and beloved; died where she had spent all her life till my crimes made her a pauper and an exile. How good it is that she got home again.

Give my love to Clara and Jean. We have that much of our fortune left.

Susy was buried in the Langdon family plot in Elmira, not far from Langdon, the older brother she had never known. Her father was too far away to attend.

AREN'T WE FUNNY ANIMALS?
AN INTERVIEW WITH HAL HOLBROOK

Few people have studied Mark Twain more closely and persistently than Hal Holbrook, who as a young actor in 1954 began developing a one-man show portraying Twain onstage. Over the course of nearly half a century, Holbrook's dedication to understanding his subject has resulted in his being able to recite more than twelve hours of Twain's writings from memory— allowing him to tailor each performance to different audiences and different times. His performances of Mark Twain Tonight! *have won Holbrook a Tony award, a special Drama Critics' Circle Award, and an Emmy nomination, and his insights into Twain have prompted scholars to make him an honorary member of the Mark Twain Circle of America. On April 17, 2000, at the Academy of Music in Northampton, Massachusetts, Ken Burns interviewed Holbrook on camera for the documentary film. The following excerpts were taken from that interview.*

Why is Mark Twain important?

Because he's talking about today as well as a hundred years ago. There's nothing really dated about Twain. I mean, if you eliminate the name of the event or the president he's talking about, it's as if he were talking about what's going on today.

There's an extraordinary lack of difference between what we're facing and what he went through in the last half of the nineteenth century. We think we've got something extraordinary going on here with the Internet and television and the airplane. But what did he have? He had the joining of the railroads across the country. He had the invention of the electric light. He had the telegraph, the telephone. He had the X-ray. He had . . . you name it! And he also had the industrialization of a pioneer society and all the inequalities and brutalities that arose out of that. He had the great fortunes. He had the greed factor.

He had the suppression of poor people. He had the beginnings of the labor movement. He had the women's suffrage movement. You name it. He had America entering into the imperialistic arena, too, and, as he said, "Now we are a world power and are happy and glad and have a seat up front with the family . . . with tacks in it."

Does Twain endure because he had some sort of special insight into the human condition?

Yeah. He was talking about the character of the human race. And as he says, "The character of the human race never changes, it is permanent." Circumstances change from time to time for better or worse, but the character of the human race never does. And then he goes out to prove it and he's right.

Is he trying to change the human race or hold up a mirror to it? What is he trying to do?

I can't speak for Mark Twain, but I would imagine that he was trying to make us see ourselves as we should see ourselves if we were being brutally honest about ourselves. The idea of trying to change us would probably send him into gales of laughter, because you can't change the human being. The human animal is the human animal. And we're going to continue to act in the same way with a different set of clothing from one century to another.

Did he love or did he hate the human race?

Well, he was one of us. That's the signal point about Mark Twain's commentary. He was one of us. He didn't exclude himself. He said, "The human race is a race of cowards and I am not only marching in that procession, I am carrying a banner."

Is the key to his humor the willingness to include himself?

Yes. One of the reasons that you can entertain an audience by doing Twain and using his words is that the joke was very often on him. When I do my show, I start out really making jokes like "When I was a young man wavering between the pulpit and the penitentiary." He sucks you in. *Roughing It* is just a funny exposition of his misadventures out west, of the tenderfoot going out west. *Innocents Abroad* is a funny portrait of the brash American going and facing up to all the glories of the European civilization, which of course in those days everyone was taught to revere. But Mark Twain wasn't about to revere anybody until he figured out who they were and what they were worth.

Talk about Twain as a performer, a stage lecturer.

In his lectures, he mostly read—or seemed to read—from *The Jumping Frog*, from *Innocents Abroad*, from *Huckleberry Finn*. It was in his speeches later in life—particularly when he was giving after-dinner speeches—that he used anecdotes and one-liners more. On the platform he was much more formal than I am, but his manner in those days was not like Dickens, for example, who stood at a lectern, wore a flower in his lapel, and, you know, *read.* Twain was much more relaxed.

He broke the rules of formal lecturing by moving around and slouching on the platform, but in today's terms what he did would seem not at all informal. So, in order to create the kind of impression he did—or something like it—I made some changes of my own. He wore a black suit; I wear white because he used to wear it going down Fifth Avenue on Sunday mornings when people were coming out of church, and it was shocking. He did not smoke a cigar on the platform; I do. And I also expanded the idea of moving around the stage.

Sir Henry Irving, the greatest English actor of the last part of the nineteenth century, said that Twain had

Hal Holbrook

the makings of a great actor. Well, he did, because he could use the pause and play with the pause to such devastating effect. And he found that a lot of the material that worked beautifully in his book wouldn't read as well on the platform. So he would alter it and improvise. "Grandfather's Old Ram" is a great example. It originally appears, I think, in *Roughing It,* but his lecture version is different, totally different—not just a few words. And that's the version that I use.

What did he expect of an audience?

He was sure hoping to get 'em laughing. Made his job easier. The major thing he was trying to do was entertain. He might want to instruct them a little, but basically he wanted to entertain them and do it through an entertaining presentation. If they got some, you know, meat out of it, fine. But anyone who spent as much time as he did rehearsing, and playing with the idea of the pause and the technique of the pause to get it just right—anyone who spent that much time working on his performance was a *performer.*

He said, "All I expect of an audience is for them to just sit there and listen for as long as they can remain conscious." See, that's where he turns the joke back on himself. That's what makes him winning. "All I expect of an audience is for them to just sit there and listen for as long as they can remain conscious." He says it straight too, he doesn't "hee, hee, hee!" You know, he doesn't have to editorialize about his joke, he just says it. Deadpan.

Do you think he liked performing?

He certainly liked performing, there's no question about that. He blossomed in front of the crowd. But he came to hate the traveling on the road. Think about how difficult it was, and take a look at his lecture schedule. I looked at his schedule recently for December and January of some year. Good grief, I think *I've* got it rough! This man was traveling and lecturing every day. The only day off was Sunday! He would travel by train on the same day that he had to give a lecture. He was tired. He was out there making money. His letters back to Livy were filled with unhappiness about the road. There is a loneliness to traveling on the road, even when you have a stage manager with you, like I do. But more often than not, he was just out there all alone.

Late in his life, it seemed that the host of every dinner in New York tried to have Mark Twain give remarks.

Well, he became the sage of the country—even the world. There's nobody today to compare him to. Whatever happened in the morning's paper, they would have a comment from Twain. Something would happen—a war would break out or somebody would do some stupid thing. Like when the Tammany Hall fellow died the night before election, you know, Twain was contacted immediately for a comment. The politico died. And Twain says, "Well, I won't attend his funeral, but I'll write a very nice letter saying that I approve of it."

In the show that I put together, I pull these one-liners out and line them up in more of a rat-a-tat-tat fashion than he would have.

Humor was his weapon. What were his targets?

Oh, you name it. Hypocrisy, pomposity, the narrow mind, the prejudiced mind, stupidity, brutality—all those things. You know that quote of his "Against the power of laughter, nothing can stand"? How you can push at an injustice, move it a little, century by century. But only laughter can blow it to rags and atoms at a blast. "Against the power of laughter, nothing can stand." When you laugh away something, you've used the most powerful instrument you can to surgically remove it and keep it from hurting you.

He's fearless.

He's fearless. He's fearless and he's dangerous. There's a quote where he says, "I suppose an honest man shines more in politics than he does elsewhere. But shouldn't a senator keep his word? Or a president?

Shouldn't he set a high example? Is keeping one's word so extraordinary a thing when the person achieving that feat is the first citizen of a civilized nation?"

Ouch.

Ouch.

He's never out of date, is he?

I have got to the point in my life and in my association with Twain where I find my own emotions, my feelings about what I don't like about what's going on in the world, in this country—I find them running down the same stream with Mark Twain's opinions and feelings and distresses. They seem to mate perfectly. I can't think of anything that's going on that he doesn't touch upon.

I just put this new material together, which I call "Get Rich." It's a routine I cobbled together. A routine, I call it—five or ten minutes long—and it might have sixteen different sources. It's all Twain, but it's not something you would have read in Twain that way. I call it "Get Rich" because we're having a greedy love affair with money. I mean, we're forgetting everything. We're just so in love with money, and everything in our society feeds into it, beginning with the television and the advertising and the commercialization of the human being. We have become a product. The human being has become a product. What a horrible conclusion to come to for the human being!

He was a master of one-liners. Do you have any favorites?

Oh, I love "Heaven for climate; hell for society." I love "The trouble is not that the world is full of fools, it's just that lightning isn't distributed right." That's one of my favorites because it covers such a wide range.

Do you know the one about lightning and the lightning bug?

Yeah. That's one: "The difference between the right word and the almost right word is the difference between the lightning and the lightning bug." That was his great literary talent: choosing just the right word. And he slipped the word a little off center sometimes. He would just cant it a bit, his phrasing, and so it took on a sort of a different dimension.

That makes him all the more subversive—he's able to reach broad numbers of people.

Yes, because he was always close to the American idiom. He made American speech something to be admired. He used the way we talk and turned it into literature.

That brings us to Huckleberry Finn. *What makes that novel so powerful?*

What makes *Huckleberry Finn* so powerful? Well, because it's the truth about what that society was like. It's a savage portrait. People think of *Huckleberry Finn* as a children's book. It's not. I mean, children understand it sometimes better than adults, because they don't complicate it. But it's a savage book about a certain society which produced some of the worst inequalities and brutalities that exist in our present society, and it's a truthful portrait.

It's a portrait done by someone who understands it because he lived it. He was there. He didn't make it up. He wasn't a Northerner writing about the South. He knew that society, and he used the lingo of that society. That's why the word *nigger* is used so often. It's a hateful word; it's like a red flag to a bull. Today, particularly. In those days, it wasn't.

But I think the reason Twain uses the word *nigger* so often in *Huckleberry Finn* is because it's like an anvil hitting you on the head. It's because the word was used constantly in that society. I mean all over America, North and South, it was used. And he wanted to hit you with it so often that after a while you said, "That's unpleasant to hear that word over and over and over. Why is he hitting me on the head with this?" He's hitting you on the head to make you understand how awful this word is and what it represents. And he's doing it to people—not the liberal minded, everybody who knows what's good and bad today— he's doing it to a society that doesn't know what they're doing. He's smashing them in the head with it.

When Huck decides against turning Jim in as a runaway slave, even though it might cost him his soul, he says, "All right, then, I'll go to hell." We, as Americans, somehow inherited at that moment a true literature. Do you have a sense that American literature started in that moment?

Well, that's what Hemingway said, so you can certainly make an argument for it. But it was a sublime moment. It was a sublime moment in American literature, because it went straight to the heart, to the very heart and core of what's good and what's bad in this country. It was honest. It was not dishonest. And it was fine. And it expressed what is in us that makes us something special. That's why it's so sad to see that special thing in us trampled and dishonored today.

And yet, for more than a century now, Huckleberry Finn *has been banned on a regular basis.*

I like Toni Morrison's assessment of the banning of *Huckleberry Finn.* She called it "elitist censorship designed to appease adults rather than educate children." Somewhere, somebody got the idea that education was supposed to be painless. Where the idea started that education was not supposed to be painful, I don't know. But it's only through the pain of learning that you learn.

Besides Adventures of Huckleberry Finn, *what other books do you like?*

Oh, I love the stuff in *Letters from the Earth.* I love his irreverent stuff. And I love so much of *Life on the Mississippi.* I think *Pudd'nhead Wilson* is a far more important book than people have yet discovered it to be. It nails us to the wall. It nails our presumption that we're better than the black man because we're white. Because he takes these two babies that were born from the same father, the plantation owner. And the two babies, one from the plantation owner and his wife, who then dies, and the other from the plantation owner and the slave Roxy, and both are the same color. And then Roxy knows what's going to happen to her slave son, and so she switches the babies in the cradle. And her son, the "black" child, is brought up as a white, rich young man and turns into a real creep. Disgusting. And the "white" child, who is now brought up as a slave, turns into a humble, subservient human being.

Ouch again.

Ouch again. *Pudd'nhead Wilson* is a wonderful book. They never call for banning *Pudd'nhead Wilson,* even though the word *nigger* is used in it a great deal and it's about the whole subject of race. They never do, because it's in the third person. *Huckleberry Finn* is told by an ignorant young boy who uses the word *nigger,* and so does everybody else in the book, because that's the society he lived in. And so you have to use your mind and your imagination when you read *Huckleberry Finn* to translate what this boy is going through and turn it upside down. When he's acting out of his good impulses, he thinks he's doing the bad thing. When he's acting out of the wrong impulses, he thinks he's doing the right thing. So we have to understand that about the society that Mark Twain is criticizing.

He had a temper, didn't he?

He had a hell of a temper. And he was an agitated man. He says, "Some people were born calm. I was born excited." And he was. He was a man whose nerve fibers must have been burning all the time. I'm sure he wasn't, you know, the classic great dad, although he did play games with his children. And he obviously had a tremendous ego—he had to. I think probably the fun had to go the way he wanted it to go, you know?

Can you tell me about Susy's death, from his point of view?

This child seemed to have been the one with whom he connected most easily. She had a talent for writing, too. She seemed to have a lot of the sensitivity of her father and understood him better than her sisters did. And so I think he grew to adore this child and expect really wonderful things from her, and when she was taken away, it was something like a death blow to him.

In his later years, after all his family tragedies, did his work really change, or do you think all that satiric bite and darkness was there from the beginning?

This was a very sensitive man. Otherwise, he could never have done what he did or written what he did. These ideas were always present in his work, but they became sharper and more pointed and more dangerous as he got older. You know *The Mysterious Stranger?* It's supposed to be the work of his old age, when he became a cynic? He started writing *The Mysterious Stranger* long before he was an old man. It was something he was writing on here and there for years. And the interesting thing is that when he was a young man of twenty-one, when he was in Cincinnati in a rooming house, he met a Scotchman who lived on the top floor, a silent, reclusive kind of guy. His name was Macfarlane. And somehow the guy took an interest in him and they talked a lot late at night up there; they talked and talked. And the philosophy of this Scotchman was very like the philosophy of *The Mysterious Stranger.*

George Bernard Shaw referred to Twain as America's Voltaire. This is something most Americans wouldn't even think of, because we still have the old attitude that he was just a humorist, kind of charming and funny and cute. As he grew up, like most of us, he began looking around at the world more deeply and more critically; he didn't like what he saw. As I say, there were all these things going on a century ago that were just as powerfully disturbing as the things that are going on now, and he began commenting on them. And it unsettled the public—the reading public, which was used to treating him as a humorist. Even his books became darker.

Help me understand the man who wrote Letters from the Earth.

Well, he starts out with a wonderfully irreverent view—irreverence was one of his strong suits—of man's idea that the world was created for him and that he's God's pet. He's the Creator's absolute pet. He says, "Man is the deity's favorite. After the house fly."

And then it turns. It turns and becomes biting. Which is very often the way his humor turned, because he was seeking to get to the heart of the truth about life and people and show us what we're doing. He used religion. This is where people get thrown off. They think he's an atheist or he was anti-religious. Well, anyone who absorbs himself in Twain's work realizes the man had a respect for the concept of a Supreme Being, because he referred to it all the time. Not always in a derogatory way. He would say, in effect, "Now, you're a good Christian, aren't you? I mean, you go to church on Sunday?" And you'd say, "Yes, I do." "Right. That's after you lynched a Negro the night before. Is that correct?" "Yeah." He pulls the rug out from under us by using religion as the mirror in which we can look at ourselves.

Hal Holbrook

By the early twentieth century, when he became more and more famous as the world's funniest man, he also seems to have been more and more alone.

I think he must have been a very lonely man. He was a soul seeking the truth, to begin with, and that's a lonely journey.

His family was a powerful surrounding force in his life, but he also was this world figure who was being pulled this way and that way to speak, pulled out of the family circle, so he probably missed many opportunities. Wasn't a great father, probably. But the deaths of people, beginning with his brother Henry, the deaths affected him deeply.

He came to be fascinated with death, really—the other world. And it's interesting that he seemed to be sort of welcoming it in many ways. Death might be a more restful journey than the one he had undertaken trying to head off the Philistines of the world. As you look around when you get older, as he must have done, you realize you can't head them all off. They're out there in force, and they are unstoppable. And that would make him lonely.

But he refused to lie down and die. He refused to take it lying down. He just kept moving forward again, getting up, going at it again. He was a life force. He was a powerful life force, a forward-moving one. And he wasn't a quitter.

Why do you find him so moving?

I don't know. It's like somebody reaching his hand out to you in comradeship, almost. Somebody who really understands what it's all about, taking you in, making you a partner in what he feels. And it's a powerful friendship to have, you know?

What's his enduring legacy? What does he have to say that keeps us returning to him again and again after so many years?

Look at us. This is who we are. We're funny, we're sad, we're foolish, we're awfully stupid sometimes. We're very mean and cruel sometimes, but we're human. This is us. It's amazing that anyone can be so critical of people and things and yet not feel hurtful.

You know, sometimes when I have not felt like reading Twain—or years ago, when I felt really lousy about things—and I pick up a book of his and I start to read a page, I say to myself: "I'll just read a page and see if I can find something." By the time I get to the top of the next page, I'm starting to enjoy it, because I see all this stuff coming back at me that says, "Hey, don't worry about it. Everybody does it. We're all nuts. We're all a little foolish or a lot foolish. Isn't that funny? Aren't we funny animals?"

CHAPTER ELEVEN

TREATMENT FOR THE DAMNED

I have been reading the morning paper. I do it every morning—well knowing that I shall find in it the usual depravities & basenesses & hypocrisies & cruelties that make up civilization, & cause me to put in the rest of the day pleading for the damnation of the human race. I cannot seem to get my prayers answered. Yet I do not despair.
—Letter to William Dean Howells, 1896

(opposite) Sam Clemens, 1897: "He was a constant surprise in his varied moods," his daughter Clara, wrote, "which dropped unheralded upon him, creating day or night for those about him by his twinkling eyes or his clouded brows. How he would be affected by this or that no one could ever foresee."

(below) Frontispiece from *Following the Equator*, 1897

After Susy's funeral, Livy, Clara, and Jean sailed back to England to rejoin Sam. They rented a furnished house on a London backstreet and told almost no one their address. They were there on December 25. "*Xmas morning,*" Clemens wrote that evening. "The square & adjacent streets are not merely quiet, they are dead. There is not a sound. At intervals, a Sunday-looking person passes along. The family have been to breakfast. We three sat and talked as usual, but the name of the day was not mentioned. It was in our minds, but we said nothing."

For several years, the family would celebrate neither Christmas nor Thanksgiving nor birthdays. "It was a long time before anyone laughed in our household, after the shock of Susy's death," Clara recalled. "Father's passionate nature expressed itself in thunderous outbursts of bitterness shading into rugged grief. He walked the floor with quick steps and there was no drawl in his speech now. . . . It was [then] that Father created the habit of vituperating the human race."

"God," he wrote in an essay he called "In My Bitterness," "gives you a wife and children whom you adore, only that through the spectacle of the . . . miseries which He will inflict upon them He may tear the palpitating heart out of your breast and slap you in the face with it. . . . He can never hurt me anymore." And he began to experiment with a series of stories in which disaster and tragedy shattered families only to turn out to have been merely bad dreams.

Work was now Clemens's only solace. He finished *Following the Equator*, wondering once again at his own ability to be funny in the midst of grief. "I don't mean that I am miserable," he wrote Howells;

no—worse than that—indifferent. Indifferent to nearly everything but work. I like that; I enjoy it, & stick to it. I do it without purpose & ambition; merely for the love of it. Indeed, I am a mud-image; &

Survivors: Clara, Livy, and Sam Clemens at Dollis Hill House just outside London in the summer of 1900

it puzzles me to know what it is in me that writes & has comedy fancies & finds pleasure in phrasing them. It is the law of our nature, of course, or it wouldn't happen; the thing in me forgets the presence of the mud-image, goes its own way wholly unconscious of it & apparently of no kinship with it.

Livy, as always, read every word Sam wrote and made meticulous notes on his manuscript, to each of which he carefully responded:

Page 1002. I don't like the "shady-principled cat that has a family in every port."
     Then I'll modify it just a little.
Page 1020. 9th line from the top. I think some other word would be better than "stench." You have used that pretty often.
     But can't I get it in *anywhere?* You've knocked it out every time.
     Out it goes again. And yet "stench" is a noble, good word.
Page 1038. I hate to have your father pictured as lashing a slave boy.
     It's out, and my father is whitewashed.
Page 1050. 2d line from the bottom. Change breech-clout. It's a word that you love and I abominate. I would take that and "offal" out of the language.
     You are steadily weakening the English tongue, Livy.

The family remained in seclusion throughout that winter, seeing only a handful of close friends. The newspapers were so accustomed to hearing from and about Mark Twain that when a rumor began to spread that he was dying, a young reporter was sent to track him down to see if it was true. When the great man himself came to the door, he recalled, the embarrassed caller showed him a telegram from his editor: "If Mark Twain very ill, five hundred words. If dead, send one thousand."

"You don't need as much as that," Clemens told him. "Just say the report of my death has been greatly exaggerated." Reported around the world, it became one of his best-remembered lines.

The family would stay abroad for nearly four more years, wandering from one city to another, living in hotels and rented homes. On August 18, 1897, the first anniversary of Susy's death, they were staying on Lake Lucerne in Switzerland. "One year today since the great disaster fell," Clemens wrote that evening. "Livy went away to be alone. She took the steamer and spent the day solitary in an inn in an unknown town up the lake. . . . I spent the day alone under the trees on the mountain-side, *writing*."

Twain hurled himself into a host of projects simultaneously, turning out thousands of pages of manuscript—most of which he never finished

WHAT TWAIN *DIDN'T* SAY

Mark Twain is probably the most quoted American of all time. It seems as if he had something memorable to say on virtually every topic. But over the years, he has also become routinely cited as the source of many remarks that in reality were someone else's. He would not have been surprised. "It is my belief that nearly any invented quotation," he once wrote, "played with confidence, stands a good chance to deceive." The following are a few well-known "Twainisms," compiled by Jim Zwick, that have not been documented as actually being Twain's words. Perhaps because they are so good, people have assumed only Mark Twain could have coined them.

- Golf is a good walk spoiled.

- The coldest winter I ever spent was a summer in San Francisco.

- If you don't like the weather, wait a minute.

- A gold miner is a liar standing next to a hole in the ground.

- When I feel the urge to exercise, I go lie down until it passes away.

- I don't exaggerate—I just remember big.

- Better to keep your mouth shut and appear stupid than to open it and remove all doubt.

- The man who does not read good books has no advantage over the man who can't read them.

- When I was a boy of fourteen, my father was so ignorant I could hardly stand to have the old man around. But when I got to be twenty-one, I was astonished at how much the old man had learned in seven years.

and much of which he did not intend to have published during his lifetime. He filled a notebook with gossipy, acid-etched portraits of 168 citizens of the Hannibal of his boyhood, started and abandoned new books about Tom Sawyer and Huckleberry Finn, began a story called "Which Was the Dream?" in which a prominent man and his family suffer a series of disasters that may or may not be part of a hideous dream from which the protagonist would one day awaken.

It was almost as if the fact of the writing had come to matter more than its meaning. "I couldn't get along without work now," he wrote Howells from Vienna the following January. "I bury myself in it up to the ears. Long hours—8 and 9 at a stretch, sometimes. All the days. . . . It isn't all for print . . . for much of it fails to suit me; 50,000 words of it in the past year. It was because of the deadness which invaded me when Susy died."

The family settled in Vienna that winter so that Clara could study music with a celebrated teacher, Theodor Leschitzky. She had spent all of her life in the shadow of the sister who had been her parents' obvious favorite; had struggled, as Susy had, to win at least a little independence from them. Susy had hoped to become a professional singer; now Clara

It Is a She

Of all of Twain's later writings dealing with biblical themes, perhaps the most enduring are the collection of works built around the story of Adam and Eve. They include Extracts from Adam's Diary, Eve's Diary, Papers of the Adams Family, Eve Speaks, and Adam's Soliloquy.

Taken together, they range from comic spoofs on the first three chapters of Genesis to blistering satires on basic Christian beliefs. But, as these excerpts from the diaries of Adam and Eve show, Twain also used them to explore the relationship between a man and a woman.

ADAM: Monday. The new creature says its name is Eve. That is all right, I have no objections. . . . It says it is not an It, it is a She. This is probably doubtful; yet it is all one to me; what she is were nothing to me if she would but go by herself and not talk.

EVE: Wednesday. We are getting along very well indeed, now, and getting better and better acquainted. . . . I have taken all the work of naming things off his hands, and this has been a great relief to him, for he has no gift in that line. . . . He can't think of a rational name to save him, but I do not let him see that I am aware of his defect. Whenever a new creature comes along, I name it before he has time to expose himself by an awkward silence. In this way I have saved him many embarrassments. . . . When the dodo came along he thought it was a wildcat—I saw it in his eye. But I saved him. And I was careful not to do it in a way that could hurt his pride. I just spoke up in a quite natural way of pleased surprise, and not as if I was dreaming of conveying information, and said, "Well, I do declare if there isn't the dodo!"

ADAM: Friday. She has taken to beseeching me to stop going over the Falls. . . . I have always done it—always like the plunge, the excitement, and the coolness. I supposed it was what the Falls were for. They have no other use that I can see, and they must have been made for something. She says they were only made for scenery—like the rhinoceros and the mastodon.

EVE: Monday. He talks very little. Perhaps it is because he is not bright, and is sensitive about it and wishes to conceal it. It is such a pity that he should feel so, for brightness is nothing; it is in the heart that the values lie.

ADAM: Wednesday. I found this place, outside the Park, and was fairly comfortable for a few days, but she found me out. . . . In fact, I was not sorry she came, for there are but meagre pickings here, and she brought some of those apples. I was obliged to eat them, I was so hungry. It was against my principles, but I find that principles have no real force except when one is well fed. . . . She says it is ordered that we work for our living hereafter. She will be useful. I will superintend.

EVE: After the Fall. When I look back, the Garden is a dream to me. . . . The Garden is lost, but I have found *him* and am content. . . . If I ask myself why I love him, I find I do not know, and do not really much care to know; so I suppose that this kind of love is not a product of reasoning and statistics, like one's love for other reptiles and animals.

ADAM: Next Year. We have named it Cain. She caught it while I was up country trapping. . . . It resembles us in some ways, and may be a relation. . . . The difference in size warrants the conclusion that it is a different and new kind of animal—a fish, perhaps, though when I put it in the water to see, it sank, and she plunged in and snatched it out before there was opportunity for the experiment to determine the matter. I still think it is a fish, but she is indifferent about what it is, and will not let me have it to try.

Ten Years Later. They are boys; we found it out long ago. It was their coming in that small, immature shape that puzzled us; we were not used to it. There are some girls now. Abel is a good boy, but if Cain had stayed a bear it would have improved him. After all these years, I see that I was mistaken about Eve in the beginning; it is better to live outside the Garden with her than inside it without her.

"Eve Reclining by Water's Edge," an illustration by Lester Ralph from the first edition of *Eve's Diary*, 1905

also hoped that a career in music—as a pianist at first and, after 1899, as a contralto—would provide her with a way to establish herself as a person in her own right, as someone more than merely "Mark Twain's daughter." Neither of her parents entirely approved. "We are very sorry indeed that she wants this public life," Livy would write a friend, and Clemens once compared Clara's decision to pursue a concert career—"performing for strangers"—as a "loss" nearly comparable to her sister's death. But they were willing to indulge her, at least for the time being. "Clara has to stay here for a year to study music," her father wrote to Henry Rogers, "and the rest of us must stay, too, for Mrs. Clemens will not hear of the family ever being divided again."

In Vienna, Clemens began to enjoy himself once more. Thanks to Rogers's shrewd investment counsel and royalties from *Following the Equator,* he had at last eliminated all his debts, news that made headlines all around the world. "It is a great thing to possess genius," said the *Boston Weekly Transcript;* "It is a greater thing to be a man of unsullied honor." ("Honest men," Clemens wrote a friend after reading a sheaf of similar tributes, "must be pretty scarce when they make so much fuss over even a defective specimen.") But, he told another friend, he had "abundant peace of mind again, no sense of burden. Work is become a pleasure—it is not labor any longer."

He began a burlesque of Mary Baker Eddy, the founder of Christian Science. "When we contemplate her and what she has achieved," he wrote, "it is blasphemy to longer deny to the Supreme Being the possession of a sense of humor." He wrote one of his finest stories, "The Man That Corrupted Hadleyburg," a novella in which the self-righteous citizens of a small town are turned into greedy hypocrites by an imaginative swindler. Angered by the Dreyfus case and disgusted by the anti-Semitism that permeated Viennese society, he wrote an essay in defense of Jews, in which he declared that he personally harbored "no race prejudices . . . nor caste prejudices nor creed prejudices. . . . I can stand any society. All

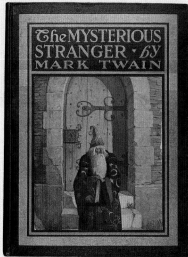

The Graben, a fashionable boulevard in the heart of old Vienna where the Clemens family lived for nearly two years. The sixty-nine-foot column in the background was set up in 1693 as a memorial to Viennese victims of the plague. While in the Austrian capital, Twain worked away at several of the stories that were posthumously published in 1916 as *The Mysterious Stranger*. The unfinished manuscript would secretly be completed by Twain's biographer Albert Bigelow Paine and his editor Frederick A. Duneka, who even added characters of their own—including the bearded astrologer handsomely rendered on the book's cover by N. C. Wyeth.

that I care to know is that a man is a human being, that is enough for me; he can't be any worse." He started "The Chronicle of Young Satan," one of several unfinished stories that his first biographer would later publish together as *The Mysterious Stranger;* they were meant, he told Howells, to "tell what I think of man, & how he is constructed, & what a shabby poor ridiculous thing he is, & how mistaken he is in his estimate of his character & powers & qualities & his place among the animals." And he began a curious little book called *What Is Man?*—a Socratic dialogue between an idealistic youth and a worldly old man who sets forth what Twain called his "gospel": his hard-won belief that man is "merely a

Sam Clemens sits for the Viennese sculptor Theresa Fedorowna Ries, 1897. His years of exile in Europe, Twain wrote, had made him "a self-appointed Ambassador-at-Large of the U.S. of America—without salary."

machine" driven by "his heredities, his habitat, his associations," and therefore incapable of independent thought or action. Livy so disliked the result that she refused to listen to him read the second half of it aloud and made him pledge not to try to have it published during her lifetime.

Clemens and Livy and their daughters were the most eagerly sought-after visitors in the city, so well known that when they found themselves cut off from their hotel by a police barrier during the public celebration of the emperor's birthday, a mounted officer ordered his men, "For God's sake let them pass. Don't you see it's Herr Mark Twain?" ("My," Sam told Clara as a big crowd watched them cross the empty street, "but that makes me feel damned good.") Artists asked to paint their portraits. They were frequent guests at court and entertained nearly every afternoon in their elegant nine-room suite at the Hotel Metropole. "Such funny combinations are here sometimes," Livy wrote: "one duke, several counts, several writers, several barons, two princes . . ."

Newspapermen called at all hours, and when one turned up while Clemens was writing in the place he liked best—bed—the writer told the butler to show him in anyway.

"Youth," Livy asked him, "don't you think it will be a little embarrassing for him, your being in bed?"

"Why, Livy, if you think so, we might have the other bed made up for him."

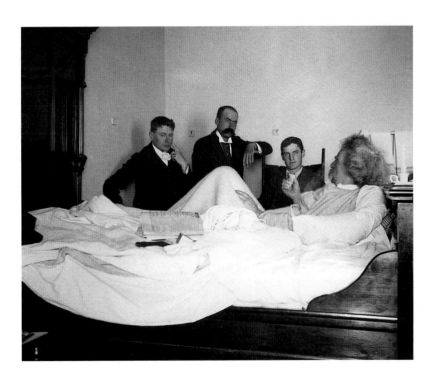

Clemens enjoyed granting audiences to the press from his bed. This photograph was made by Colonel J. B. Pond at the beginning of the 1895 round-the-world tour, but the scene was repeated frequently on both sides of the Atlantic. "I have never taken any exercise," Clemens once explained, "except sleeping and resting, and I never intend to take any. Exercise is loathsome. And it cannot be any benefit when you are tired; and I was always tired."

Sam Clemens at Dollis Hill House, 1900. "I should like to call back Will Bowen," he wrote from here to the widow of his boyhood friend, "& John Garth & the others & live the life, & be as we were, & make holiday until 15, and then all drown together."

Sam and Livy Clemens on the lawn at Dollis Hill

After two winters in Austria, the family moved on. Clemens was weary of what he would call his "everlasting exile," and was wealthy enough that he had begun again to invest large sums in vaporous business schemes—including a carpet-weaving machine that he thought would revolutionize the industry precisely as he'd been certain the Paige type-setter would transform the printing business; and a food supplement called Plasmon, made from skim milk, which he had convinced himself would end famine forever, everywhere in the world.

But he still did not go home to America. The ambitions of his oldest surviving daughter had kept the family in Vienna. Now it would be his youngest daughter who kept them overseas. Jean was lovely but delicate. She had suffered a blow to the head as a child that, her father remembered, had left her with "capricious changes of disposition which we could not account for," and it may have caused the epileptic seizures that began after Susy's death and from which she would never be entirely free. By 1899 she was suffering two grand mal seizures a day. Her parents kept her condition from all but a handful of friends—epilepsy was then considered shameful. But, desperate to find a cure, the family traveled first to London, where Clemens had heard of a Swedish doctor named Henrik Kellgren, who claimed success in treating people who suffered seizures; then to Kellgren's spa at Sanna, Sweden, for the summer. There they all eventually underwent what was called the Swedish Movement Cure. Clemens enjoyed the daily massage ("it is vigorous exercise," he told Howells, *"and other people do it for you"*), admired the prolonged Swedish sunsets, and liked watching his daughter whirl and spin in Swedish folk dances. Otherwise, as a letter to Clara—who joined the family late in the season—makes clear, he hated it:

Hell, July/99
This is the daily itinerary:
8 to 10 a.m. Inferior London coffee for the damned.
10 to 12 a.m. "Treatment" for the damned.
12 to 2. Pant and gasp and fight the flies.
2 Dinner for the damned.
3 till 8 p.m. Pant and gasp and fight the flies.
8 Supper and flies for the damned.
9 till 11 Flies, fans and profanity.
11 p.m. Bed. Tallow candles. Flies. No night—dim, pale-blue daylight all night. . . . Cool, and might be pleasant, but the flies stand watch and persecute the damned all night. . . . Rooms the size of a tiger's cage. Not a bath-room in the whole settlement. A great lake but not near by. Open fields all around the damned—no woods. Row-boats on the simmering puddle—none on the lake. Make your peace with Satan and come along. Leave your clothes behind. Fly-paper is all you need.

> *Exhausted.*
> *With a power of love,*
> *Father*

When Dr. Kellgren returned to London for the winter of 1899–1900, the Clemenses followed him, settling first into an apartment not far from Sam's British publishers, and then moving to a handsome brick country home called Dollis Hill, just outside the city, where they spent a tranquil summer. "Jean has a hammock swung between two . . . great trees," Livy wrote, "& on the other side of a little pond . . . *full* of white & yellow pond-lilies, there is tall grass & trees & Clara & Jean go there in the afternoons, spread down a rug on the grass in the shade & read & sleep." Dollis Hill was "nearer to being a paradise than any other home I ever occupied," Clemens wrote as autumn approached, but when Dr. Kellgren assured him that there were now trained osteopaths in New York equipped to help Jean, he rejoiced. He was sixty-four years old and could go home at last. "If I ever get ashore [in New York]," he told a reporter, "I am going to break both my legs so I can't get away again."

Jean Clemens, 1901

CHAPTER TWELVE

I WILL HAVE MY SAY

*I have always preached . . . if the humor came of its accord and
uninvited I have allowed it a place in my sermon, but I was
not writing the sermon for the sake of the humor. I should have
written the sermon just the same whether any humor applied for
admission or not.*

— Mark Twain, autobiographical dictation from 1906

**Samuel Clemens, 1903. "Yes you are
right," he wrote to a friend. "I am a moral-
ist in disguise; it gets me into heaps of
trouble when I go thrashing around in
political questions."**

**In 1905, Mark Twain agreed to serve
as vice president of the Congo Reform
Association, which published this pam-
phlet to protest Belgian brutality toward
her African subjects.**

After nine long years abroad, Mark Twain landed in New York on October
15, 1900, to a tumultuous welcome. The whole country had sympathized
with his sorrow at Susy's death, and everyone now admired him for having
worked himself out of debt. "Our friend entered the fiery furnace a man,"
Andrew Carnegie said, "and emerged a hero." "The average American
loves his family," said Thomas Alva Edison. "If he has any love left over
for some other person, he generally selects Mark Twain." Reporters from
all the country's leading newspapers crowded the gangplank. "There was
the familiar bushy hair," said a front-page story in the *New York World*,
"the twinkling, semi-mysterious eyes, the peculiar drawling voice, half
Yankee, half Southern, the very low turn-down collar of the West and the
immaculate shiny silk hat and long frock coat of the effete East. He
looked as young as he did twenty years ago, and younger than he did
when he shook American dust off his feet in 1891."

The family moved into a furnished house at 14 West Tenth Street, just
off Fifth Avenue; they could not bear the thought of going back to the
Hartford house where Susy had died. ("Do you think we can live through
the first going into the house in Hartford?" Livy had asked her sister from
England. "I feel if we had gotten through the first three months all might
be well, but consider the first night.") A steady stream of reporters came
knocking at the door, seeking Twain's opinions on every imaginable topic.
"It always puzzled me how Mark Twain could manage to have an opinion
on every incident, accident, invention or disease in the world," Clara
remembered. "Every day was like some great festive occasion. One felt
that a large party was going on and that by and by the guests would be
leaving. But there was no leaving. More and more came."

They continued to come, and for the first time in his life, Twain began speaking out directly on political issues, including the most divisive
issue of the day: whether or not the United States should follow the
example of the Great Powers of Europe and establish its own empire.

"I am an anti-imperialist," he told the press. "I am opposed to having the eagle put its talons on any other land." On New Year's Eve he published in the *New York Herald* a brief, bitter GREETING FROM THE NINETEENTH TO THE TWENTIETH CENTURY:

> *I bring you the stately matron named Christendom, returning, bedraggled, besmirched and dishonored from pirate raids in Kiao-Chou, Manchuria, South Africa and the Philippines, with her soul full of meanness, her pocket full of boodle, and her mouth full of pious hypocrisies. Give her soap and a towel, but hide the looking-glass.*

That was only the beginning. Twain had always seen himself as more than a "humorist." But his more serious messages—his effort to portray black Americans as human beings, for example—had until now largely been disguised as fiction. Now the wraps were off. Over the next few years he would publish "To the Person Sitting in Darkness," an assault on what he called "the Blessings-of-Civilization-Trust": American missionaries whose presence in China had helped to bring on the Boxer Rebellion. He attacked Britain for waging war on the Boers in South Africa, and the United States for turning a war to free the Philippines from Spain into the brutal conquest of the Filipinos. When his friend Joe Twichell urged him to tone down his rhetoric, he answered with unusual asperity. As a clergyman, Twichell should be ashamed of himself, Clemens wrote: "This nation is like all the others that have been spewed upon the earth—ready to shout for any cause that will tickle its vanity or fill its pocket. What a hell of a heaven it will be, when they get all these hypocrites assembled there!" He went on to express support for votes for women, for Booker T. Washington's efforts to uplift his race, for the first Russian Revolution. He spoke on behalf of an anti-Tammany candidate for mayor of New York—and when his man won, cheerfully claimed all the credit—and he so violently denounced King Leopold of Belgium for his savagery in the Congo that his own publisher refused to print his comments.

Friends continued to warn him that the public would be offended by his anti-imperialist fervor. He didn't seem to mind. "I'm not expecting anything but kicks and scoffing and . . . a diminution of my bread and butter," he told a friend, "but if Livy will let me, I will have my say." In fact, nothing Twain said seemed to dim his popularity. During his first winter in New York, he was given testimonial dinners by the most exclusive men's clubs in the city and ate and drank and spoke at so many formal banquets that he made himself ill. "What a fame and a force he is!" William Dean Howells wrote to a mutual friend. "It's

King Leopold's Soliloquy by "Mark Twain"

PRICE, TWENTY FIVE CENTS

THIS Congo parable proves his humor a power for righteousness, - - an international force." Boston Transcript.

"A startling piece of scathing denunciation." Evangelical Messenger.

"To read the Soliloquy makes one ask why the nations permit this king to maintain this hell." Syracuse Herald.

"King Leopold's Soliloquy," Mark Twain's indictment of the Belgian king, published in 1905 by the Congo Reform Association when Twain's own publisher turned it down

astonishing how he holds out, but I hate to have him eating so many dinners, and writing so few books."

Livy continued to let her husband have his say. "He receives more letters of approval than of disapproval," she told a friend, "ten to one I should think." But according to Clara, "It was pathetic to see the effect [the hostile mail] had on Mother." The controversy—and the frenetic pace of her husband's life—took its toll, and her health again began to fail. To ease her burdens, Clemens moved his family half an hour north to a big riverside house in the quiet Bronx neighborhood of Riverdale.

But life there was hectic, too: in a single week, the Clemenses had guests at seventeen out of twenty-one meals. Nor was the head of the household's unpredictable temperament always held in check. After

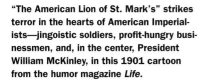

"The American Lion of St. Mark's" strikes terror in the hearts of American Imperialists—jingoistic soldiers, profit-hungry businessmen, and, in the center, President William McKinley, in this 1901 cartoon from the humor magazine *Life.*

The War Prayer

In 1905, Twain wrote a piece called "The War Prayer," an attack on enthusiasm for war so scathing that it would not be published until after his death. In it, young troops about to march off to battle gather in a church, where the minister prays for their victory.

But then a stranger enters, wearing a white robe, and tells the congregation he has been sent from God to say He has heard their prayer and is willing to grant it—but only after the messenger explains what it really means.

God has actually received two prayers from the group, the stranger says: the one that the preacher spoke, but also a second, silent one that was in their hearts when they asked for victory. Then the messenger puts the unspoken prayer into words:

"O Lord our Father, our young patriots, idols of our hearts, go forth to battle—be Thou near them! With them—in spirit—we also go forth from the sweet peace of our beloved firesides to smite the foe.

"O Lord our God, help us to tear their soldiers to bloody shreds with our shells; help us to cover their smiling fields with the pale forms of their patriot dead; help us to drown the thunder of their guns with the wounded, writhing in pain; help us to lay waste their humble homes with a hurricane of fire; help us to wring the hearts of their unoffending widows with unavailing grief; help us to turn them out roofless with their little children to wander unfriended through wastes of their desolated land in rags & hunger & thirst, sport of the sun-flames of summer & the icy winds of winter, broken in spirit, worn with travail, imploring Thee for the refuge of the grave & denied it—for our sakes, who adore Thee, Lord, blast their hopes, blight their lives, protract their bitter pilgrimage, make heavy their steps, water their way with their tears, stain the white snow with the blood of their wounded feet! We ask of one who is the Spirit of love & who is the ever-faithful refuge & friend of all that are sore beset, & seek His aid with humble & contrite hearts. Grant our prayer, O Lord, & Thine shall be the praise & honor & glory now & ever, Amen."

(After a pause.) "Ye have prayed it; if ye still desire it, speak!—the messenger of the Most High waits."

Mark Twain (seated directly behind the speaker) lends his support to Booker T. Washington at the twenty-fifth anniversary of the Tuskegee Institute at New York's Carnegie Hall, January 22, 1906

writing a scathing letter to a young woman poet, he received a rare reprimand from his wife:

I am absolutely wretched today on account of your state of mind—your state of intellect—why don't you let the better side of you work? . . . Where is the mind that wrote the Prince & the P., Jeanne d'Arc, the Yankee, &c. &c. &c. Bring it back! You can if you will—if you wish to. Think of the side that I know: the sweet, dear, tender side—that I love so. . . . Does it help the world to always rail at it? There is great and noble Work, being done. Why not sometimes recognize that? You always dwell on the evil until those who live beside you are crushed to the earth and you seem almost like a monomaniac. Oh I love you so and wish you would listen and take heed.

The Clemens family vacationing at Saranac Lake in the summer of 1901. While staying there, Twain began writing an all-out book-length assault on racial violence to be called "The United States of Lyncherdom," then sheepishly abandoned it for fear of losing loyal readers in the South. He was a lightning bug, not an industrious bee, he once explained. "I scatter from one interest to another, lingering nowhere."

There were other tensions in Riverdale as well. "One day, Mrs. Clemens and I were mourning for our lost little ones," Clemens wrote of the family's time there.

Not that they were dead, but lost to us all the same. Gone out of our lives forever—as little children. *They were still with us, but they were become women, and they walked with us upon our own level. There was a wide gulf, a gulf as wide as the horizons, between these children and those. We were always having vague dream-glimpses of them as they used to be in the long-vanished years—glimpses of them playing and romping, with short frocks on and spindle legs, and hair-tails down their backs—and always they were far and dim, and we could not hear their shouts and their laughter. How we longed to gather them to our arms! But they were only dainty and darling specters, and they faded away and vanished, and left us desolate.*

The Clemenses' surviving daughters were indeed women now, women with minds—and difficulties—of their own. Jean continued to suffer frightening seizures for which there seemed to be neither cause nor cure. Clara remained determined to pursue a career in music. When she made her debut in Washington, D.C., in 1901, her father did not bother to attend; and when her parents objected to her plans to pursue further studies in Paris, out from under their protective care and in dangerous proximity to a young pianist named Ossip Gabrilowitsch, with whom she had fallen in love, she defied them and sailed for Europe anyway.

It all evidently became too much for Livy. The family was vacationing at York Harbor, Maine, in August of 1902 when she was struck by heart

The house at York Harbor, Maine, where Livy fell ill in the summer of 1902

Wave Hill, the Bronx home of the Clemens family home from October 1901 through July 1903

palpitations and asthma attacks that left her gasping for air, unable even to lie down for fear of suffocating. "She believed she was dying," Sam reported to Henry Rogers. "I also believed it." Her doctors insisted that neither her mercurial husband nor her seizure-haunted younger daughter be allowed into her sickroom for fear of adding to her anxiety and further damaging her heart. Nurses were summoned, but it fell to Clara, twenty-eight now and back from Paris, to set aside her plans for a concert career and oversee the household, act as "assistant nurse," and try to keep her volatile father calm. "I wouldn't go in to see your mother, even if the doctor permitted it," Clemens assured her, "for I would surely give out some startling yarn that would make the hair of a wolf stand on end." Livy laughed to learn that Sam had pinned notes to the trees outside her window, warning the birds not to sing for fear of disturbing her rest. But he felt his banishment keenly. Livy was his sounding board as well as his wife, his editor, and his main source of psychological support; without her he was bereft. He tried writing a new novel in which Tom Sawyer and Huck Finn, now grown old, returned to their boyhood home. "Life has been a failure," he wrote in his notebook; "all that was lovable, all that was beautiful is under the mould. They die together." He wrote some thirty-eight thousand words but could not seem to make the story work and eventually destroyed the manuscript.

In October, Livy was taken by special train to Riverdale, where the butler carried her upstairs to her room. She would remain there for eight months. There was a new diagnosis now: "nervous prostration." "Our dear prisoner is where she is through overwork," Clemens wrote, "day and night devotion to the children & me. We did not know how to value it. We do now." It was a bitter, difficult winter. Jean suffered repeated seizures, then developed pneumonia, facts that had to be kept from Livy. A secretary, thirty-seven-year-old Isabel Lyon, was hired to help out, handling Livy's correspondence, but Clara remained in charge.

Sam was forbidden to see his wife for more than two minutes in the evening. "With a word," he told Joe Twichell, "I could freeze the blood in her veins!" But he was still allowed to communicate with her in writing. "Two or three times a day," Clara recalled, "Mother's face would light up eagerly when the nurse approached the bed with a little slip of paper in her hand. These greetings to Mother from her husband were rainbows during the storm, and the colors were never the same."

Isabel Lyon, 1908

Good morning, sweetheart, it is bright and beautiful and I love you most deeply. This dining-room is a paradise with the flooding sunshine, the fire of big logs, the white expanse of cushioned snow and the incomparable river. I wish you were down here sweetheart.

Y[outh].

Youth my own precious Darling,
I feel so frightfully banished. Couldn't you write in my boudoir? Then I could hear you clear your throat and it would be such joy to feel you near. I miss you sadly, sadly. Your note in the morning gave me support for the day, the one at night, peace for the night. With the deepest love of my heart,

Livy

Good morning, dear heart & thank you for your dear greeting. I think of you all the time, & it was for you that I was awake till after midnight arranging for this snow-storm & trying to get it at fair & honest rates—which I couldn't, but if you will take a handful of the snow & examine it you will realize that you have never seen any that could approach this for fineness of quality, & peculiar delicacy of make & finish, and unqualified whiteness, except in the Emperor's back-yard in Vienna.

I love you most dearly and continuously & constantly, Livy dearest.

Y.

In January, the Clemenses sold their Hartford house. It had become clear now that they would never resume life there again. Livy slowly improved and by summer was well enough to travel with the family to Quarry Farm, where, Clemens wrote happily, she was "mostly very gay, not very often depressed . . . & in the matter of superintending every-

AN EXPERT IN CATS

"Papa is very fond of animals, particularly of cats," young Susy Clemens wrote in her secret biography of her father. "The difference between papa and mama," she added, "is that mama loves morals and papa loves cats."

It was a fondness Clemens inherited from his mother and which would last him a lifetime. From boyhood to old age, he loved having them around—especially kittens, whose curiosity and playfulness were a constant source of joy to him. "Next to a wife whom I idolize," he wrote to Livy early in their marriage, "give me a cat—an *old* cat, with kittens." As their family grew, Clemens made sure his young daughters were surrounded by cats in Hartford and at his sister-in-law's summer home at Quarry Farm. He seemed to revel in giving them all names: Stray Kit, Abner, Frauelein, Lazy, Sour Mash, Cleveland, Buffalo Bill, a black mother cat named Satan, and her black kitten Sin.

As his girls grew older—and more distant from their father—Clemens's interest in kittens seemed to intensify. In 1906, during a summer in Dublin, New Hampshire, he actually rented three kittens from a farmer's wife to keep him company, promising to return them when he went back to New York. He called the gray one Ashes; the other two were black and so much alike that he named them *both* Sackcloth, since "when you call one, the other is likely to answer, because they cannot tell each other apart." He spent afternoons on the porch watching them chase grasshoppers and but-

Sam Clemens plays with his cat Tammany and her kittens at Redding, Connecticut, in 1908. When she died, he called her "the most beautiful of her race, admired, beloved & now lamented by all who knew her."

terflies—and eventually working them into his autobiography:

> I believe I have never seen such intelligent cats as these before. They are full of the nicest discriminations. When I read German aloud they weep. . . . It shows what pathos there is in the German tongue.
>
> French is not a familiar tongue to me, and the pronunciation is difficult, and comes out of me encumbered with a Missouri accent; but the cats like it, and when I make impassioned speeches in that language they sit in a row and put up their paws, palm to palm, and frantically give thanks.
>
> Hardly any cats are affected by music, but these are; when I sing they go reverently away, showing how deeply they feel it.

Later, at his grand but isolated home in Redding, Connecticut, he made sure that families of cats and kittens were always on hand. His favorite was a gray mother cat named Tammany that had several lively offspring. "One of them," he wrote in a letter to an admirer, "likes to be crammed into a corner-pocket of the billiard table—which he fits snugly as does a finger in a glove, and then he watches the game (and obstructs it) by the hour, and spoils many a shot by putting out his paw and changing the direction of a passing ball."

By the end of his life, Mark Twain could write, "I am an expert in cats," and not be accused of his usual hyperbole. Perhaps he saw something of himself in their spirit: "Of all God's creatures there is only one that cannot be made the slave of the lash. That one is the cat. If man could be crossed with the cat it would improve the man, but it would deteriorate the cat."

Sam Clemens on the steps to his hilltop
study during what turned out to be
his final visit to Quarry Farm in 1903

Sam and Livy at Quarry Farm, 1903. "I must confess to a great feeling of pathos and sadness," Livy wrote Clara during their visit. "Everything here is so full of the past—the cherry tree, the air, the odors, the sounds of summer, everything is so suggestive of a time long ago, that one feels overwhelmed with a cloud of sorrows."

thing & everybody, has resumed business at the old stand." Her doctors urged that she spend the winter in Florence, where the warm climate and calm atmosphere would help her to fully regain her health, just as they had eleven years before.

Things did not work out that way. The weather in Florence turned cold and dank. Clemens did not like the villa they had rented sight unseen. It was "a monster accumulation of bricks . . . built for fuss & show & irruptions of fashion, not for a home," he wrote Howells; there were some sixty rooms, "yet if you were to come I could not find you a comfortable & satisfactory place." The landlady, the capricious American-born widow of an Italian count, seemed bent on making her tenants' lives still more difficult: she sometimes refused to open the gates to Livy's doctors, cut off water to the villa for a time, even allowed a vicious donkey to roam the gardens, so frightening Isabel Lyon that she took to her bed.

Livy's condition soon worsened again. She accidentally burned herself with carbolic acid not long after she arrived, then developed tonsil-
itis, suffered more "breathless spells," sometimes seemed unable to
think clearly. Clemens, too, was bedridden for a time with bronchitis
and afterward could not seem to shake his cough. At Livy's urging, he
tried to lose himself in work, dictating fragments of autobiography to
Isabel Lyon for an hour or so each morning. By returning in his mind to
his boyhood on the Mississippi, he seemed to be trying to blot out what
was happening to the person who mattered most to him.

> *I can call back the solemn twilight and mystery of the deep woods,*
> *the earthy smells, the faint odors of the wild flowers, the sheen*
> *of rain-washed foliage, the rattling clatter of drops when the wind*
> *shook the trees, the far-off hammering of wood-peckers and the*
> *muffled drumming of wood-pheasants in the remoteness of the*
> *forest, the snap-shot glimpses of disturbed wild creatures scurrying*
> *through the grass, —I can call it all back and make it as real as*
> *it ever was. I can call back the prairie, and its loneliness and peace,*
> *and a vast hawk hanging motionless in the sky with his wings*
> *spread wide and the blue of the vault showing through the fringes*
> *of their end-feathers. I can see the woods in their autumn dress, the*
> *oaks purple, the hickories washed with gold, the maples and the*

The Villa di Quarto at Florence (opposite page) and Clara Clemens momentarily at rest in its garden, 1904

sumacs, luminous with crimson fires, and I can hear the rustle made by the fallen leaves as we ploughed through them.

"You will never know how much enjoyment you have lost until you get to dictating your autobiography," he assured Howells that winter. "You will be astonished (& charmed) to see how like *talk* it is, & how real it sounds . . . & what a dewy & breezy & woodsy freshness it has & what a darling & worshipful absence of the signs of starch & flat iron & labor & fuss & the other artificialities. Mrs. Clemens is an exacting critic, but I have not talked a sentence yet that she has wanted altered."

Livy had good days and bad—once Clemens reported happily that she was "editing the hellfire out of 2 new stories"—but she remained confined to her room. Her husband and youngest daughter were again barred from her bedside for more than a few minutes a day. On February 2, 1904, the Clemenses' wedding anniversary, Sam sent in a note:

It's a long time ago, my darling, but the 33 years have been richly profitable to us, through love— a love which has grown, not diminished, and is worth more each year than it was the year before. And so it will be always, dearest old Sweetheart of my youth.

Goodnight, and sleep well.

A few days later, the pressure of life in the Villa Quarto overwhelmed Clara Clemens. Still responsible for her mother's care and expected to smooth the way for her excitable father while trying to find the time to prepare for a series of spring recitals, she "reached the very lowest stage a human being can drop," she later confessed to a friend. "I don't know why I was so suddenly seized but at any rate I was seized by something & began to scream & curse & knocked down the furniture . . . till everyone of course came running & in my father's presence I said I hated him hated my mother hoped they would all die & if they didn't . . . soon I would kill them."

From her bedroom, Livy heard Clara shrieking. Someone, perhaps Katy Leary, tried to calm her by saying that Clara was simply "overwrought," but Livy suffered another heart attack. Clara was certain she had caused her mother's collapse; like her father, she saw herself always at the center of things.

Tensions within the villa remained high. On April 8, Clemens attended Clara's recital and pronounced it "a triumph." That night, Livy was stricken again. This time, according to Clemens, "her pulse rose to 192 & there was a collapse. Great alarm. Subcutaneous injection of brandy brought her back to life." A week later a visitor noticed that Clemens's right eye was inflamed and his right cheek twitched spasmodically. When he and Clara ventured out together to a café one afternoon and he saw several men gazing at his daughter—who happened to be wearing a hat decorated with artificial fruits and flowers—he hustled her home, seized the hat, and furiously snipped off all the decorations. She was then nearly thirty years old; he insisted she continue to be chaperoned wherever she went.

Then the weather at last began to change and Livy's health seemed to improve with it. "After 20 months of bedridden solitude & bodily misery," Clemens wrote to friends back home in mid-May, "she all of a sudden ceases to be a pallid, shrunken shadow, & looks bright & young & pretty."

On June 5, Livy appeared so much stronger that Clemens was allowed to spend half an hour in her room at dinnertime, describing the new villa he planned to buy for the family. Her "eyes danced with pleasure," he remembered, because "she said she wanted a *home*—a home of her own; that she was tired and wanted to rest, and could not rest and be in comfort and peace while she was homeless."

She seemed so well, he remembered, that "I did a thing which I have hardly done since we lost our incomparable Susy. . . . I went to the piano and sang the old songs, the quaint Negro hymns which no one cared for when I sang them except Susy and her mother. When I sang them, Susy always came and listened; when she died, my interest in them passed away; I could not put force and feeling into them without the inspiration of her approving presence." This time, as Clemens sang, Jean slipped into the room to listen, startling her father. "Now," he wrote, "the force and feeling were all back in full strength, and it was as if eight years had fallen from me." He played "Go Chain the Lion Down," then "Swing Low, Sweet Chariot."

The sound drifted downstairs, and Livy smiled in her sickroom. "He is singing a good-night carol to me," she told Katy Leary.

A few minutes later, Clara remembered, "the agitated voice of Katy rose above all other sounds: 'Miss Clara! Miss Clara!'" Clemens and his daughters rushed downstairs and into Livy's room.

Aftermath: Sam Clemens's telegram informing Susan Crane of Livy's death; and (below) the printed card he sent out to scores of people who wrote to him when they heard the sad news

Form No. 168. **THE WESTERN UNION TELEGRAPH COMPANY.**
INCORPORATED
21,000 OFFICES IN AMERICA.   CABLE SERVICE TO ALL THE WORLD.

THOS. T. ECKERT, President and General Manager.

RECEIVED at Cor. Baldwin and Carroll Sts., Elmira, N. Y.

19 NY EH B 9   Cable

Firenze

Langdon   Elmira NY

She passed peacefully away last night

Cable and Money Order Office.   Open Day and Night.   Messenger Service.

To whom this shall come:

For what you have said, I thank you more than I can tell. If I could, I would thank with my own hand and pen each friend who has remembered me and mine with a kindly word of sympathy in this heavy time, but I am not able to do it. Therefore I beg that this general acknowledgment may be accepted as a token of the gratitude, unexpressed & inexpressible, which is in my heart.

SL Clemens

Florence, Italy June 1904.

We that are left, send love,
SLC

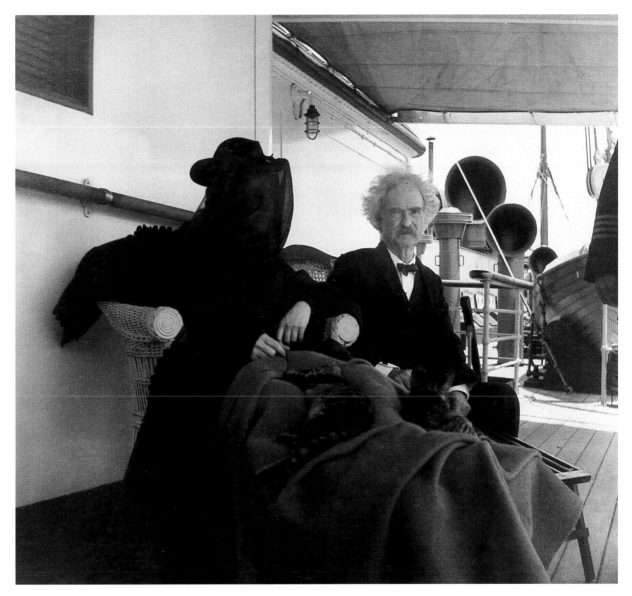

Clara Clemens, veiled in mourning, and her father aboard the *Prince Oscar,* which brought Livy's body home from Europe. "She was all our riches and she is gone," he wrote a friend. "She was our breath, she was our life, and now we are nothing."

She was dead. "It was a pitiful thing to see her there," Leary said, "and him looking at her. Oh, he cried all that time, and Clara and Jean. They put their arms around their father's neck and they cried, the three of them, as though their hearts would break."

"An hour ago," Clemens wrote to a friend that night, "the best heart that ever beat for me and mine was carried silent out of this house and I am as one who wanders and has lost his way." "Our life is wrecked," he told another; "we have no plans for the future; she always made the plans, none of us was capable. We shall carry her home and bury her with her dead, at Elmira. Beyond that, we have no plans. The children must decide. I have no head."

The children had no head either. Clara, apparently convinced that her violent outburst earlier that spring had brought on her mother's death, threw herself onto her mother's bed as soon as Livy's body was taken from it, then locked herself in her room and refused either to move from it or to speak for four days. Jean soon suffered a seizure—the first in thirteen months.

It was left to Isabel Lyon to arrange for the family to take Livy's body home aboard the *Prince Oscar*. Clemens kept a desultory journal of the voyage.

> *June 29, 1904. Sailed last night at 10. The bugle-call to breakfast. I recognized the notes and was distressed. When I heard them last Livy heard them with me; now they fall upon her ear unheeded. In my life there have been sixty-eight Junes—but how faded and color-less sixty-seven of them are, contrasted with the deep blackness of this one! . . .*

> *July 2, 1904. In these thirty-four years we have made many voyages together, Livy dear—and now we are making our last, you down below and lonely; I above with the crowd and lonely.*

> *July 3, 1904. Ship-time, 8 a.m. In thirteen hours and a quarter it will be four weeks since Livy died.*

> *July 10, 1904. Tonight it will be five weeks. But to me it remains yesterday.*

> *July 14, 1904. (Elmira.) Funeral private in the house of Livy's young maidenhood. Where she stood as a bride thirty-four years ago there her coffin rested; and over it the same voice that had made her a wife then, committed her departed spirit to God now.*

Joe Twichell, who had married Sam and Livy and buried both little Langdon and Susy, officiated at the funeral. Clara, who had now suffered what her father called "two-thirds of a nervous breakdown," had to be restrained from hurling herself into her mother's open grave and soon thereafter checked herself into a New York sanitarium. A week or so later, after Jean was injured in a carriage accident, Clemens rushed to tell Clara about it in person. Though her doctors warned him to be gentle, he could not resist dramatizing the event; storming into her room, he waved a lurid headline about the accident before telling her that Jean had not actually been badly hurt. Clara sent him away. Her doctors insisted he not try to contact her again for the foreseeable future; even telephone calls were banned. She would remain bedridden and discon-solate, unable even to read her mail, for more than seven months—and would not see her family again for nearly a year. Meanwhile, Jean had

Joseph Twichell and Mark Twain,
photographed by Jean Clemens in 1905

seizures more frequent and severe than ever before and began to act more and more strangely in between them. Her father struggled to reconcile himself to the fact that she was "heavily afflicted by that unearned, undeserved & hellish disease & is not strictly responsible for her disposition & her acts."

The "very happy family" Susy had once described had been shattered. Sam Clemens would spend the rest of his life looking for some way to put some semblance of it back together again.

"There is *nothing*," he wrote Joe Twichell that summer.

There is no God and no universe; . . . there is only empty space, and in it a lost and homeless and wandering and companionless and indestructible Thought. And . . . I am that thought. And God, and the Universe, and Time, and Life, and Death, and Joy and Sorrow and Pain only a grotesque and brutal dream, evolved from the frantic imagination and that insane Thought.

Eventually, Twain would publish a slim volume called *The Diaries of Adam and Eve,* whose last line was his tribute to Livy: "Wherever she was, *there* was Eden."

OUT AT THE EDGES

RUSSELL BANKS

It's not often said of those who make literature, but it strikes me that Mark Twain was an enormous force for social good. He was not, and still is not, a writer read only by other writers or academics or critics; he has always been a writer read by ordinary, everyday folks. And in the end, that's where true and meaningful social change occurs, in the lives of everyday folks. There is a saying—actually, I first heard it from the novelist Doris Lessing—that, yes, literature changes things, but not at the center, because nothing changes at the center. Change occurs only at the edges and then works its way in. And surely Mark Twain, of all American writers, made changes out at the edges that have by now worked their way into the center.

When, for example, a novel alters a white or black kid's understanding of race, and that kid goes out and becomes a teacher, a journalist, a dentist or plumber, another mere adult American citizen living a life out at the edge him- or herself, he or she will in turn change the views of people who touch his or her life, too. And thus the altered edge moves another degree toward the center. Starting in the lecture halls, parlors, and bedrooms of Victorian America and continuing even to today, in the classrooms of every school and university in the land, on subways, in libraries, in waiting rooms, wherever his books are read, Twain alters people's view of the world and of themselves. More than a national treasure, Mark Twain was and is a national necessity.

How, in the twenty-first century, nearly a hundred years after Twain's death, is this possible? It is important to note that he is persistently, almost uniquely among our nineteenth-century authors, modern. He refuses to age. On the one hand, he is as Hemingway said, "the headwater of American fiction," the father of all our literary fathers and mothers. But on the other, it seems as though he started writing yesterday and is writing about today. Perhaps they are the same,

for in a sense all American fiction that matters got started only yesterday and is inescapably about today.

But there are crucial ways in which Twain differs from both his predecessors and those who came after. He's the writer who above all others took the first dip and then the deepest dive into the American vernacular and made it possible for the rest of us to swim there. And he swam so deeply and skillfully in it from the start that you simply can't write modern fiction without in some important way imitating him. There is in every sentence written by Twain a fresh feeling of intimacy that can only come from his language, which is plainspoken American English. He has an easy, comfortable, private, almost erotic relationship with the English language, not as it is written by Americans, but as it is *spoken* by them—urban and rural, Northern, Southern, and Western, African-Americans, Euro-Americans, working-class, upper-class, and middle-class Americans. Twain was the first among us to tell stories in the language that we use to tell our secrets to one another and to make love with and to express our pain, rage, and delight.

Beyond that, he feels modern—like our contemporary, almost—because of a genre of fiction, the moral fable, that he practically invented alone, and that we Americans characteristically rely upon for our "true" stories today. We require, it seems, stories that are rooted in our everyday lives, that are conveyed to us and dramatized for us in American vernacular speech, but that nonetheless help us know what it is to be truly human, for better or worse. Twain invented for us a form that is hyperreal, in which the characters are slightly exaggerated but not to the point of becoming stereotypes or clichéd; he clothes them in the garments that we all wear every day of our lives and puts them down in a recognizable world (even if it's called King Arthur's court), where they eat and drink and get up in the morning and work at their jobs and worry about money; and all the time he lets them speak to us in a voice that is intimate and immediately familiar to us.

The genius of Twain may also be that for him other human beings were more real than he was himself. "I am *the* American," he declared. Paradoxically, despite its apparent grandiosity, it's an extremely modest statement. It's an expression of deep affection for Americans, plural. He's really talking about his love object. When you truly love someone, you in a sense become that person. You move toward him or her, and you bring him or her toward you, and that's what he's describing: his love for *all* Americans.

There is a sense in which he was the first writer to have discovered America from inside America, rather than from someplace else. All his travel writings, so-called, were really about going out to the margins of the world from the center, rather than to its center from a marginal place. Until Twain, American writers—Hawthorne in England and Italy, Melville in Europe and the Holy Land, Emerson in England—went abroad to visit and view the source. By reversing that old polarity, Twain established the American point of view. And from then on, you rarely see an American writer approach Europe or Asia or Africa or any other place on the planet from any other point of view, not even Henry James.

"Thinking"; Huck ponders whether or not to betray his friend Jim, in an illustration by Edward Kemble from the first edition of *Adventures of Huckleberry Finn.*

It's a great invention, America at the center, and it didn't exist before Twain's *Innocents Abroad* and *A Tramp Abroad.* We are not simply descended from Europeans and the English, nor are we their country cousins. We are utterly and significantly different from them. And when he describes himself as *the* American, he's making that declaration on the basis of a belief that his own contradictions are in some way large enough to represent those that are inherent in our culture and history. As a people and as a culture, we're filled with these same contradictions. Like Mark Twain, we are African-Americans and Euro-Americans, we're immigrants and we're natives, we're rural and we're urban, we're Western and Eastern, Northern and Southern. We're expansionists and we're isolationists, we're radical rebuilders and we're reactionary conservatives, and we approach every problem, every crisis in our history and our personal lives, it sometimes seems, just as Twain did, by deploying exactly these contradictions.

It was those contradictions, which often took the form of deep, abiding inner conflicts, that provided a kind of engine that drove Twain and powered him, allowing him to overcome and keep on working in the face of terrible personal tragedy and loss. Especially the loss of his wife, Livy, the love of his life, and the loss of his children. And one must include the shocking loss of his fortune. Throughout his middle and late years, he endured one catastrophe after another, events that would have driven most human beings into despair, depression, suicide even. And indeed Twain despaired, grew depressed, contemplated suicide. Yet he kept on driving on into the night that seemed increasingly to surround him. No matter how dark that night became, he kept his eyes wide open.

Hemingway was right, possibly more right than even he thought. It all goes back, not only to one writer, but to one book, *Huckleberry Finn.* I think that *Huckleberry Finn* is our Homeric epic, or the basis for one. It stands in relation to our literature as *The Iliad* and *The Odyssey* stand to Greek and European literature. Twain's operating premise in all his work was that we are, as a people, radically different from Europeans, despite our common threads of history. And the elements that make us different are essentially two: race and space. *Huckleberry Finn*, more than any other of Twain's books, and certainly more than the work of any writer before him and probably more than that of any writer since, embraces those two facts. It makes possible an American literature that otherwise was not possible. Even Melville, in his great extremity, while he accepted the central fact of space, was a little more ambiguous and ambivalent about race. Twain made it central.

Nothing human shocked him, except slavery and racism. Whenever he deals with race or the history of slavery and its residue in his own time, there's a simple, but nonjudgmental, horror that runs through it. It's as if he's physically repelled, thrown back upon himself. And the story that, after several abandoned efforts, he finally tells through *Huckleberry Finn* is possibly the only way he could step back from that shock and come to moral grips with his horror—without being didactic, boring, or self-righteous—and still be as inclusive in his work of everything that is human as he was in his personal life.

Huck's momentous decision—a single sentence that creates the moral climax of the book: "All right, then, I'll *go* to hell"—makes the hair on the back of my neck stand up. In the interests of justice, Huck makes himself a race traitor, regardless of the price he may end up paying. When I think about that sentence and its context, I see it as the great moral moment, the moral awakening, one might say, for white Americans. There is, from that moment on, the possibility of redemption for what Twain saw, and what most of us today still see, as the great sin at our inception, the twinned sins of slavery and racism. If we can say, with Huck and his creator, "All right, then, I'll *go* to hell," the possibility of redemption exists.

At the heart of Twain's work, and it may be his essential, guiding insight into American life, was that you couldn't tell a truth about American life unless you talked directly and perhaps even endlessly about race. That he took race to be a central fact of American life and history and the ongoing culture was as courageous as it was unusual. Very few writers of his time—no white writer of his century, in fact, and only a few of ours—have operated from that premise.

It was something that came straight from his childhood and youth in Hannibal, Missouri—that borderline area between East and West, North and South, a region where you couldn't get away from the fact of race and couldn't rationalize or compartmentalize it, so that you simply could not live a day without being aware of the permanent presence of African-Americans the way you could in the Northeast or other parts of the country. But what is unusual about Twain, both as a writer and as a man, is that as the circumstances of his life changed, as he moved increasingly in a white, bourgeois world and even into a European, cosmopolitan world, he never forgot that basic fact. It had come home to him in his early childhood and adolescent years, and he remembered it in his old age with the clarity of someone who'd learned it yesterday.

It was as though he never lost his deepest connection to that boy, no matter how far in time and society he traveled from him. Memory for Twain was essential, probably as essential as it has been for any novelist. But not the conscious, narrative memory that one relies on to recollect one's experiences and then retell them. Twain's reliance was on the kind of unconscious memory that retains isolated, felt experiences—the jackrabbit crossing the road or the shift in the sound of the leaves when the wind changes direction or the smell of wood smoke from a chimney across the valley—and allows those remembered long-ago perceptions to carry into the present their original resonance and emotional meaning. For most writers, and Twain is exemplary in this, there is a free-floating memory that limns every day and every new experience with meaning; that gives to one's days and nights a precious luminosity. It's not difficult for a young writer to have access to the sort of memories that lend a numinous quality to everyday experiences; he or she is still pretty close to the initial, and initiating, experiences. But it's much harder as one grows older to hold on to the perceptions of reality that one received as a child and a youth. Twain was gifted with maintaining this ability even into old age, well into his years of gloom and pessimism.

That all his life he was such a purely funny man, on the page and in person, from the first time he appears in public until the very end, shouldn't surprise us. His father was a dour and probably depressed man, and the children of depressives tend to be tap dancers and joke tellers, attention-getters, slightly manic diverters. Part of it is out of a fear that if they don't make the old man or Mother laugh, things are just going to bear down harder and eventually will smother them with a gloom they can't escape. Twain's need to read the world through the prism of humor was perhaps the only way it was tolerable for him. There was likely no other option for him, given what he knew of the world, besides fantasy or suicide. It's not just a man who's trying to entertain us; it's a man who is trying to keep from killing himself.

He was above all else and from the very beginning an unflinching realist, not as a writer, technically speaking, but in philosophical terms. It was his great struggle all his life not to delude himself in any way about the nature of the world that surrounded him. This is a difficult mission, because it implies that the more you learn about the world that surrounds you, the sadder you're going to get. You aren't protected by fantasies or dreams or delusions. And it was true in his case. The more he learned about the world, about human beings in America and abroad, the more he traveled, the more people he knew, the more human venality and cruelty and selfishness that he met, the darker he necessarily became. And the more rigorous and disciplined his humor became. To me, the late Twain is the funniest and most appealing. It's cosmic humor, the dark laughter of a god. The tones and notes that run through Samuel Beckett can be heard in every sentence of the late Twain. More than ever in his long life, at the end of it he was still looking mortality straight in the face, staring cruelty and greed down, gazing at humanity and not once wincing from the sight.

As Twain gets older, you can see the lights going out. He begins his career as a writer standing on a brightly lit stage, reciting from the early journalism and *Innocents Abroad*, the wise guy with the depth and profundity of a great and wise man, a wise guy who actually sounds wise. And then as he grows older and the personal tragedies start to strike one after the other, you can see the lights that illuminate the stage going out one by one. Until late in life, he's standing up there all by himself with just one little reading light reflecting upward from the podium and shining on his face. That light still shines today and will likely shine for centuries to come.

When Twain died, the people who lost something crucial to their lives were those who knew him personally and loved him. But because his work goes on altering our consciousness of the world today fully as much as if we, too, had known him personally, we ourselves didn't really lose anything when he died. This is what any writer hopes will happen, that the work will go on altering human consciousness after his or her death. We're a strange species, we humans. We're unique on this planet, yes, but only insofar as we have to learn over and over again what it is actually to be human. Unlike all other species, we have to learn with each generation how to be ourselves. And Twain, like all the great writers, reminds us, and by reminding teaches us, what it is to be human, the worst of it and the best of it. This is the great gift of Mark Twain the man in his lifetime, and it is the gift of his work today. A hundred years after his death, in order to be true to our own species, to be true to ourselves, we require that work.

Huck and Jim and the river, by Edward Kemble

CHAPTER THIRTEEN

THE MOST CONSPICUOUS PERSON

I am the human race compacted and crammed into a single suit of clothes but quite able to represent its entire massed multitude in all its moods and inspirations.

—Letter to Helen Picard, February 11, 1902

Sam Clemens and Clara pretend not to notice the stir their passage causes along a Manhattan street. "Fame," Twain wrote, is "what a boy or a youth longs for more than any other thing. He would be a clown in a circus, he would be a pirate, he would sell himself to Satan, in order to attract attention and be talked about and envied. True, it is the same with every grown-up person."

The New York house at 21 Fifth Avenue in which Sam Clemens spent the lonely winters from 1904 to 1908

Clemens settled into a brownstone on Fifth Avenue. Isabel Lyon, forty-one years old, attractive, capable, and almost worshipful of the employer she called "the King," now presided over the household, doing her best to do all that Livy had done for him. She acted as Twain's escort and hostess, kept his accounts, supervised the servants, took dictation from him in his bedroom, even rounded up friends with whom he could play billiards in the evenings. "All my days are hallowed by Mr. Clemens's wonderful presence," she confided to her journal, and she seems to have harbored hopes of marrying him: "I've known of several men who have married several times—they couldn't live without the companionship and sympathy of a woman and I like the thought of it."

Despite his grief, Clemens continued to work, contributing short essays to *Harper's Weekly* and other publications, beginning—and giving up on—two more novels, and dictating more chapters of his autobiography, which soon began appearing in the *North American Review*. (Twain liked them well enough, Howells recalled his saying, though "as to veracity it was a failure; he had begun to lie, and that if no man ever yet told the truth about himself it was because no man ever could.")

In early January of 1906, another outsider moved into the Clemens house: Albert Bigelow Paine. A young man who had talked the older one into letting him write an authorized biography, Paine rooted through Clemens's correspondence, listened to him talk. "He was not to be learned in a day," Paine wrote, "or a week, or a month; some of those who knew him longest did not learn him at all."

Meanwhile, Jean's condition worsened, as Isabel Lyon noted in her journal:

January 27, 1906. This was a tragic day. . . . When I went to [Jean's] room for tea, she told me that . . . in a burst of unreasoning rage she struck Katy [Leary] a heavy blow in the face. . . . She described the wave of passion that swept over her as being that of an

Overspeeding

Born and brought up in the age of steam, Mark Twain lived long enough to write about the age of the automobile, as in this October 18, 1905, letter written from Dublin, New Hampshire, to the editor of Harper's Weekly.

Sir,—Equal laws for all. It is good in theory, and I believe it would prove good in practice, if fairly and dispassionately tried. The law dresses a convict in a garb which makes him easily distinguishable from any moving thing in the world at a hundred and twenty-five yards, except a zebra. If he escapes in those clothes, he cannot get far. Could not this principle be extended to include his brother criminal the Overspeeder, thus making the pair fairly and righteously equal before the law? Every day, throughout America, the Overspeeder runs over somebody and "escapes." That is the way it reads. At present the 'mobile numbers are so small that ordinary eyes cannot read them, upon a swiftly receding machine, at a distance of a hundred feet— a distance which the machine has covered before the spectator can adjust his focus. I think I would amend the law. I would enlarge the figures, and make them readable at a hundred yards. For overspeeding—first offense— I would enlarge the figures again, and make them readable at three hundred yards—this in place of a fine, and as a warning to pedestrians to climb a tree. This enlargement to continue two months, with privilege of resuming the smaller figures after the first thirty days upon payment of $500. For each subsequent offense, reenlargement for six months, with privilege of resuming the smaller figures upon payment of $1000 at the end of three. With auto numbers readable as far as one could tell a convict from a barber-pole none of these criminals could run over a person and "escape."

Two months ago a touring 'mobile came within an indeterminable fraction of killing a member of my family; and its number was out of sight-range before the sharpest eyes present could make it out, it was so small and the spectators so dazed by momentary fright. I have had two narrow escapes in New York, and so has everybody else. None of us has succeeded in capturing the auto number. I feel a sort of personal interest in this suggested reform.

I am, sir, M.T.

Sam and Jean at Dublin, New Hampshire, in the summer of 1906. "There seems to be a tragic something hanging near," Isabel Lyon wrote that summer. "Some fate that is coursing along in their blood, and waiting to drop with a clutch at their hearts."

insane person. She had to strike, she knew she couldn't stop & she said she wanted to kill & was sorry she had not killed Katy. . . .

February 2, 1906. Today Jean has [again] been ill—and this morning I had to have a plain talk with Mr. Clemens about her condition. . . . The dreadfulness of it all swept over Mr. Clemens as I knew it would, and with that fiercest of all his looks . . . he blazed out against "the swindle of life" & "the treachery of God that can create disease & misery & crime—create things that men would be condemned for creating—that men would be ashamed to create."

The following autumn, after a second attempt on Katy Leary's life, Jean would be sent away to the first of a series of sanitariums in America and Europe. Again and again over the coming years, she would beg to be allowed to come home. Her father, fearing that he was not up to the job of caring for her, always said no, and she became convinced that he was "glad to have me away."

Meanwhile, in spite of the presence of Lyon and Paine, Clemens felt more and more alone. Clara left the hospital and moved in with her

Katy Leary, photographed by Jean Clemens in 1905. She served the family as nursemaid, seamstress, nanny, traveling companion, and sometime nurse, from 1880 until October 1910. "She had a heart of Irish warmth," Twain wrote, "quick Irish wit, and a good store of that veiled and shimmering and half-surreptitious humor which is the best feature of the 'American' brand—or of any brand, for that matter."

The guest of honor's table at Mark Twain's seventieth birthday party, held at Delmonico's Restaurant in Manhattan. His guests, all close friends, included Joe Twichell (third from the left) and Henry H. Rogers (far right).

A Severely Moral Life

Called upon to speak at a dinner at Delmonico's Restaurant in New York City on December 5, 1905, to celebrate his seventieth birthday, Mark Twain drew lessons from his long life.

I have had a great many birthdays in my time. I remember the first one very well, and I always think of it with indignation; everything was so crude, unaesthetic, primeval. Nothing like this at all. No proper appreciative preparation made; nothing really ready. Now, for a person born with high and delicate instincts—why, even the cradle wasn't whitewashed—nothing ready at all. I hadn't any hair, I hadn't any teeth, I hadn't any clothes, I had to go to my first banquet just like that. . . .

It's a long stretch between that first birthday speech and this one. That was my cradle-song, and this is my swan-song, I suppose. I am used to swan-songs; I have sung them several times. . . .

I have achieved my seventy years in the usual way: by sticking strictly to a scheme of life which would kill anybody else. It sounds like an exaggeration, but that is really the common rule for attaining to old age. When we examine the programme of any of these garrulous old people we always find that the habits which have preserved them would have decayed us; that the way of life which enabled them to live upon the property of their heirs so long, as Mr. Choate says, would have put us out of commission ahead of time. I will offer here, as a sound maxim, this: that we can't reach old age by another man's road. . . .

We have no permanent habits until we are forty. Then they begin to harden, presently they petrify, then business begins. Since forty I have been regular about going to bed and getting up—and that is one of the main things. I have made it a rule to go to bed when there wasn't anybody left to sit up with; and I have made it a rule to get up when I had to. This has resulted in an unswerving regularity of irregularity. It has saved me sound, but it would injure another person.

In the matter of diet—which is another main thing—I have been persistently strict in sticking to the things which didn't agree with me until one or the other of us got the best of it. Until lately I got the best of it myself. But last spring I stopped frolicking with mince-pie after midnight; up to then I had always believed it wasn't loaded. For thirty years I have taken coffee and bread at eight in the morning, and no bite nor sup until seven-thirty in the evening. Eleven hours. That is all right for me, and is wholesome, because I have never had a headache in my life, but headachy people would not reach seventy comfortably by that road, and they would be foolish to try it. And I wish to urge upon you this—which I think is wisdom—that if you find you can't make seventy by any but an uncomfortable road, don't you go. When they take off the Pullman and retire you to the rancid smoker, put on your things, count your checks, and get out at the first way station where there's a cemetery.

I have made it a rule never to smoke more than one cigar at a time. I have no other restriction as regards smoking. I do not know just when I began to smoke, I only know that it was in my father's lifetime, and that I was discreet. He passed from this life early in 1847, when I was a shade past eleven; ever since then I have smoked publicly. As an example to others, and not that I care for moderation myself, it has always been my rule never to smoke when asleep, and never to refrain when awake. It is a good rule. I mean, for me; but some of you know quite well that it wouldn't answer for every-body that's trying to get to be seventy. . . .

As for drinking, I have no rule about that. When the others drink I like to help; otherwise I remain dry, by habit and preference. This dryness does not hurt me, but it could easily hurt you, because you are different. You let it alone. . . .

I have never taken any exercise, except sleeping and resting, and I never intend to take any. Exercise is loathsome. And it cannot be any benefit when you are tired; and I was always tired. But let another person try my way, and see where he will come out.

I desire now to repeat and emphasize that maxim: We can't reach old age by another man's road. My habits protect my life, but they would assassinate you.

I have lived a severely moral life. But it would be a mistake for other people to try that, or for me to recommend it. Very few would succeed: you have to have a perfectly colossal stock of morals; and you can't get them on a margin; you have to have the whole thing, and put them in your box. Morals are an acquirement—like music, like a foreign language, like piety, poker, paralysis—no man is born with them. I wasn't myself, I started poor. I hadn't a single moral. There is hardly a man in this house that is poorer than I was then. Yes, I started like that—the world before me, not a moral in the slot. Not even an insurance moral. I can remember the first one I ever got. I can remember the landscape, the weather, the—I can remember how everything looked. It was an old moral, an old second-hand moral, all out of repair, and didn't fit, anyway. But if you are careful with a thing like that, and keep it in a dry place, and save it for processions, and Chautauquas, and World's Fairs, and so on, and disin-fect it now and then, and give it a fresh coat of whitewash once in a while, you will be surprised to see how well she will last and how long she will keep sweet, or at least inoffensive. When I got that mouldy old moral, she had stopped growing, because she hadn't any exercise; but I worked her hard, I worked her Sundays and all. Under this cultivation she waxed in might and stature beyond belief, and served me well and was my pride and joy for sixty-three years; then she got to associating with insurance presidents, and lost flesh and character, and was a sorrow to look at and no longer com-petent for business. She was a great loss to me. . . .

Threescore years and ten!

It is the Scriptural statute of limitations. After that, you owe no active duties; for you the strenuous life is over. You are a time-expired man, to use Kipling's military phrase: you have served your term, well or less well, and you are mustered out. You are become an honorary member of the republic, you are emancipated, compulsions are not for you, nor any bugle-call but "lights out."

. . . But I am seventy; seventy, and would nestle in the chimney-corner, and smoke my pipe, and read my book, and take my rest, wishing you well in all affection, and that when you in your return shall arrive at pier No. 70 you may step aboard your waiting ship with a reconciled spirit, and lay your course toward the sinking sun with a contented heart.

father, but spent as little time as she could in his company. "This is the wretched day," Isabel Lyon noted on March 24, 1906,

> *when Mr. Clemens went down to the living room & there wasn't anyone there. For half an hour he waited for a human being, & none came to stay. [Clara] looked in upon him as she passed out of the house & then a cold bedeviled loneliness swept over him & made him hate his life. [She] was late for luncheon, & Mr. Clemens loathed the meal. He dropped his . . . hard water-biscuit with a bang on the mahogany table—in a cursing wave of bitterness. These are the agony days when he knows Mrs. Clemens is gone.*

Sam Clemens performs for a photographer while Clara and Marie Nicols, a violinist with whom she sometimes toured, look on, 1906.

Relations continued to be difficult between father and elder daughter. He agreed to attend a New York concert, then tried to lead Clara onstage over her protests, and when she had finished singing gave a twenty-minute speech from the stage that drew more press attention than her music had. At a New Year's party in 1907, she embarrassed her father in front of some sixty guests by loudly refusing to play charades with him. That summer, when Clara suggested he arrange for her to sing in Tuxedo Park, the village where he was vacationing among some of New York's wealthiest families, he told her he'd leave rather than agree to have her come; and when she insisted on giving a recital at 21 Fifth Avenue the following January, he remained upstairs, the angry clicking of his billiard balls clearly audible to the guests as she sang.

As the relationship between Clemens and his daughters grew more torturous, he began to seek the uncomplicated adoration they had once provided him by cultivating friendships with a group of young girls, aged ten to sixteen, whom he came to call his "Angelfish." He flooded them with letters, encouraged them and their mothers to call, openly sought their praise and affection. "My heart . . . is a treasure place of little people whom I worship," he explained. "In grandchildren I am the richest man that lives today: for I *select* my grandchildren, whereas all other grandfathers have to take them as they come, good, bad, and indifferent."

He kept writing, too. Full-length works of fiction no longer seemed possible for him, but he continued to labor over short stories, essays, and

Clemens reclines at the right with Ralph Ashcroft and Isabel Lyon; the young man at the left is a stenographer, W. E. Grumman.

"Pity the Poor Sailors"

Twain testified before Congress in 1906 to support a new copyright law. Most of his speech to the committee was deadly serious, but he ended with this story, which sent the senators and congressmen into gales of laughter.

I do seem to be extraordinarily interested in a whole lot of arts and things that I have got nothing to do with. It is a part of my generous, liberal nature; I can't help it. I feel the same sort of charity to everybody that was manifested by a gentleman who arrived at home at two o'clock in the morning from the club and was feeling so perfectly satisfied with life, so happy, and so comfortable, and there was his house weaving, weaving, weaving around. He watched his chance, and by and by when the steps got in his neighborhood he made a jump and climbed up and got on the portico.

And the house went on weaving and weaving and weaving, but he watched the door, and when it came around his way he plunged through it. He got to the stairs, and when he went up on all fours the house was so unsteady that he could hardly make his way, but at last he got to the top and raised his foot and put it on the top step. But only the toe hitched on the step, and he rolled down and fetched up on the bottom step, with his arm around the newel-post, and he said: "God pity the poor sailors out at sea on a night like this."

after-dinner speeches, and he saw to it that *What Is Man?*—the book Livy had loathed—was finally published anonymously in a printing of just 250 copies.

Celebrity was now his chief source of solace. He took to wearing scarlet socks and all-white suits year-round—his "don'tcareadam suits," he called them, "very beautiful and conspicuous"—and on Sunday mornings he paraded up and down Broadway just as church let out to draw still more attention to himself. "He was the object on which every passing eye turned," wrote Paine, "the presence to which every hat was lifted." His mere appearance at a billiards tournament at Madison Square Garden brought the crowd to its feet. A woman begged to kiss his hand, saying, "How God must love you." "I hope so," he answered, but as soon as she was out of earshot he murmured, "I guess she hasn't heard of our strained relations." Mail flooded in from all over the world, including one letter addressed simply to "Mark Twain, Godknowswhere." A friend called him "the Belle of New York," and he reveled in the name; he was now, he boasted, "the most conspicuous person on the planet." When an energetic young British-born entrepreneur named Ralph Ashcroft persuaded Clemens to trademark his pen name in order to protect his copyrights and established the Mark Twain Company to oversee the expected profits, the grateful author gave Ashcroft and Isabel Lyon his power of attorney.

MARK TWAIN AT PLAY

When he was a young reporter in Virginia City, Nevada, Twain encountered a stranger at a billiard parlor who proposed a game for half a dollar—even offered to play left-handed after watching Twain warm up. "I determined," Twain wrote later, "to teach him a lesson." But the stranger won the first shot, cleared the table, took Twain's money, "and all I got was the opportunity to chalk my cue."

"If you can play like that with your left hand," Twain said, "I'd like to see you play with your right."

"I can't," the stranger answered. "I'm left-handed."

Whether the incident ever actually occurred—it has the hallmark of a good Twain yarn—there's no question that Sam Clemens enjoyed games of all kinds.

He took up bowling during his time in San Francisco. Years later, when his family was summering at Bateman's Point, Rhode Island, he devoted his entire vacation to bowling with a man named Higgins on a dilapidated alley that "consisted of a rolling stretch of elevations and depressions, and neither of us could, by any art known to us, persuade a ball to stay on the alley until it should accomplish something." The balls, he claimed, ranged in size from that of a grapefruit to ones almost too big to lift. But they stayed at it for days (and sometimes nights, playing by candlelight), concocting new games that made the most of the faulty equipment. In one game, they each got to roll thirty-five balls to see if they could knock something down; in another, called "cocked hat," they set up three pins and struggled to hit them with the smallest balls. One day they snookered a young army officer into a wager and then watched him bowl nearly two hundred balls with-

Albert Bigelow Paine and Sam Clemens at billiards, which Twain loved, although, he said, it "has destroyed my naturally sweet disposition"

out hitting anything. "We easily got out of that old alley five times the fun that anybody could have gotten out of the best alley in New York," he said later. "It compelled skill; it provided the opportunity for bets; and if you could get a stranger to do the bowling for you, there was more and wholesomer and delightfuler entertainment to be gotten out of his industries than out of the finest game by the best expert."

At Quarry Farm, he enjoyed playing charades and cards with his family after a day of writing. He dreamed up a game to teach Susy and Clara the history of England, planting stakes in the ground, each stake representing a different monarch and each foot separating them counting as a year's reign. Then the girls would race up the hill, calling out each ruler's name at each stake. (Clemens toyed with the notion of turning this into a board game and marketing it—even contacted his brother Orion to do the historical research—but eventually dropped the idea.)

One summer, he decided to learn how to ride a bicycle. The expert he hired to teach him "said that the dismounting was perhaps the hardest thing to learn, and so we would leave that to the last," he wrote of the experience. "But he was in error there. He found, to his surprise and joy, that all he needed to do was to get me on to the machine and stand out of the way; I could get off, myself. Although I was wholly inexperienced, I dismounted in the best time on record."

Many days—and bruises—later, Clemens had conquered the bicycle, only to find himself at the mercy of the dogs that chased him down the street:

I have seen it stated that no expert is quick enough to run over a dog; that a dog is always able to skip out of his way. I think that that may be true: but I think that the reason he couldn't run over the dog was because he was trying to. I did not try to run over any dog. But I ran over every dog that came along. I think it makes a great deal of difference. If you try to run over the dog he knows how to calculate, but if you are trying to miss him he does not know how to calculate, and is liable to jump the wrong way every time. It was always so in my experience. Even when I could not hit a wagon I could hit a dog that came to see me practice.

But billiards remained his favorite pastime. At his home in Hartford, friends would gather once a week in his third-floor office for the "Friday Evening Club," to drink, smoke cigars, tell stories, and play billiards on the big table dominating the room. Clemens usually adjusted the rules to make the games livelier—and increase his odds of winning.

As an old man living at Stormfield, where he sometimes whiled away an afternoon playing hearts with the girls he called his "Angelfish," his greatest joy came with a pool cue in hand. "The billiard table," he wrote to Henry Rogers's wife, is "better than the doctor's." Albert Bigelow Paine, his young biographer, found himself playing billiards with his subject constantly, sometimes for eight or nine hours at a stretch and often into the early hours of the morning. The two celebrated Clemens's seventy-first birthday together at Stormfield by playing billiards the entire day, breaking only for dinner before starting up again. Clemens invented new rules with nearly every shot, and when they finally quit, Paine said he hoped they'd still be playing billiards on Clemens's eighty-first birthday. "Yes," the old man said, "still playing the best game on earth."

New York humorists, cartoonists, and comic-strip artists gather for a beef dinner at Reisenweber's Restaurant on Columbus Circle in New York to honor Mark Twain and his friend Henry Rogers. The honorees (standing together against the wall) accepted their invitations on the strict understanding that neither would be required to make a speech.

In the spring of 1907, Oxford University offered Twain an honorary doctorate of letters. He eagerly set sail for England; an Oxford degree, he said, was "worth twenty-five of any other [university's,] whether foreign or domestic." At a garden party at Windsor Castle, he chatted with the king and queen (who allowed him, alone among the guests, to keep his hat on). He met George Bernard Shaw, who proclaimed himself a "Huckamaniac." And he made headlines by strolling across the street from Brown's Hotel in London to a public bath wearing his bathrobe, which produced an anxious telegram from Clara. "Much alarmed," it said. "Remember the Proprieties." At Oxford, he found himself in the most distinguished company possible: Rudyard Kipling, Auguste Rodin, Camille Saint-Saëns, and General William Booth, founder of the Salvation Army, were all to be given degrees at the same ceremony. And he was especially pleased that—after the chancellor, Lord Curzon, had addressed him in Latin as "Most amiable and charming and playful sir, you shake the sides of the whole world with your merriment"—the

British reporters surround Clemens aboard the steamer after she docked at Tilbury. When he went ashore he was cheered by the stevedores—"the very people of all people in the world whom I would have chosen," he wrote, "a hundred men of my own class—grimy sons of labor, the real builders of empires and civilizations. . . . They stood in a body on the dock and charged their masculine lungs, and gave me a welcome which went to the marrow of me."

(opposite) Mark Twain, wearing his Oxford robes, enjoys a cigar in a 1908 autochrome by Alvin Langdon Coburn. "I know a bad cigar better than anybody else," he wrote. "I judge by the price only. If it costs above five cents I know it to be either foreign or half-foreign, and unsmokeable. By me."

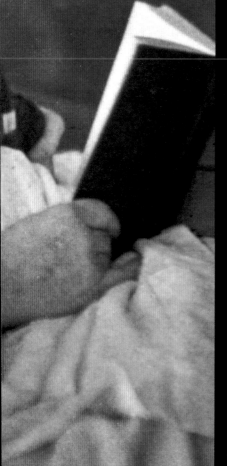

sailors, her hull burdened to the Plimsoll line with a rich freightage of precious spices, lading the breezes with gracious and mysterious odors of the Orient. It was a noble spectacle, a sublime spectacle! Of course the little skipper popped into the shrouds and squeaked out a hail, "Ship ahoy! What ship is that? And whence and whither?" In a deep and thundering bass the answer came back through the speaking-trumpet, "The *Begum of Bengal*—142 days out from Canton—homeward bound! What ship is that?" Well, it just crushed that poor little creature's vanity flat, and he squeaked back most humbly, "Only the *Mary Ann,* fourteen hours out from Boston, bound for Kittery Point—with nothing to speak of!" Oh, what an eloquent word that "only," to express the depths of his humbleness! That is just my case. During just one hour in the twenty-four—not more— I pause and reflect in the stillness of the night with the echoes of your English welcome still lingering in my ears, and then I am humble. Then I am properly meek, and for that little while I am only the *Mary Ann,* fourteen hours out, cargoed with vegetables and tinware; but during all the other twenty-three hours my vain self-complacency rides high on the white crests of your approval, and then I am a stately Indiaman, plowing the great seas under a cloud of canvas and laden with the kindest words that have ever been vouchsafed to any wandering alien in this world, I think; then my twenty-six fortunate days on this old mother soil seem to be multiplied by six, and *I* am the *Begum of Bengal,* 142 days out from Canton, homeward bound!

Clemens at rest, 1908

Isabel Lyon accompanied her employer to Bermuda in 1908 and snapped these pictures of him surrounded by friends, including Woodrow Wilson (leaning against the pillar), and alone on the beach.

"veritable cyclone of applause" that followed the mention of his name was louder and longer than the cheers that greeted those of his fellow honorees.

With British applause still ringing in his ears, Twain returned to the dark, silent New York house he now called The Valley of the Shadow. "Nobody thrives in this house," Clemens complained. "Nobody profits by our sojourn in it except the doctors. . . . We must move out and find a home with some sunshine in it." Before leaving for England, he had bought 248 acres of farmland for a new home near Redding, Connecticut, and asked John Howells, the architect son of his old friend William Dean Howells, to design and build it. Isabel Lyon volunteered to see to all the details, just as Livy had when she and her husband were building their home in Hartford. "I don't want to see it," Twain said, "until the cat is purring on the hearth."

As work proceeded on his new house, Twain began spending time in Bermuda. "There are no newspa-

Clemens in Bermuda with two of his "Angelfish," Maude Blackmer (above) and Irene Gerken

pers," he wrote a friend, "no telegrams, . . . no trolleys, no trains, no tramps, no railways, no theatres, no noise, no lectures, no riots, no murders, no fires, no burglaries, no offenses of any kind, no follies but church, and I don't go there. . . . *You* go to heaven if you want to—I'd druther stay here."

Twain moved into his new home on June 18, 1908. Isabel Lyon, with Clara's help, had carefully designed it to be a museum of his memories. Waiting beneath the porte cochere was the carriage Livy's father had given him and his bride on their wedding day, its polished-wood interior nicked and scarred by the hundreds of matches he had scratched to light his pipes and cigars over the years. The mantelpiece from the old Hartford house had been installed in the new living room. Nearby stood the *orchestrelle* that had delighted the family's dinner guests with its familiar airs. The great carved bed he had shared with Livy now served him alone. Twain pronounced it "a perfect house—perfect, so far as I can see, in every detail. It might have been here always." He called it Innocence at Home at first, and then Stormfield, after the hero of "Captain Stormfield's Visit to Heaven," one of the many stories he could no longer quite complete. He hoped—everyone hoped—that somehow it would come to seem as warm and welcoming as his Hartford home had been.

Stormfield, Samuel Clemens's last home, in Redding, Connecticut. It was an Italian-style villa something like the ones in which the Clemens family had lived in Florence, but it included precious details from the beloved Hartford house like the mantelpiece seen in the photograph at right, the same one that had provided Clemens with the setting for bedtime stories when his grown daughters had been little girls.

"I came in with Halley's comet in 1835," Twain wrote in 1909. "It is coming again next year, and I expect to go out with it. It will be the greatest disappointment of my life if I don't go out with Halley's comet. The Almighty has said, no doubt: 'Now here are these two unaccountable freaks; they came in together, they must go out together.'" Twain was seventy-four now, frail, sometimes befuddled, and suffering from chest pains, the first signs of heart disease. He called it "tobacco heart," cut back from forty cigars a day to four, and continued to play billiards with Paine every night despite recurring pain that sometimes bent him double. But he knew he was beginning "a holiday," he said, "whose other end is the cemetery."

He loved showing off his new house—the only film footage of him known to exist shows him striding proudly out its front door in one of his fourteen white suits—but the little world that had been so painfully reconstructed for him there did not last long.

Clara may have quarreled loudly and often with the father who still seemed determined to thwart her every bid for independence, but she would also brook no rivals for his attention. Isabel Lyon had initially been her ally, but in Clara's mind she always remained an employee, not part of the family, and in July, when the *New York Herald* reported that her father was planning to marry Lyon—a false rumor, which he swiftly denied—Clara was appalled. Lyon married Ralph Ashcroft later that summer, at least in part to quiet such rumors—the newlyweds are said to have slept in separate bedrooms—but when the two gently suggested to Clemens that too much of his money was being spent on Clara's career, she exploded, charging the couple with thievery and demanding that her father fire them both. The ailing old man, perpetually suspicious of anyone who tried to do business with him and perhaps fearful of further alienating his temperamental daughter, did as he was told, denounced Lyon and Ashcroft to the press as "professional traitors and forgers," and then prepared for Howells a four-hundred-page document setting forth their supposed crimes.

Clemens was now virtually alone again—Clara still stayed away most of the time; Paine and the servants were his only companions—and when Jean, now twenty-nine, once again asked to be allowed to come home, her father agreed. "Dear child," he wrote to her, "you will be as welcome as if it were your mother herself calling you home from exile!" She quickly found herself in charge of Stormfield—and Sam Clemens. Father and

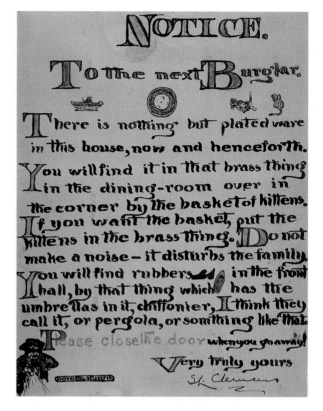

During the night of September 18, 1908, two burglars broke into Stormfield—only to flee in terror after the butler fired a shot at them. The sheriff had them locked up within a few hours. Clemens was delighted by all the excitement. He wrote and illuminated the "Notice to the Next Burglar" above, and cheerfully brandished the butler's pistol for the camera (opposite). "We are buying a couple of bulldogs," he told one of his Angelfish, "& hoping [the thieves] will call again."

daughter rediscovered each other. "Jean is a surprise and a wonder," he wrote. "She has plenty of wisdom, judgement, penetration, practical good sense—like her mother." And Jean relished caring for her father, she said—even though, "when he has an idea in his head, it's like melting marble with a piece of ice to make him change his mind."

Twain still worked every day, publishing an elegant essay about his own career, "The Turning Point in My Life," and starting a series of "Letters from the Earth," which would eventually add up to a zestful attack on the brand of Christianity he had first heard echoing from the Presbyterian pulpit of his mother's church seventy years before:

> *Man is a marvelous curiosity. When he is at his very very best he is a sort of low grade, nickel-plated angel; at his worst he is unspeakable, unimaginable; and first and last and all the time he is a sarcasm. Yet he blandly and in all sincerity calls himself the "noblest work of God."... And this is not a new idea with him, he has talked it through all the ages and believes it. Believed it, and found nobody among all his race to laugh at it....*
>
> *[The Bible] is full of interest. It has noble poetry in it; and some clever fables; and some blood-drenched history; and some good morals; and some execrable morals; and a wealth of obscenity; and upwards of a thousand lies....*

> *Now here is a curious thing. It is believed by everybody that while [God] was in heaven he was stern, hard, resentful, jealous and cruel; but that when he came down to earth and assumed the name Jesus Christ, he became the opposite of what he was before: that is to say, he became sweet, and gentle, merciful, forgiving, and all harshness disappeared from his nature and a deep, yearning love for his poor human children took its place. Whereas it was as Jesus Christ that he devised hell and proclaimed it! Which is to say, that as the meek and gentle Savior he was a thousand billion times crueler than ever he was in the Old Testament—oh, incomparably more atrocious than ever he was at his very worst in those old days!*

That September, Clara and Ossip Gabrilowitsch returned together to Stormfield for a benefit concert for the local public library and became officially engaged. In October, they were married on her father's lawn. Whatever Clemens thought of the now prominent pianist he insisted on calling "Gossip," he

Clara Clemens's wedding party at Storm-field, October 6, 1908: (left to right) the father of the bride in his Oxford robes; his nephew, Jervis Langdon; Jean Clemens; the groom, Ossip Gabrilowitsch; the bride; and the Rev. Joseph Twichell

(opposite) Jean Clemens and the interior of Stormfield decorated for Christmas

was privately delighted that marriage would likely "squelch" his daughter's career, and on her wedding day he did his best to steal the show by wearing his crimson and gray Oxford robes to give the bride away. The newlyweds set sail for Europe as soon as they could, and Clemens undertook another sojourn in Bermuda, returning just a few days before Christmas.

Christmas had been the highlight of the Clemenses' year in Hartford, but, Jean told a friend, her father was now "utterly disinterested" in it, and she was determined to cheer him by re-creating for him something like the holidays they had once known together. She wound the Stormfield mantelpiece with garlands of evergreen, trimmed a tree, piled brightly wrapped packages around its base.

During dinner on the evening of December 23, a newspaperman telephoned to inquire about the old man's health: a rumor was going around that he was near death. Clemens scribbled out a good-humored reply and had Jean call it in to the manager of the Associated Press:

I hear the newspapers say I am dying. The charge is not true.
I would not do such a thing at my time of life. . . .
Merry Christmas to everybody!
Mark Twain

His daughter rose early the next morning and drew her bath. It was Christmas Eve, and she still had a lot to do. An hour or so later, Katy Leary knocked on the bathroom door. There was no answer. She looked in. Jean Clemens lay dead in the bathtub, the victim of a heart attack evidently brought on by a seizure. "We were together," Clemens wrote that evening; "*we were a family!* The dream had come true—oh, preciously true, contentedly true, satisfyingly true! And remained true two whole days."

He felt too frail to go to Jean's funeral in Elmira, but he asked Paine to play the *orchestrelle* as her body was carried away from Stormfield.

At six o'clock the hearse drew up to the door to bear away its
pathetic burden. Paine played Schubert's "Impromptu," which was
Jean's favorite. Then he played the Intermezzo, that was for Susy;
then he played the Largo, that was for their mother.

From my windows I saw the hearse and the carriages wind along
the road and gradually grow vague and spectral in the falling
snow, and presently disappear. Jean was gone out of my life, and
would not come back any more.

Somehow, within the next few days, Twain once again summoned the
strength to turn sorrow into art, writing "The Death of Jean." It was the
"final chapter" of his autobiography, he told Paine, and the last manuscript he would complete.

Stormfield was now unbearable to Clemens. He asked to be taken back
to Bermuda. Life there had always done wonders for his spirits. "My
ship has gone down," he wrote a friend not long after getting there, "but
my raft has landed me in the Islands of the Blest, and I am as happy as
any other shipwrecked sailor ever was." He enjoyed long drives in the
company of some of his Angelfish, and, wearing a mourning band on his
sleeve in memory of the latest of his losses, he played miniature golf
with the president of Princeton University, Woodrow Wilson—who, he
predicted, would one day be president of the United States.

The newspapers reported on his failing health, and well-wishers inun-
dated him with homegrown cures. "Dear Sir (or Madam)," he wrote to
one. "I try every remedy sent to me. I am now on No. 87. Yours is 2,653.
I am looking forward to its beneficial results." And he prepared some
playful advice for those hoping to pass through the Pearly Gates:

Upon arrival do not speak to St. Peter until spoken to. It is not your
place to begin. . . .

When applying for a ticket avoid trying to make conversation. If
you must talk let the weather alone. St. Peter cares not a damn for
the weather. And don't ask him what time the 4:30 train goes; there
aren't any trains except through trains, and the less information you
get about them the better for you.

You can ask him for his autograph—there is no harm in that—
but be careful and don't remark that it is one of the penalties of
greatness. He has heard that before.

Don't try to kodak him. Hell is full of people who have made that
mistake.

Leave your dog outside. Heaven goes by favor. If it went by merit
you would stay out and the dog would go on in.

Sam Clemens comes home to New York
for the last time, April 14, 1910: "It is a
losing race," he had told Albert Bigelow
Paine on the voyage from Bermuda, "no
ship can outsail death."

His angina grew steadily worse: "I had a picturesque night," he told a friend. "Every pain I had was on exhibition. . . . I am losing enough sleep to supply a worn-out army." Injections of morphine helped dull the pain. Nothing else could be done for him.

In late March 1910, his doctors wrote Paine to say that Clemens was failing. Paine wired Clara to sail for America as soon as she could, then hurried south in early April to escort his subject home. The old man had difficulty breathing during the forty-eight-hour voyage and had to be wheeled down the gangplank in New York, but he managed to totter through Stormfield's front door, greeting Katy Leary and the other servants with a courtly handshake before agreeing to be carried upstairs to his big carved bed.

Clara and her husband arrived three days later and began what amounted to a deathwatch. When her father asked her to sing him three Scottish songs he especially loved Clara tearfully complied.

On April 21, she remembered,

he awoke with mental clarity and vigor but not inclined to converse. Then he dozed off. I was sitting by the bedside, when suddenly he opened his eyes, took my hand, and looked steadily into my face. Faintly he murmured, "Goodbye dear, if we meet . . ." After that he sank into sleep that deepened and possessed him wholly. While the sun dimmed, the great soul of Mark Twain melted into that speechless state of majesty and calm he had so fervently yearned for. His face was illumined with smiling peace.

Sam Clemens died at 6:22 in the evening. As he slept away, the bright glow of Halley's comet could just be made out above the horizon.

More than three thousand mourners turned out a few days later at the Brick Presbyterian Church in New York City to say goodbye to Mark Twain. Joe Twichell presided once again, and Clemens's old friend Howells was among those who shuffled past his open coffin. "I looked a moment at the face I knew so well," he remembered, "and it was patient with the patience I had so often seen in it: something of a puzzle, a great silent dignity, an assent to what must be from the depths of a nature whose tragical seriousness broke in the laughter which the unwise took for the whole of him. Emerson, Longfellow, Lowell, Holmes—I knew them all and all the rest of our sages, poets, seers, critics, humorists; they were like one another and like other literary men; but Clemens was sole, incomparable, the Lincoln of our literature."

A blur of admirers shuffles past Mark Twain's open coffin at the Brick Presbyterian Church in New York City.

Samuel Clemens at the Hannibal depot with a bouquet presented to him by old friends during his last visit to his boyhood home in June 1902

ACKNOWLEDGMENTS

"A successful book," Mark Twain once said, "is not made of what is in it, but what is left out of it." The same, we have learned, can be said of documentary films. Few topics we have undertaken have proven more of a challenge in deciding what to take out and what to leave in than the protean character of Samuel Langhorne Clemens, better known to the world as Mark Twain. He lived too eventful a life, he gleefully embodied too many human contradictions, and he had too much to say about the world he experienced to capture it all in a single book or a single film. And so we were forced to make thousands of painful choices in carving out what—we are the first to admit—is not an exhaustively comprehensive biography but one we hope nonetheless successfully captures something of the essence of this essential American.

To the extent we succeeded, the credit goes to many talented people and dedicated organizations. Without them, neither the film nor this book would exist.

Erik Ewers and Craig Mellish edited the film, ably assisted by Christine Rose Lyon and Margaret Shepardson-Legere. Their remarkable skills brought both clarity and grace to the final products. Their work, in turn, depended to a large degree on the stunning visual images gathered over the course of several years. Buddy Squires and Allen Moore—with Roger Haydock's assistance—once again proved why we consider them the best cinematographers in America. Stephen Petegorsky and Robert Sargent Fay provided an added bonus with their exquisite black-and-white photographs of Twain sites. And in culling through the thousands of archival photographs of "the most conspicuous person on the planet" to find the perfect ones to tell Mark Twain's story, Susanna Steisel and Pam Tubridy Baucom displayed not just keen eyes but incredible diligence. So, too, the other members of the Florentine Films family contributed mightily:

Brenda Heath, Patty Lawlor, Susan Yeaton Butler, and Debra Keller.

Two superb actors were particularly indispensable to this project. Kevin Conway has been a versatile "voice" in many of our previous documentaries, but in this one he was central to it. Reading Mark Twain's words—his jokes, his despairing letters, his piercing observations on human nature—Kevin demonstrated both an acute intelligence and an emotional range we think Clemens himself would have appreciated. Keith David's narration could be authoritative when necessary, or it could verbally "wink" when the story required it. Likewise, we're grateful to the others who breathed life into voices from the past: Philip Bosco, Tim Clark, Blythe Danner, Ann Duquesnay, Carolyn McCormick, Amy Madigan, and Cynthia Nixon.

Another great actor played an essential role in this project—by playing himself. In his on-camera interview, the incomparable Hal Holbrook offered insights on Twain gleaned from nearly a half-century of portraying him on stage; and behind the scenes, his understanding of Twain's life and work helped us at many turns. We were fortunate to find a wealth of people who, like Hal, were willing to share their thoughts with us about Twain: Arthur Miller, Russell Banks, Ron Powers, David Bradley, Hamlin Hill, William Styron, John Boyer, Shelley Fisher Fishkin, Laura Skandera-Trombley, Jocelyn Chadwick, Dick Gregory, Chuck Jones, Roy Blount Jr., Justin Kaplan, Jim Cox, David Lionel Smith, and Louis Budd. Some of those interviewees also contributed essays for this book; and some of them served as consultants to the film, along with Paul Barnes, Lynn Novick, Julie Dunfey, Robert Hirst, Gretchen Sharlow, Henry H. Sweets III, and Jim Zwick.

Our quest to understand Mark Twain took us to many of the important places in his life and in turn introduced us to some remarkable people who are devoted to preserving them. In no place did we find the presence of Clemens more palpable than the Mark Twain House in Hartford, Connecticut. It was the first home this restless American could truly call his own, the symbol of his boundless aspirations, the scene of the most happy and productive years of his life, and the site of one of the hardest personal tragedies he had to endure. Every aspect of Twain's kaleidoscopic personality is on display there on Farmington Avenue—and fortunately open for the public to experience for themselves. John Boyer and his dedicated staff made us feel at home there, and our profound thanks can best be expressed by encouraging everyone else to make a visit. More information on visiting the Mark Twain House is available from the Connecticut Office of Tourism at 1-800-CTBOUND or www.CTBOUND.org. At the Twain House, Marianne Curling and Karen Hibbitt were enormously helpful in providing pictures for both book and film.

In Hannibal, Missouri, where young Sammy Clemens stored up the memories he would later turn into great art, we are grateful to Henry Sweets and his staff at the Mark Twain Home Foundation, which manages the buildings of Twain's childhood and operates a wonderful museum not far from the Mississippi shore. John Huffman at the Mark Twain Birthplace State Historic Site in nearby Florida, Missouri, was also helpful; and Faye Bleigh of the Hannibal Convention & Visitors Bureau went out of her way to make our time there as productive and enjoyable as possible.

Elmira, New York, is the home of the Center for Mark Twain Studies, where Gretchen Sharlow showed us Quarry Farm, the Clemens family's summer retreat of many years, and the octagonal study in which some of America's greatest literature was written. The Center has been active in advancing Twain scholarship, as well as managing the important Elmira sites, and helped us at every turn. We also thank Jervis Langdon, proud descendant of the Langdon line in Elmira, for his assistance in explaining its influence on Twain's evolution as a man and an author.

At the Bancroft Library in Berkeley, California, Robert Hirst and the other members of the Mark Twain Project have been diligently editing and publishing the voluminous letters and journals of Mark Twain for many years, striving to make more and more of his work public, not just for scholars but for general readers, too. It is a daunting but absolutely critical undertaking. Besides editing the letters and manuscripts, the Project also oversees a wealth of Twain photographs and artifacts. For granting us access to them, we're grateful to the Project and the Mark Twain Foundation. And for her untiring assistance, we'd like to thank Neda Salem.

For this book, special thanks also go to its editor, Ashbel Green; to our agents, Gerry McCauley, Carl Brandt, and Chuck Verrill; and, once again, to our superb designer, Wendy Byrne.

Our film could not have been made without the generous financial support of General Motors; the Corporation for Public Broadcasting and the Public Broadcasting System; the Pew Charitable Trusts; the Arthur Vining Davis Foundations; the Park Foundation; the Connecticut Tourism Council & the Connecticut Office of Tourism. Our good friends at WETA-TV, especially Sharon Rockefeller, David Thompson, and Karen Kenton, were equally instrumental in making the film possible.

Finally, any investigation of Mark Twain's life quickly reveals how important his family was to his creative work. We wish to avoid any direct comparison between our own creative powers and Twain's, but we unabashedly proclaim that no one ever owed more thanks to their families than we do. To Sarah and Lilly Burns; Dianne, Emmy, and Will Duncan; and Diane Ward we offer this paraphrase of Twain's feelings for Livy: wheresoever you are, *there* is Eden.

Ken Burns
Geoffrey C. Ward
Dayton Duncan

SELECTED BIBLIOGRAPHY

Mark Twain's words in this book and the film it accompanies were drawn mainly from two multivolume sources: The Mark Twain Papers, *the ongoing series of Twain's letters, journals, and other previously unpublished materials being edited under the supervision of Robert Hirst by the Mark Twain Project at the University of California at Berkeley and published by the University of California Press; and* The Oxford Mark Twain, *edited by Shelley Fisher Fishkin and published by Oxford University Press—twenty-nine volumes of facsimile first editions of Twain's works. We enthusiastically recommend both projects to readers who want more from Twain himself. We also drew upon the following sources:*

Anderson, Frederick, et al., eds. *Mark Twain's Notebook & Journals.* 3 vols. Berkeley, Calif., 1975–1979.

Baetzhold, Howard G., and Joseph B. McCullough, eds. *The Bible According to Mark Twain.* New York, 1995.

Cardwell, Guy. *The Man Who Was Mark Twain.* New Haven, 1991.

Chadwick, Jocelyn. *The Jim Dilemma: Reading Race in "Huckleberry Finn."* Jackson, Miss., 1998.

Clemens, Clara. *My Father, Mark Twain.* New York, 1931.

Cooley, John, ed. *Mark Twain's Aquarium: The Samuel Clemens Angelfish Correspondence 1905–1910.* Athens, Ga., 1991.

Cooper, Robert. *Around the World with Mark Twain.* New York, 2000.

Cox, James M. *Mark Twain: The Fate of Humor.* Princeton, 1966.

DeVoto, Bernard. *Mark Twain's America and Mark Twain at Work.* Boston, 1977.

———, ed. *Mark Twain in Eruption.* New York, 1922.

Emerson, Everett. *Mark Twain: A Literary Life.* Philadelphia, 2000.

Fatout, Paul. *Mark Twain on the Lecture Circuit.* Bloomington, Ind., 1960.

Fisher Fishkin, Shelley. *Lighting Out for the Territory: Reflections on Mark Twain and American Culture.* New York, 1997.

———. *Was Huck Black?* New York, 1993.

———, ed. *The Oxford Mark Twain.* 29 vols. New York, 1996.

Geismar, Maxwell. *Mark Twain: An American Prophet.* Boston, 1970.

Gribben, Alan, and Niek Karanovich, eds. *Overland with Mark Twain: James B. Pond's Photographs and Journal of the North American Lecture Tour of 1895.* Elmira, N.Y. , 1992.

Harnsberger, Caroline Thomas. *Mark Twain at Your Fingertips.* New York, 1948.

Hill, Hamlin. *Mark Twain: God's Fool.* New York, 1973.

Hoffman, Andrew. *Inventing Mark Twain: The Lives of Samuel Langhorne Clemens.* New York, 1997.

Howells, William Dean. *My Mark Twain.* Mineola, N.Y., 1997.

Kaplan, Justin. *Mr. Clemens and Mark Twain.* New York, 1966.

———. *Mark Twain and His World.* New York, 1974.

Lauber, John. *The Making of Mark Twain.* Boston, 1985.

Lawton, Mary. *A Lifetime with Mark Twain: The Memories of Katy Leary.* New York, 1925.

LeMaster, J. R., and James D. Wilson, eds. *The Mark Twain Encyclopedia.* New York, 1993.

Mark Twain Project, eds. *Mark Twain's Letters.* 5 vols. Berkeley, Calif., 1988.

Meltzer, Milton. *Mark Twain Himself.* New York, 1960.

Neider, Charles, ed. *The Autobiography of Mark Twain.* New York, 1959.

———. *The Selected Letters of Mark Twain.* New York, 1982.

———. *Papa: An Intimate Biography of Mark Twain by His Thirteen-Year-Old Daughter Susy.* New York, 1985.

Paine, Albert Bigelow. *Mark Twain: A Biography.* New York, 1912.

Powers, Ron. *White Town Drowsing.* New York, 1986.

———. *Dangerous Water: A Biography of the Boy Who Became Mark Twain.* New York, 1999.

Quick, Dorothy. *Mark Twain and Me.* Norman, Okla., 1961.

Rasmussen, R. Kent. *Mark Twain A to Z.* New York, 1995.

———, ed. *The Quotable Mark Twain: His Essential Aphorisms, Witticisms & Concise Opinions.* Chicago, 1997.

Salsbury, Edith Colgate, ed. *Susy and Mark Twain: Family Dialogues.* Mattituck, N.Y., 1965.

Sanborn, Margaret. *Mark Twain: The Bachelor Years.* New York, 1990.

Skandera-Trombley, Laura. *Mark Twain in the Company of Women.* Philadelphia, 1994.

Steinbrink, Jeffrey. *Getting to Be Mark Twain.* Berkeley, Calif., 1991.

Webster, Samuel Charles, ed. *Mark Twain, Businessman.* Boston, 1946.

Wecter, Dixon. *Sam Clemens of Hannibal.* Boston, 1952.

———, ed. *The Love Letters of Mark Twain.* New York, 1947.

Willis, Resa. *Mark and Livy: The Love Story of Mark Twain and the Woman Who Almost Tamed Him.* New York, 1992.

Zwick, Jim. *Mark Twain's Weapon of Satire: Anti-Imperialist Writings on the Philippine-American War.* Syracuse, N.Y., 1992.

INDEX

Laura Hawkins, the model for Tom Sawyer's first love, Becky Thatcher, outlived her childhood friend to preside at the 1922 Hannibal premiere of a silent Hollywood version of *A Connecticut Yankee.*

Poland, 1959

ILLUSTRATION CREDITS

Archive Abbreviations

LOC: Library of Congress

MTH: The Mark Twain House, Hartford, Connecticut

MTM: Mark Twain Museum, Hannibal, Missouri

MTP: The Mark Twain Project, Bancroft Library, Berkeley, California

NK: Nick Karanovich

Endpapers

Geoff Chester, Oak Shade Observatory

a: Jim Zwick

Frontispiece

ii: NK

Preface:
The Right Word

vii: MTH,1900 #10; **viii–ix**: MTH, 1903 #15

Prologue

xiii: MTP, 1902.7 Dunlay; **xiv–xv**: MTM; **1**: MTP, 1902.7 Dunlay

Chapter One:
A Boy's Paradise

2: MTP; **3**: MTM; **4**: Nevada Historical Society; **5**: **top left** MTH; **top right** MTP; **bottom** MTP, Appert Coll./Autobiography p.249; **6**: MTH, Houses/Hannibal #2; **8–9**: LOC, G4164.H2A3 1869; **10**: MTP; **11**: Mark Twain Birthplace State Historical Site, courtesy MTP; **12**: **top** Nevada Historical Society, C-106; **bottom** State Historical Society of Missouri; **13**: **top** MTM, courtesy MTP; **bottom** State Historical Society of Missouri; **14**: MTH, 1835-60 #6; **15**: Glenn C. Meister Collection

Chapter Two:
Life on the Mississippi

16: Kansas State Historical Society, FM8; **17**: MTH; **18–19**: LOC, G4042.M5 1862 L53 Fil260; **20**: **top** MTM, HB.35.11696.1; **bottom** American Antiquarian Society; **21** Mariners' Museum, P2975; **22–23** Museum of the City of New York, 58.300.24; **25**: **top** MTH, Riverboats #34; **26 left** MTH; **right** Special Collections, Vassar College Libraries, 3.1249; **27**: LOC, LCUSZC4-7996

Hannibal's Sam Clemens

31: MTH

Chapter Three:
Roughing It

32: Wells Fargo Historical Services; **33**: MTH; **34**: MTP; **35**: MTP, 1864.1; **37**: Wells Fargo Historical Services; **38–39**: **both** Nevada Historical Society, **top** ST-463, **bottom** ST-1925; **40**: MTH, Cyril Clemens Coll./ Box II; **41**: **top** MTP, Scrapbook#4 1864-67; **bottom** MTP; **42–43**: LOC, PGA-Deroy-Ports de mer d'Amerique **45**: California Historical Society, FN-04071; X57-113-1-2; **46**: **both** Society of California Pioneers, **top** C003100 #20416, **bottom** C008285 #12364; **49**: **top** Bishop Museum, CP30905; **bottom** MTH; **50–51**: Hawaiian Mission Children's Society, N1412; **52**: **top** Hawaiian Mission Children's Society, N-1413; **bottom** Bishop Museum, CP45401-XS 34773; **53**: **both** Bishop Museum, **top** XC76912; **bottom** CP59717; **54**: **bottom** Society of California Pioneers

Chapter Four:
Innocents Abroad

56: Daniel Wolf, Inc., Greece-E38 #55; **57**: Lightfoot Collection; **58–59**: Museum of the City of New York, 29.100. 2373; **60**: **left** MTH; **right** MTP; **61**: Mariners' Museum, APB 15v75; **62**: **top left** MTP; **top right** MTP, May–July 1867/Notebook #8; **bottom** Professor W.E. James Collection, courtesy Randolph James; **63**: MTP, Denny Album; **64**: MTP, 1867.1; **65**: **top** NK; **bottom left** MTH, Misc. Friends #62, **bottom right** Professor W.E. James Collection, courtesy Randolph James; **66–67** Professor W.E. James Collection, courtesy Randolph James; **68**: MTH, Cyril Clemens/Box IV; **69**: MTP

Chapter Five: The Best
Girl in All the World

70: MTM, HB.35.11696.2; **71**: MTP, 1868.3; **72**: MTH, Houses/Elmira #2; **73**: **both** MTP; **74**: MTP, Nov. 28, 1868, p.14, **75**: MTH, Houses/ Elmira, **left** #10, **right** #23; **77**: MTP; **78**: Yale University Library, courtesy MTP; **79**: **top** Brown Brothers; **bottom** MTH, Friends #1; **80**: **top** MTH, Watkinson/SLC/Susan 1867-73 #3398.78; **bottom** Buffalo and Erie County Historical Society; **81**: Buffalo and Erie County Historical Society; **82**: **left** Harriet Beecher Stowe Center; **right** MTH, Friends #7; **83**: **top left** MTH, 1861-70 #13; **top right and bottom** MTH; **84–85**: Connecticut Historical Society, 1959.81.15A; **insets**:

Harriet Beecher Stowe Center; **86**: Robert Slotta/Admirablebooks.com; **87**: **left** MTH, OLC #3; **right** MTH, 1872-80 #3

Hartford's Mark Twain
89–91: MTH

Chapter Six:
The Gilded Age

92: MTH, 1874-81 #9; **94**: **left top** MTH, Family #6.1; **left bottom** Paine Bio. p.1290; **right both** NK; **95**: **left** MTH; **right** LOC, LCUSZC4-5606; **96**: MTH, Quarry Farm #3; **97**: **top** Center for Mark Twain Studies, Elmira College; **bottom** MTH, Quarry Farm #18; **99**: **left** MTH, Employees #13; **right** MTH; **100**: **top** MTP; **bottom** MTH; **101**: **all** Heritage Press/MBI Inc.; **103**: **left** MTH; **right** MTH, Family Groups #10; **104**: MTH, 1882-1903 #14; **105**: MTH, OLCw/children #4; **107–111** **all** Florentine Films/photo by Stephen Petegorsky

Chapter Seven: Truth

112: MTP, 1880.01; **113**: MTH; **114**: **both** MTP; **117**: **both** MTH; **118**: MTP, ms. *A Tramp Abroad*, p.2123; **119**: MTH, OLCw/children #3; **120**: **top** MTH; **bottom** MTH, Watkinson/OLC 1877 #3180.77; **121**: **top** MTH; **bottom both** Heritage Press/MBI Inc.; **122**: **left both** Robert Slotta/Admirablebooks.com; **right** American Antiquarian Society; **123**: **left** Special Collections, Vassar College Libraries, courtesy MTP; **right** LOC, USZ62-7607; **124**: MTH, Cyril Clemens/Box IV; **126**: NK; **127**: LOC, LCUSZC4-4294

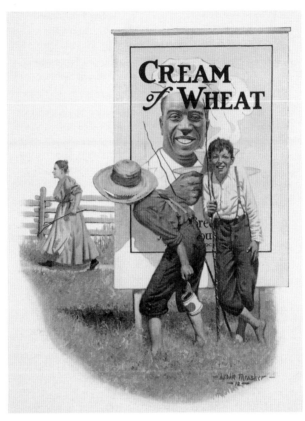

Tom Sawyer, Huck Finn, and Aunt Polly join forces to sell breakfast cereal in a 1913 advertisement, painted by Leslie Thresher

FILM CREDITS

A Film Directed by
KEN BURNS

Written by
DAYTON DUNCAN
and
GEOFFREY C. WARD

Produced by
DAYTON DUNCAN
and
KEN BURNS

Edited by
ERIK W. EWERS
and
CRAIG MELLISH

Cinematography
BUDDY SQUIRES
ALLEN MOORE
KEN BURNS

Associate Producer
SUSANNA STEISEL

Coordinating Producer
PAM TUBRIDY BAUCOM

Narrated by
KEITH DAVID

The Voice of Mark Twain
KEVIN CONWAY

Other Voices
PHILIP BOSCO
TIM CLARK
BLYTHE DANNER
ANN DUQUESNAY
CAROLYN McCORMICK
AMY MADIGAN
CYNTHIA NIXON

**Assistant Editor/
Associate Editor**
CHRISTINE ROSE LYON

Post-Production Associate
MARGARET SHEPARDSON-
LEGERE

Senior Creative Consultant
GEOFFREY C. WARD

Program Advisers
PAUL BARNES
JOHN BOYER
JOCELYN CHADWICK
TIM CLARK
JULIE DUNFEY
SHELLEY FISHER FISHKIN
ROBERT HIRST
LYNN NOVICK
RON POWERS
GRETCHEN SHARLOW
LAURA SKANDERA-
TROMBLEY
HENRY H. SWEETS III
JIM ZWICK

Chief Financial Officer
BRENDA HEATH

Administrative Assistants
PATTY LAWLOR
SUSAN YEATON BUTLER
DEBRA KELLER
MEG ANNE SCHINDLER

Sound Effects Editor
ERIK W. EWERS

Dialog Editor
PAUL BARNES

Music Editor
CRAIG MELLISH

Assistant Sound Editor
CHRISTINE ROSE LYON

Sound Post-Production
SOUND ONE

Re-Recording Mixer
DOMINICK TAVELLA
LEE DICHTER

**Additional
Cinematography**
ROGER HAYDOCK
STEPHEN LIGHTHILL

Assistant Camera
ROGER HAYDOCK
FORREST THURMAN
PAUL MARBURY
ANTHONY SAVINI

Grip
MARCUS HAMILTON
GORDON DAIGLE

**Animation Stand
Photography**
THE FRAME SHOP
Edward Joyce and
Edward Searles

Still Photography
STEPHEN PETEGORSKY
ROBERT SARGENT FAY

Voice-Over Recording
Lou Verrico
FULL HOUSE PRODUCTIONS

**Other Voice-Over
Recording**
WAVES, Hollywood, CA

Sound Recording
ERIK W. EWERS
CRAIG MELLISH
JEFF KENTON
DEAN SARJEANT
CHUCK FITZPATRICK

Post-Production Assistants
THOR NEURITER
FORREST THURMAN
ALEX WEBB
JENNIFER WARYAS

Post-Production Interns
RODRIGO BRANDAO
DESDEMONA BURGIN
BRANNEN BERGERON
STACEY CHEENEY
TIM DUNBAR
JEREMY FRAIZER
MELINDA GARRETT
BRIAN GRANDISON
LOUISA HUNKER
LISA JASON
MAUREEN McDOUGALL
KELEHER
DANIEL LETIZA
DAVE LIEBOWITZ
JEREMY MORRISSETTE
BRANDON NORMAN
BRANDY PAVLOSKY
ANDREA RYAN
MICAH TENNEY
BETSY TIMBERS
LINDSEY WARREN

Research Intern
LINCOLN FARR

Kine Camera Operator
DAVID FAULKNER

Negative Matching
NOELLE PENRAAT

Title Design
JAMES MADDEN

Color
DUART FILM LABS

**Spirit Data
Cine Film Transfer**
THE TAPE HOUSE
John J. Dowdell III

On-Line Editing
THE TAPE HOUSE
Joe Salleres

Digital Imaging
TIM THRASHER

Film Editing Equipment
THE BOSTON CONNECTION
Dwight Cody

Legal Services
ROBERT N. GOLD

**Instrumentalist and
Studio Arrangements**
BOBBY HORTON

Traditional Music
JACQUELINE SCHWAB, piano

**Additional
Traditional Music**
JAY UNGAR
MOLLY MASON
TEESE GOHL

Music Recorded at
SOUNDESIGN
Brattleboro, Vermont

Music Engineers
BILLY SHAW
ALAN STOCKWELL

Locations
THE MARK TWAIN HOUSE,
Hartford, Connecticut
THE CENTER FOR
MARK TWAIN STUDIES,
Elmira, New York

THE MARK TWAIN MUSEUM,
Hannibal, Missouri
MARK TWAIN BIRTHPLACE
STATE HISTORIC SITE,
Florida, Missouri
ELMIRA COLLEGE,
Elmira, New York

Extra Special Thanks
Judy Hu
Phil Risinger
Dennis Bolen
Peg Holmes
Skip Roberts
The Mark Twain Foundation

Special Thanks
The People of Walpole,
New Hampshire
The Academy of Music,
Northampton, MA
The Colonial Theatre,
Keene, NH
Dartmouth College Libraries
The Delta Queen
Steamboat Co.
Greater Falls Travel
Hannibal Convention &
Visitors Bureau
Golden Eagle Distributing
Co., Hannibal, MO
Johns Hopkins University
Keokuk Public Library
Insignia Films
Keene State College,
Mason Library
The MacDowell Colony
Mark Twain Riverboat,
Hannibal, MO
Missouri Division of Tourism
Oxford University Press
The Park Hyatt,
Washington, DC
Steeplechase Films
Walpole Public Library

Anne Ames
Roy Blount Jr.
Louis Budd
James Cox

Marianne Curling
Jan Grenci
Michael Hager
Karen Hibbitt
Sean Huff
John Huffman
Justin Kaplan
Nick Karanovich
Jan Kather
Lois Merry
Debra Petke
George Plimpton
Allen Reuben
Neda Salem
David Lionel Smith
Chase Twichell
Amy Wilson
Mark Woodhouse

———

Robert Bain
Faye Bleigh
Anh Bui
Sarah Botstein
George Briggs
Dr. & Mrs. William Brody
DeSota Brown
Lee Philip Brumbaugh
Carol Butler
Brenda Coker
Mike Conner
Philip Cronenwett
John Crowley
Diane Curry
Debra Dearborn
Jeanne Dickerman
Robin Espinola
Dr. William Esicar
Kricket Fellows
Nancy Finlay
John Froats
Wayne Gallup
Les Gardner
Victoria Gohl
Joanna Groning
George Hansen
Ellen Harding
Susan Haas
Jon Haug
Doug Holleley

Chris Jennings
Claudia Jew
Jervis Langdon
Milford Lawrence
Erin Lester
Janice Madhu
Patrick Martin
Ronald W. May
Jacqueline McKiernan
Dave McMahon
Peter Miller
Jon Minard
Eileen K. Morales
Carol Murray
Milton J. Nieuwsma
Charles Orcutt
Lili Ott
Will Perez
William Perry
Stephen Rice
Rich Riesenbeck
Linda Ritter
Marilyn Reppun
Duane Robinson
Tracy Sayles
Ken Sanderson
Rob Schoeberlin
Robbi Siegel
Claire Schlesser
James Skofield
Susan Snyder
Kurt Steelman
Nancy Stiner
Thomas Tenney
Captain Steven Terry
Charles Wehrenberg
Robin Weekes
Nicole Wells
Morgan Wesson
Roger Whitehouse

National Publicity
DAN KLORES
COMMUNICATIONS

**Produced in
Association with**
WETA, WASHINGTON, DC

**Executive in Charge of
Production for WETA**
DALTON DELAN

**Project Director
for WETA**
DAVID S. THOMPSON

**Associate Producer
for WETA**
KAREN KENTON

Publicity for WETA
DEWEY BLANTON

SHARON ROCKEFELLER,
President and CEO

**A Production of
Florentine Films**
Executive Producer
KEN BURNS

Funding Provided By
General Motors Corporation
The Pew Charitable Trusts
Public Broadcasting Service
Connecticut Office of Tourism
Corporation for Public
Broadcasting
The Arthur Vining Davis
Foundations
Park Foundation